wild ink

**Success Secrets to
Writing and Publishing
in the Young Adult Market**

TRANSIT

This item needs to be routed to
DCTPLD:
Danville-Center Township Public
Library - Danville

Barcode: 32604000168485
Title: Wild ink : success secrets to
writing and publishing in the young
adult market
Author: Hanley, Victoria.

Slip Date: 2014-11-20 20:06
Sent from MCPLMV

Second Edition

wild ink

Success Secrets to Writing and Publishing in the Young Adult Market

Victoria Hanley

PRUFROCK PRESS INC.
WACO, TEXAS

Library of Congress Cataloging-in-Publication Data

Hanley, Victoria.
 Wild ink : success secrets to writing and publishing in the young adult market / by Victoria
Hanley. -- 2nd ed.
    pages cm
Includes bibliographical references.
ISBN 978-1-59363-864-1 (pbk.)
1. Young adult fiction--Authorship. 2. Young adult literature--Authorship. I. Title.
PN3377.H36 2012
808.06'83--dc23
                          2011050344

Edited by Lacy Compton

Cover and layout design by Raquel Trevino

ISBN-13: 978-1-59363-864-1

Printed in the United States of America.

At the time of this book's publication, all facts and figures cited are the most current available.
All telephone numbers, addresses, and website URLs are accurate and active. All publications,
organizations, websites, and other resources exist as described in the book, and all have been
verified. The author and Prufrock Press Inc. make no warranty or guarantee concerning the
information and materials given out by organizations or content found at websites, and we are
not responsible for any changes that occur after this book's publication. If you find an error,
please contact Prufrock Press Inc.

Prufrock Press Inc.
P.O. Box 8813
Waco, TX 76714-8813
Phone: (800) 998-2208
Fax: (800) 240-0333
http://www.prufrock.com

dedication

To you—and your success as a writer

acknowledgments

Great thanks to my editors, Lacy Compton and Cheryl Miller Thurston. Thanks to Raquel Trevino for designing the cover. Big gratitude to my husband Tim, who put up with all the weekends and holidays I spent writing. Thanks to my kids, Emrys and Rose, for being a perpetual source of inspiration and the gleam in my eye. Thanks also to workshop participants far and wide, for providing buckets of fun and motivation. And gratitude beyond measure for my friends Rebecca Rowley, Lisa Pere, and Jeannie Mobley, who read over drafts of this book and contributed insights. Katharine Gregory, Laurel Lagoni, Bob McDonnell, and Elissa Tivona also read excerpts and offered helpful comments. Thank you Diane Tuccillo, Sue-Ellen Jones, and Mary McCarthy, for using your skills as teen librarians to assist me with reference questions, and your skills as remarkable human beings to bring a sense of possibility to this project. And to all of the wonderful writers, editors, and agents who contributed interviews and excerpts for this book—thank you for your time, your expertise, and your help.

table of contents

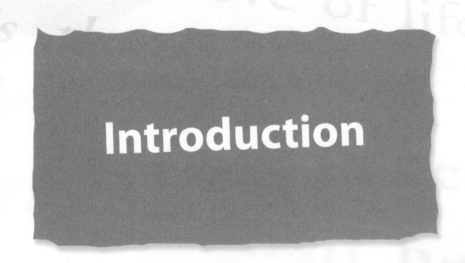

Introduction

This edition of *Wild Ink* has three new chapters: two on novel writing and another on writing YA nonfiction. Other chapters have been revised and updated, and additional interviews with authors, editors, and agents are included.

Originally, this book grew out of workshops I've given at writing conferences. The young adult (YA) market is flourishing, and eager workshop participants have been full of questions—so many questions it would take a book to answer them all.

If you've been wondering whether writing for the YA market is for you, by the end of this book I hope you'll have a good idea of whether the answer is "yes" or "no." Besides offering plenty of down-to-earth tips, *Wild Ink* aims to help you explore unknown territory, tread risky ground, and bring buried dreams into the open.

Write that book!

Victoria Hanley

Chapter 1

The YA Genre and You

*Tell the truth as you know it and
let it fall where it falls.*

—Chris Crutcher

Is it me, or is the world changing at a blistering pace? Inventions, innovations, discoveries! Much that we take for granted today would have been considered out of this world a short while ago. Things move so fast that when boarding the light rail for a trip across Denver, I sometimes wonder if I'll end up on a spaceship circling the Milky Way.

So how do we keep up? How do we write books relevant to today's young people?

I often remind myself that although the world changes, the spirit of youth is a universal constant. The desire to explore, the need to create new things and new experiences, the urge to express, to discover, to venture into the unknown—these are the marks of youth. Great stories for young adults bring forth that spirit, no matter the setting or circumstances.

Naturally, there are as many reasons to write in the young adult (YA) genre as there are writers who do so. Numerous subgenres—which we'll explore in this chapter—make room for scads of stories. The sky—or is it the galaxy?—is the limit.

That's where you come in.

who reads young adult fiction?

The target market for books labeled young adult is ages 13–16. However, it may surprise you to learn that people ages 9–99 read teen books. Seriously. Now, more than ever, YA is not only for teenagers.

A hefty number of adults gravitate to teen fiction because they love the excitement of a well-written book with powerful storylines. Take a look at these statistics from 2010:

> According to surveys by the Codex Group, a consultant to the publishing industry, 47 percent of 18- to 24-year-old women and 24 percent of same-aged men say most of the books they buy are classified as young adult. The percentage of female Y.A. fans between the ages of 25 and 44 has nearly doubled in the past four

years. Today, nearly one in five 35- to 44-year-olds say they most frequently buy Y.A. books. For themselves. (Paul, 2010, para. 5)

The reading trends reported in Paul's essay still pertain. If anything, the percentage of adults reading and buying YA books has increased. Current indications from librarians, fellow authors, and my own e-mails say that it's at least 50% now.

Not only that, but avid readers ages 9–12 are also eager for stories that go beyond the middle grade (MG) category. This group forms an enthusiastic but smaller cheering section for YA novels.

With such a wide readership, what really distinguishes the young adult genre from books found in the main section of the library or bookstore?

definition of ya fiction

In general, YA novels move at a brisk pace. Everything's a bit more condensed and intense than in traditional adult novels. As a writer, you'll want to aim for a style that moves forward quickly and emphasizes voice. (More about voice in Chapter 3.)

Word Count

Page requirements for teen titles used to be strict. Between 50,000 and 60,000 words was the norm, but those requirements have loosened up, and now teen books can range from just short of 100 pages to more than 600. A quick look at page counts in my latest stack of YA novels checked out from the library reveals that the average is 325. The shortest book is 135 pages, and the longest is 405. A 325-page book is approximately 80,000 words, depending on how much dialogue is included. By comparison, the average adult novel has more than 100,000 words.

Categories of Reader Age

The young adult category has divisions within itself, marked by the designated age of the expected reader. It's a ratings system of sorts, based on content, sex, and language usage. But as of now, no consistent rubric is shared by publishers, reviewers, and authors. Review publications such as *Kirkus*, *School Library Journal*, and *Publishers Weekly* each have their own way of notating and arriving at suggested reader age. The same book may receive a "12 up" rating from *Publishers Weekly*, a "Grade 8 up" rating from *School Library Journal*, and a "14 & up" rating from *Kirkus*. Individual educators and parents apply their own standards. All of this can be confusing for writers, especially because these categories and others (explained below) can all show up as just plain "young adult" on shelves or online listings.

Age 12+. The original and most traditional age category for YA readers is age 12 and up. Parameters include:

➤ *Language.* Books in this category may include mild profanity (unless you're writing in the subgenre of religion-based fiction—especially Christian—which considers any crude language or sex to be off limits).

➤ *Sex.* Romance is everywhere in this category of YA. Kissing and caressing is par. Sex is sometimes referred to, but with the details left out.

➤ *Violence.* Fights that include smashing things and punching people are common, as are knives, guns, and other weapons. These fights may result in injuries and death. Cruel characters may inflict psychological violence, too. However, graphic violence with descriptions full of gore will move a book to the adult shelves.

Age 14+. This designation means a novel that's a step closer to the genre of adult fiction. Parameters include:

➤ *Language.* May include profanity and swearing; no word is off limits. (Religion-based fiction would not have titles in this category.)

➤ *Sex.* There's a presumption that the reader is well-acquainted with the facts of life. There is probably at least one sex scene, although the sex will not be graphic.

> ➤ *Violence.* As far as I can determine, books land in the 14+ category rather than 12+ due to profanity or sex, not violence.

Age 10–14. Books designated for age 10–14 readers are closer to the category of middle grade. Parameters include:
> ➤ *Language.* No swearing.
> ➤ *Sex.* No sex, but possibly a hug or a first kiss.
> ➤ *Violence.* Fighting or injury, including death, are allowed if such incidents fit the story, but graphic details are not presented.

These novels may—or may not—be defined 10–14 in online listings, or they may be listed as simply young adult. They may be found in either the "young readers" section of a library or bookstore or on the teen shelves. (Yes, it's mysterious how such decisions are made.) The protagonist is usually 12–14. The coming-of-age theme, so prevalent in YA, still applies, but story events aren't as wrenching as those found in the other YA categories.

Crossover adult. Sometimes teens gobble up a book that's written for adults. And sometimes a book crosses from the YA market into the adult market to the point that many more adults than teens have bought it and read it. This is more of a sales category than a true ratings category.

Age of Protagonist

Protagonists of teen books are usually teens themselves, most often closer to 17 than 13. Does this mean you should worry if your protagonist is 12 or 20? Not always. The story comes first—and there have been wildly successful YA books with protagonists who are 12 or 20. But most often, if your story calls for a 12-year-old, you're probably writing a book for ages 9–12, also known as middle graders (MG). And if your protagonist is already 20 in Chapter 1, it would take a breathtakingly original plot or voice to convince a contemporary editor that your book is truly YA and not adult.

Vocabulary

Do you restrict vocabulary when writing YA, using only words that your readers are sure to be familiar with? No. Naturally, you want to keep your overall style engaging, so don't pack your prose with heavy academic terms. However, you can use whichever words your story calls for, whether those words have two syllables or five. As for profanity, some YA authors use no profanity; some use occasional mild profanity; some use quite a bit of profanity. Word choice is determined by the story and characters.

Technology, Fashion, and Slang

What about keeping up with technology, fashion, and slang? It's a valid question, considering that the website http://www.urban dictionary.com has more than a million entries and counting. When writing about gadgets, outfits, or ways of speaking, it's disconcerting to realize how fast they can slide into the past.

My best advice for this problem is to focus on the story first, remembering that the essence of a person's life—or story about it—will never be defined by the latest tech-toy, style, or slang. It's neither necessary nor possible for our writing to reflect every reader's up-to-the-minute environment. Most books are published years after being submitted by the author, during which time technology will have advanced, styles will have changed, and slang will have fallen out of favor. If the story's good, however, readers won't fixate on whether the book is totally current. Trends may go in and out, but stories are forever.

Coming of Age

The overarching theme in young adult novels is coming of age, which is defined as the attainment of maturity and loss of innocence. Put that way, it almost sounds easy. Ha! It isn't easy at all, which is part of why coming of age is a timeless theme, endlessly appealing to young and old, and one that can be woven into a wide variety of plots. (More about plots in Chapter 2.) There are so many levels and layers to coming of age, affecting not only the body but also the mind and emotions. The profound miseries and joys that come with childhood's end are felt in all domains of life.

Protagonists in YA novels encounter situations beyond the scope of anything they've handled before. Challenges arise from which there is no escape. The shelters of childhood can't protect or defend them from what's happening, and a child-like perspective won't cut it anymore. As tension mounts, these young characters must find within themselves what is needed to deal with people and events. It's time to step up or lose out. By the end of the book, eyes are opened, scales have fallen away, and innocence is irretrievably lost. A young adult emerges.

Authors writing YA do not smooth over jagged edges. We confront the frustrations, disappointments, mistakes, and unwanted realizations that are part of growing up.

Breakdown and Breakthrough Are Part of the Picture

Haven't we all been through meltdown moments when things seemed truly terrible—when our sense of perspective was dim and skewed, and when hopes and dreams collapsed? And then there's breakthrough: The "aha" moments that enable fresh understanding, the sudden giggle as we laugh at ourselves, the mysterious inner change giving us a second wind at the end of our strength.

Breakdowns and breakthroughs seem to be more frequent in the lives of young people. Learning curves are steep and fast. Hormones are racing. Inner life is stretching and reaching for what's next. Much is outgrown, and much more grown into—and then outgrown again. New tastes are discovered and discarded. Dire dejection meets outrageous comedy. Hope and angst. Idealism, cynicism.

Everything is going on.

And this is the stuff of marvelous stories! Think about it—would you rather read about someone who walked through an open door, or some-one who found an open door after crashing into seven walls? Would you rather read about a romance that runs a smooth course from week to week, or a romance that falls like a massive meteorite, opening a lava pit from which the hero must crawl to find a new love that heals the day?

Passion

Adolescence is a time of big emotions. Remember?

Whether teens show their feelings or not, most can go from eager to apathetic, easygoing to raging, buoyant to downcast, all in the course of a day. You name it, teens have felt it.

The emotional core of a YA novel colors every action and situation taking place in the plot. It forms the basis for character experiences and character growth.

Each of us is an expert on at least a few emotions. Whether it's fear, triumph, despair, denial, hope, anger, embarrassment, surprise, regret, sorrow, bliss . . . we've all felt some emotions more than others. By drawing on our own experiences, we can infuse fictional characters with feelings of their own, making them unforgettable.

In the YA genre, tame is lame. So write with passion. If you're a passionate person, more power to you—and more joy, fury, tenderness, thrills, chills, and fire.

Honesty

Want the truth? Blunt, in-your-face, stripped-down truth? Ask a teen.

Ruthless, brutal honesty may be hard to take sometimes, but overall it's enlivening. Teen literary voices are ideally suited to communicate raw and personal observations of people and the world. Novels in the YA genre take full advantage of this, using character voices to reveal thoughts and emotions at a level rarely seen in fiction for adults.

Independence

Adolescents reaching for adulthood are seeking independence. They can't get there by letting adults handle their problems. Confronting and resolving their own conflicts, enduring their own heartaches, and recovering from their own stumbles is empowering. Books that show the painful joy of moving from dependence to self-reliance are likewise empowering.

Whatever the trouble is, let the young characters deal with it. Can they occasionally consult a wise mentor? Sure. But the answers they receive should not be easy to apply. Let your fictional mentors use riddles or give advice that's quickly forgotten or seems impossible to follow. Sometimes the advice may be wrong altogether—or the mentor who is supposed to save the day will be called away at a crucial moment.

Rebellion

Adolescent rebellion goes hand in hand with the urge for independence. Teens rebelling against authority don't see themselves as typical "rebellious teenagers." For them, it's all about a fresh perspective and throwing off arbitrary rules. Why should they do something a certain way just because it's been done that way a hundred times before? Why should they bow to an authority they don't respect? Why allow anyone to tell them what to do?

Themes of rebellion against unreasonable or tyrannical people and situations are always popular in YA books. Readers identify with teen protagonists who break free.

Wild Exploration

For many, our wildest and craziest actions are taken during our teen years or early twenties. Neurologists tell us the adolescent brain is a work in progress, a stage of life guided by emotion more than reason, when bouts of recklessness are likely. Human history tells us that adolescence is a time of exploration.

Some explorations work out fantastically well. The rush of discovery, of breaking new ground, of rising to a challenge, can help launch fulfilling journeys, splendid careers, or profound relationships.

At the other end of the spectrum, some explorations result in lasting injury. We've all known—or been—people who took risks involving drugs, alcohol, sex, speeding, fighting, and so on.

In YA novels, teens experience the parts of life that are dark and sad as well as uplifting. People die sometimes. Things change so drastically that nothing will ever be the same. Love is tested against the world, and hope must survive reality. Wounds leave scars.

Prices are paid.

If you have a fast–paced book with a teen protagonist coming of age who is experiencing breakdowns and breakthroughs, struggles for independence, wild times, honesty, and passion, you're writing a novel in the YA genre.

ya subgenres

There's an important "you factor" in writing. It's why you care to create a story in the first place, what you bring to your writing from your life and times, the subjects that interest you, the types of scenarios you invent for your characters, and the way you go about the work of writing itself. This all ties in to your choice of subgenres, because some will fit you, and some will not.

Several zillion subgenres exist in the young adult category, from contemporary realistic to speculative fiction to nonfiction. (By the time this book is published, there may be more.) We'll look at a variety of subgenres to give you a sense of which type(s) may best suit your writing style. Each has its own characteristics and its own fans, and each requires something a little different from writers.

Contemporary Realistic

Contemporary realistic YA is the broadest of the subgenre categories, encompassing characters in the real world who face just about every issue you can name. As always, the overarching theme is coming of age. Set in the modern world, contemporary books most often emphasize character growth in a context of relationship with others, with one's self, and with the world.

In the area of personal relationships, you'll find teen protagonists interacting with friends, teachers, parents, siblings, relatives, stepfamilies, and love interests. Characters may find themselves growing away from friends who were once close or living in a family where the parents are ready to divorce. They may fight with their siblings, hate their teachers, or feel the pain of betrayal by a loved one. At the end of the book, some of the conflict will be resolved as characters grow and change. They may find new friends, discover a mentor, ease a tense relationship with a parent or stepparent, begin to value the sibling they used to fight with daily, or get over a broken heart.

Regarding relationships with self, teen characters may be shown struggling to sort out matters of identity, including racial, cultural, or gender identity or sexual orientation. They may be seeking an absent parent or exploring what it means to them to be adopted. They may be struggling with issues of peer pressure, conscience, personality, or self-esteem. Another popular theme is dreams and ambitions in stories of talented teen musicians, actors, dancers, painters, writers, and athletes. Issues involving health and well-being have also found their way into contemporary novels for young adults, showing teens who are dealing with diseases, handicaps, injuries, stress, depression, suicide, self-mutilation, and problems with drug and alcohol addictions.

Experiences with the outer world in its harshest or most challenging forms are also explored. Stories can detail great hardships, including being involved in intense competition, getting bullied or treated like an outcast, suffering physical and/or sexual abuse, and enduring gang wars, terrorism, or environmental disasters.

And, of course, there are stories that highlight dating, awakening sexuality, and everything that goes along with surging hormones, from feverish excitement over a single kiss to unplanned pregnancies.

The themes listed in the above paragraphs show how many experiences teen protagonists may have in the course of a contemporary novel. It's a long list, and by no means complete. When deciding whether to write in this subgenre, your own passionate interests will guide you. You can draw on your understanding of life. If your father was an alcoholic and you started sneaking booze as a teenager, then you can mine the experience to create a novel where alcoholism is part of the story. If you've been active in politics, then your book could have a student running for office. If you've been in the foster care system, then you can tell it like it is. No matter where your life has led, it can enrich your writing.

Multicultural

Teens coming to terms with cultural differences create a perfect forum for stories that show characters learning about themselves, where they come from, who they are, and where they're going. Sometimes the emphasis of a multicultural story is on clashes between parents who want to preserve the customs of their culture of origin and teenage children who don't. Sometimes it's on learning to value a heritage that has almost been lost. It might be concerned with feelings of displacement or loneliness within a community where the protagonist is not welcome. It might be about dating someone from a different ethnic group or religion. The possibilities are endless.

African American, Native American, Asian American, and Latino American multicultural stories have some representation in YA literature—although not enough. And there's a lot of diversity among immigrant populations that isn't yet represented at the YA table at all.

Besides ethnic groups, multicultural literature can also address differences in religious backgrounds. There's wide territory here for writing books that give readers more awareness. In the U.S., more and more children of marriages that unite people of different faiths or races are growing up. These young people are eager to find voices that reflect their experience. If you have a background in or an affinity with any of these diverse groups, you can add your perspective to the growing body of multicultural literature within YA.

Gay and Lesbian (GLBTQ)

The market for quality YA novels with gay and lesbian protagonists has expanded, and publishers are adding more titles in this subgenre. In addition, libraries and publishers recognize the category known as GLBTQ: gay, lesbian, bisexual, transgender, queer or questioning. Books in this category of YA literature highlight characters who are gay or lesbian, characters who are bisexual, characters who identify with the opposite gender, or those who are simply questioning their sexual identity. Readers seek out stories about protagonists they can relate to, protagonists finding self-acceptance and living life fully.

When you imagine your protagonist, do you imagine someone from the GLBTQ community? You could be the perfect person to write the next YA story in this subgenre.

Action-Adventure

Wilderness adventures, war stories, spy thrillers, pirate escapades, and martial arts scenarios fall under the action-adventure subgenre. Teen protagonists are busy fending off life-threatening disasters, using their wits and resourcefulness to survive while coping with privation and injury. Survival is key, and coming of age is the theme.

Violence in some form is built into the structure of this subgenre, whether that violence is due to nature (e.g., avalanches, raging rapids, earthquakes, marauding animals) or clashes with humans (e.g., soldiers, gang members, spies).

Action leads, so the pace is relentless and fast. But what distinguishes this subgenre is not only the pace but also the tone: The focus is on external events, and introspection occurs only in rare moments, although those moments may be turning points for the character.

If you've traveled wide and journeyed far; if you have a military, martial arts, or wilderness-preparedness background; if you enjoy risk-taking, bold moves, and real danger, you could translate your experience into a YA action-adventure novel.

Speculative Fiction

The term *speculative fiction* is attributed to author Robert Heinlein. It encompasses all of the following categories: fantasy, paranormal, angels and demons, horror, science fiction, dystopias, and alternate history. Whereas realistic fiction attempts to convey the verities and realities of life as we know it, writers of speculative fiction take liberties with reality, employing imagination to alter it.

All genres require the writer to successfully suspend the reader's disbelief, but your job as a writer of speculative fiction involves extra work. Along with a good story you must weave a convincing cosmology where characters and circumstances behave in ways not seen in normal life.

Fantasy. Fantasies are set in imaginary worlds or introduce imaginary elements into the world we know. In traditional fantasy, the world is created by the author, although it may contain elements drawn from historical times on Earth. Urban fantasy can be set in modern cities or in futuristic places.

Fantasy books usually include plenty of adventure. Magicians, enchantresses, elves, fairies, genies, pixies, sprites, super-powered heroes and arch villains, dragons, goblins, trolls, and other fantastic beings can populate the pages. Crystal balls, magic wands, special swords, and enchanted islands or forests play their parts. Anything is possible—any creature can come to life, any item can store special powers. Wizards, sorcerers, seers, and the like often interact with regular humans. Magic is portrayed as part of ordinary reality.

If technology is present, it is secondary to the central action and is never used to solve the central conflict. This is an important identifying mark of fantasy. Spiritual insight, magical power, or strong character traits must solve the central conflict. (This contrasts with science fiction, a genre in which the right piece of technology or the right scientific formula may well solve the central problem.)

Modern coming-of-age issues can be treated in an allegorical way in YA fantasy. For example, the story of a hero who has lost his father, kingdom, sword, and freedom is the story of any young person whose world has been turned upside down. The plight of a gifted young woman in a fantasy realm who is shunned because of her background applies to modern teens who are treated as outcasts.

I write fantasy (with romance thrown in). When I was a teenager, every week I came up with some new daydream about other worlds. In school I'd hide books like Tolkien's *The Lord of the Rings* inside my chemistry book. How about you? Does your mind take you on similar excursions? Would you like to bring other people with you? The magic of words is your ticket.

Paranormal. This subgenre has fantasy elements, but rather than wizards and magic wands, it's more likely to have ghosts or mythical creatures such as vampires, zombies, werewolves, and other shape shifters. Paranormal romance, featuring love between humans and paranormal beings, has many devoted fans.

Angels and demons. A popular subset of speculative fiction is stories involving angels and demons, seraphim and imps, the blessed and the damned. These novels explore light and darkness, the sublime and the fallen, immortal goodness and eternal corruption. Everything is on a grand scale.

Horror. In this subgenre, teen protagonists confront dire super-natural forces or horrific events such as nuclear winter or plagues. The assorted monsters found in horror may overlap with those found in fantasy or the paranormal. Miscellaneous beasts created by the author may join forces with zombies, ghosts, or vampires. And there are strange unions between science and fantasy, of which the original was *Franken-stein* by Mary Shelley.

Although readers of horror expect to be frightened into nightmares, the coming-of-age theme still prevails. Are you good at describing ter-rifying episodes? Does your mind spin dark disasters? Horror draws on archetypal fears for maximal reaction.

Science fiction. In the adult fiction section of libraries, sci-fi books are shelved spine to spine with fantasy. Both are in the category of specu-lative fiction; in both, the author creates worlds that do not actually exist. But the worlds found in sci-fi novels are linked to scientific principles: robots instead of sorcerers, radar instead of telepathy, and statistical analysis instead of crystal balls. Science fiction is almost always set in the future, with technology central to the action.

Hard sci-fi is based firmly on scientific knowledge. The stories writ-ten by hard sci-fi writers may fly through outer space or travel through time or perhaps into a parallel universe—but only because the author believes that such travels are logical extensions of today's scientific achievements.

In YA sci-fi, teen protagonists must keep their nerve in the face of daunting circumstances—they must use their thinking powers to dis-cover solutions. In the hands of an ingenious writer, the coming-of-age theme works well within a sci-fi story.

It takes a particular personality to come up with believable future scenarios, inventive technologies, and sweeping ideas. Is this you? Are you always reading up on the latest discoveries and dreaming of where humanity will go next? You could be successful writing YA science fiction.

Sometimes sci-fi and fantasy blend together: Wizards may battle extraordinary machines, dragons may breathe fire over a settlement on a foreign world, or a teen who can shape shift may be fitted with a nano-chip that inhibits her powers.

Dystopias. If a utopian society is an ideal state imbued with harmony, equality, freedom, and justice, a dystopian society is the opposite: a realm where oppression prevails. Most often set in the future, dystopian societies may be presented to their inhabitants as utopian places or have utopian elements as part of their facade. But this presentation is false, a cover for states where extreme control is exerted by those in power. Deprivations and punishments—physical, mental, and emotional—are used as a means of perpetuating this control. The characters in dystopian worlds struggle against this oppression, seeking freedom under conditions designed to prevent it.

What better environment to write about coming of age? Teen protagonists rebel against the regimes imprisoning them and discover ingenious and dangerous ways to outsmart their oppressors. The subgenre of dystopian YA novels is thriving, so if you have dystopian visions, start writing!

Alternate history. If you're human, you've probably wondered, "What if 9/11 had never happened?" "What if nuclear weapons had never been invented?" or "What if cars had always been electric?" There are hundreds of questions that history poses, questions speculating about what would have turned out differently for whom. Writers of alternate history use imagination to answer such questions. They rewrite the history of a specific era, putting their characters into a timeline that might have been. As such, they are part of speculative fiction, but they are also powered by research into actual history: They know exactly how and when their fiction diverges from what is recorded.

Historical Fiction

History provides rich opportunities to create teen protagonists. So much history has been lived by young adults through the ages. How many were sailors, soldiers, pioneers, brides, husbands, parents, slaves, indentured servants, artists, or travelers?

Do you research history in your spare time for fun? Do you find yourself hanging around older relatives, asking questions about what it was like to be a teenager growing up in a different era? When you think of stories, are they about people from World War II, early America, or ancient Greece or Rome? Are you drawn to books about the Dark Ages, the pharaohs of old, or feudal Japan? If so, let your imagination lead you further into those distant times and create a living, breathing tale peopled with teens who play important roles.

Magical Realism

In stories of magical realism, the supernatural view is accepted as legitimate, and it's woven into the fabric of the story. Dreams, visions, or mythology interpret the meaning of physical events. Reality is depicted as the result of human perception rather than a set of physical laws that can be studied in a lab. In magical realism, one event can be experienced in completely different ways by two people with different views. For example, a suburban American teenager might view a mugging as a piece of bad luck arising from being in the wrong place at the wrong time. However, a *curandera* (female healer in the Hispanic tradition) could interpret the same mugging as something arranged by the teenager's spirit, a spirit urging that teen to look deeper and value life more.

Have you studied mythologies or cultural mysticism? Are you interested in the meaning of dreams? Do you like to ponder how differently two people will interpret the same episode? Do you seek visions to help you understand life? Magical realism could be your niche.

Humor

Humor can be an enhancing part of any novel. We all need to laugh, right? Many YA authors put humorous moments into their books with great success, combining laughs with poignant understanding of adolescent struggles.

Do your words hit readers' funny bones? Do people chuckle when they read your account of the date that went bad, the school assignment that failed, the private blog that went public? If so, keep smiling—and writing.

Satire is also an option. Perhaps you'd like to use exaggeration and mockery to draw attention to an aspect of popular culture. Maybe you've got a knack for sarcasm and you understand how to set up events in a novel to bring about social commentary and snickering.

Mystery-Detective

The young adult mystery-detective novel is leaner and less gory than some adult mysteries. And of course, the teen protagonist solves the crimes and puzzling circumstances. (Adults stepping in with solutions would ruin everything.) This subgenre requires excellent plotting skills. Red herrings, misdirection, and intrigues abound, with interesting characters who showcase human motivations.

Are you an incorrigible sleuth who loves to read mysteries? Are you a student of human nature? Do you enjoy subjects like forensic psychology? Do you have an idea for a teen investigator who could solve a series of clever crimes or unravel a delightfully tangled web of lies? Write a great mystery.

Religion-Based Fiction

In this genre, coming of age in a particular faith is the main story, whether about sudden conversion or a slowly deepening relationship with a higher power. Storylines may include resurrecting one's faith after losing it during a period of trauma, learning to resist temptations toward violence or self-destruction, finding satisfaction in service to others, gaining compassion for someone who's been getting under a character's skin . . . the possibilities are many.

Maybe your own faith is so central to your life that you want to give it a central place in your fiction. If so, you can incorporate what's meaningful to you into the stories you write.

Romance

First love, anyone?

Romance is a huge favorite among readers. And why not? Romance adds verve to just about any story and crosses all of the other subgenres. Love and kisses are always popular, whether they occur in contemporary realistic novels, mysteries, speculative fiction, graphic novels, or other subgenres.

In multicultural books, young adults falling in love take on added fascination when members of the pair come from divergent backgrounds or when parents disapprove.

Young people will walk through fire for each other. They will transform themselves from spoiled to selfless, from haughty to humble, from wimps to wonders. They struggle to be taken seriously, to get a grip on powerful emotions, to find the time or place to be together at all. Feeling so much for someone else can be consuming.

Do you keenly remember the feeling of first love? Do you create characters who whisper of passion and sacrifice? Love stories will be treasured forever and ever, so if romance calls to you, let yourself answer with head-over-heels enthusiasm.

Graphic Format

There's a surging movement to incorporate illustrations into books of all types, called graphic format. Once upon a time, graphic format was confined to traditional comic books—action-adventure stories about superheroes, with the bonus of fantastic illustrations. But now, any and all of the subgenres (and nonfiction books) listed above can be done in graphic format. Graphics are being incorporated into more and more books, including those with large amounts of text. As this genre continues to grow, there will doubtless be new categories and subcategories emerging.

Classic graphic novels have very little text. The story is told largely through the combination of illustrations and dialogue. Although there may be short sections of highly abbreviated narrative, the lion's share of narration falls to the illustrations. This sort of novel is ideal for you if you can visualize frames of characters exchanging dialogue, with bits of strategic narration thrown in. To gain a sense of what's involved in writing graphic format books, read them. You may be surprised by the variety and creativity you'll find.

You don't have to be an illustrator to write graphic novels. If you come up with excellent text, a publisher will put you together with an artist. But if you have a flair for illustration, by all means get started with sketches and dialogue boxes.

Because graphic-format books are really taking off, here's an interview with an expert to give you more information.

Graphic Format Expert: John Shableski

Bio: John Shableski is an internationally recognized expert on the world of graphic novels. He's been a featured speaker and panelist at industry trade shows and professional conferences throughout North America. He has served as a member of the Book Expo America Advisory Committee and was a judge for the 2009 Eisner Awards at Comic Con International. He has also created professional development programs about graphic novels for Miami Book Fair International, the American Library Association, New York Comic Con, Comic Con International, Book Expo America, and the Texas Library Association.

What is the difference between the terms "graphic novel" and "graphic format"? What else can you tell us about this exploding publishing phenomenon?

Graphic novel is really a misnomer, as it was meant to be an elegant and literary-sounding way to disguise the comics medium for storytelling. Graphic format essentially describes a long-form comic book. Other descriptors can then be added such as memoir, romance, science fiction, nonfiction, etc. The irony here is that the teen audience simply calls them what they are: books. We in publishing and non-comics-reading industry types are the ones who need some sort of tag that allows us a way to categorize the product.

Graphic novels have grown exponentially over the past decade, and much of that growth has surprisingly come from the traditional houses. Oddly enough, a great percentage of the comics publishers like Marvel, DC, and the like have been more intent on creating comic books for the traditional fan base. In the meantime, the major houses have been making serious developments in the graphic novel category.

What is the publishing climate for writers of young adult titles in graphic format?

We are now seeing 6,000 new titles published in the graphic format annually, and that's way up from the 500–600 titles in the 2002–2003 time frame. Of these, about 35% are titles for teens, and it's growing.

The YA and tween markets are the best opportunity for publishing in the graphic format. This audience is already in tune to its sense of visual literacy, whereas adults (at least most of us) have been programmed for prose-only format. Interestingly enough, I've met author after author who say that if they could draw, they'd use the graphic format to show you exactly how they imagine their stories would look. Many credit their love of comics as the initial source for their love of reading.

What suggestions do you have for writing in graphic format?

You could read the following books: *Understanding Comics* by Scott McCloud, *Making Comics* by Scott McCloud, *Drawing Words and Writing Pictures* by Jessica Abel and Matt Madden, and last but not least, *Adventures in Cartooning* by James Sturm, Alexis Frederick-Frost, and Andrew Arnold. If you haven't ever written a screenplay or worked in the comics medium, these books will help you to understand the complexity and beauty of comics. You will also want to find a comics artist who has the right feel for your story. It's the same thing as putting together a band. If the band feels the music, it'll sound great. If it just plays the notes on the page, it will sound okay, but you'll always know it could have been a lot better. The artist has to feel what you feel about the story.

What avenues exist for publishing in this genre?

It all depends on how hard you are willing to work and how creative you are. Some of the best success stories have come from webcomics. *Smile: A Dental Drama* by Raina Telgemeier began as a webcomic and sold really well for Scholastic. Jeff Kinney developed *Diary of a Wimpy Kid* as a webcomic first before he landed his book deal. The thing is, the audience these two generated with their webcomics certainly helped convince their publishers that there was a great audience for the stories. They had established an audience without risking money on printing books first.

Cross-Genre

Books that combine more than one genre are called cross-genre. For example, romance is frequently paired with other subgenres, because it easily spices up any YA fiction, whether speculative or realistic. But romance isn't the only option in the cross-genre category. Paranormal satire, anyone? And, as mentioned above, sci-fi and fantasy often come together. But what about a dystopian graphic novel, or magical realism combined with detective work? Anything's possible as long as you make it work.

Nonfiction

Nonfiction for teens is booming. This genre is expanded on in Chapter 4, Writing YA Nonfiction.

Your Book

Publishers like to know up front what genre they're looking at, so it makes sense to study the categories outlined above so that you can accurately designate your book's subgenre in a query letter (see Chapter 7, Submitting Your Manuscript). For a more in-depth understanding, consult your library or teen librarian and bookstore shelves. Your best education lies in reading many titles from each category.

The type of book you write is important. Once you establish a following, those who love your work will seek out everything you've written in a similar subgenre. Few readers will cross from one subgenre to another and back again; most will stick devotedly to their chosen preference, whether dystopian, sci-fi, multicultural, or something else.

what about market trends?

We've all witnessed the way a given subgenre can take off. For a couple of years fantasy might dominate the YA market. Then paranormal. Then something else. How do these market trends affect you? Should you consider them when writing your novel?

I've met a number of aspiring writers who have stopped writing about what truly interests them and taken up a substitute interest they think has more market appeal; "Everyone wants to read about _____, so I'll write about _____ to be successful," they say.

Publishers sometimes unknowingly contribute to this problem by talking about what's hot and what's not:

➤ "We're not publishing historical fiction this year."
➤ "We're looking for a great detective novel with a female protagonist."
➤ "Fantasy is on the way out."
➤ "What the teen market needs now is more dystopian novels."
➤ "We won't consider books written from a third person viewpoint."

Trends come and go, but your best work will always be your most authentic work, and this will not be determined by market forces.

Wouldn't it be sad if your voice cried out to write a dazzling historical novel, but because you'd heard that such a book would never be published, you quashed the idea and wrote sci-fi? Your sci-fi could easily be rejected as "not right for us at this time"—and a year later you might see historical fiction go leaping full force into the marketplace. It's far more satisfying to write the book you really want to write and then wait for the market to change in your favor than to put your time and effort into a "coattail" title that gets lost in the flurry of transient popularity within a different subgenre.

The market is ever changing. You can count on it. Ultimately, your greatest market appeal will come from writing something captivating and enlivening. You're bound to write in a more captivating, enlivening way if you write about what truly calls to you. Your heart knows what kinds of stories will inspire you to create a novel that pulses with life. Pay attention.

When writing a book, comparing yourself to others is not only unhelpful but misleading. Remember the Ugly Duckling? The poor "duckling" was reviled, cast out, and left to die because he didn't look like other ducklings. Yet somehow he survived to grow up—only to discover he was really a glorious swan.

The duckling did not *turn into* a swan. He was a swan all along but didn't know it. Moral of the story? Know what sort of bird you are. You're the best at being you. You'll be the best at telling the stories you have to tell.

drawing from your life to create fictional characters

Teen readers—and adult readers of teen books—love the feeling of finding fictional characters they can relate to, characters who get under their skin, characters they wish they could meet.

So where do those characters come from?

Everyone you've ever met has given you material for character creation. You observe traits wherever you go and whatever you're doing. Then you mix them up, exaggerate them, distort them, or reinvent them to create characters with personalities of their own. Observation is key to feeding your creative mind what it needs to make memorable characters. But I think it's equally important to let go of formulaic notions when it comes to creating those characters. Fictional beings are not assembled piece by piece from individual traits—they're not like lawnmowers or Mr. Potato Head. I recommend simply allowing your creative mind to get to work and make up a whole person.

I don't know exactly how fictional characters come to life, but they do. And they're more likely to be worth knowing if we get our greasy, analytical fingers off of them, and let them come into being on their own.

Once they're fully created, talking and taking action and full of natural spunk, *after* that first draft has been completed, then—and only then—it's time to invite the critical thinking brain to get involved.

That's what Chapter 2 is all about.

Getting Your Book In Shape:
Novel Writing, Part 1

The key, I have found, is to find whatever ways you can to get to the end.

—T. A. Barron

Writing any book is quite a process, a delightful, infuriating, discouraging, and inspiring process. In fact, pick an emotion. Whatever it is, you're sure to come across it multiple times somewhere between the beginning and the end of your writing endeavor. Just remember that difficult emotions are not a reason to stop writing. They're normal, natural, and to be expected.

Although it's true that you might get through whole sections of your book with ease and sunshine, it's also true that you're bound to hit the sucky swamp and wonder why you ever started writing in the first place. And what's easy for you might feel like an endless bog to the next writer. For example, I detest writing first drafts, but to me there's no finer treat than doing final revisions. My writing buddy Jeannie Mobley feels the opposite way. She gets excited about first drafts and loathes revising.

Depending on your temperament, many different elements of writing can trigger sweaty panic: first drafts, beginnings, middles, endings, conflict, setting, characterization, dialogue, plotting, voice, point of view, showing and telling, and revisions. We're about to go over every one of these areas with an emphasis on writing YA. But before we do, I'd like to point out that *Wild Ink* is not designed to get you started from scratch. If it were, these chapters on getting your novel in shape would be twice as long. So if you're brand new to novel writing, please take advantage of the many books and resources out there to help you hone your craft. (You'll find a partial list in Chapter 6.) There are plenty of marvelous writing guides for beginners! (I've written one called *Seize the Story*.) But the writing advice here is directed at those who have already written at least half of a novel.

Ready? Off we go!

first drafts

If you think first drafts are shiny and fun, please accept my congratulations and then skip ahead to the next section—about beginnings.

The rest of you, hang in with me.

First drafts. Sigh. Really, the only way to get through a first draft is to get through it. Bleah! And furthermore, ack. Not to mention, bleah-ack.

Sketchy at Best

First drafts are to writers as sketches are to artists. They're not meant to be the final artwork. They're meant to allow you to get some communication going between yourself and your story. And unlike doing revisions and polishing your pages, writing a first draft is about letting things be messy and uncertain. You're exploring a story idea. Explorers do not know in advance what they will discover, nor do they know exactly where they're going when they set out.

Should You Outline?

Should you outline before writing your first draft? That's a question only you can answer. My informal polling of fiction writers reports that only about a third of them outline their books before writing. And those who do always diverge from their outline as soon as their characters show any spunk. The consensus: *There will be times when all you can do is wander around lost.* That's when it's easiest to give up and most important to keep going.

Many authors develop rituals to help keep up their momentum. Write 500 words, stand up, brew some coffee or tea, go a few rounds with a hula hoop, talk to the cat, write another 500 words. Whatever works for you, rituals can provide a framework to keep you on track.

Set word-count goals for each day and keep them. Ideally, your goals will be high enough to challenge you but not so high that you're bound to fail. The idea is to develop consistency and momentum. It's perfectly fine to start small. Even 200 words a day, 6 days a week is 62,400 words in a year, which is a reasonable length for a YA novel's first draft.

National Novel Writing Month

Have you heard of National Novel Writing Month, which happens each November? Affectionately known as NaNoWriMo, or NaNo for short, this program has helped thousands of people gain enough momentum to get through a first draft. The goal for NaNo is to write 50,000 words in a month. That's 1,667 words a day for 30 days, or it's 2,500 words 5 days a week for 4 weeks—or whatever combination

---

you customize. The mindset is one of cranking those words out. Pay no attention to careful wording, exquisite characterization, or nuanced subplots. Quantity over quality. Just get it done! And there's something about joining other people who have the same goal as you do that creates an atmosphere: All participants get to feed off the energy of the totality. If you haven't already tried NaNo, why not sign up for the next round? Just go to http://www.nanowrimo.org to learn more.

Critique groups or writing buddies can help keep you accountable with your word count goals throughout the year. Sometimes I'll meet with a writing buddy just to sit across the table from each other and write. I also meet with my critique group once a week. Knowing that they're going to be there with pages and expect me to be there, keeps me from weaseling out of writing.

In short, get that first draft written! When it's done, admire it in all of its abominable glory. Once you have a draft, you get to start over again—from the beginning.

beginnings

Have you started at the beginning? Just so you know, most writers do not. (This morning, I cut out the beginning of a novel I'd been working on for a year and a half.) Why is this? Because there's a tendency to cover too much of the backstory in the first chapters without realizing it.

How do you know where a story begins? You want to be *in media res*, which means "in the middle of things." Think of your own favorite YA books. Where do they start?

Let's look at two popular YA level books, one classic and one modern, both with wide readerships: *Pride and Prejudice* by Jane Austen (1813/1996) and *The Hunger Games* by Suzanne Collins (2008). *Pride and Prejudice* has demonstrated lasting appeal: Although it was first published in 1813, it has continued to captivate new fans in each succeeding generation. *The Hunger Games* is also likely to reach new readers for years to come; as of now, there are millions of copies in print.

The beginning of *Pride and Prejudice* shows that Jane Austen really understood the concept of *in media res*. She didn't start her novel with the birth of Jane Bennet and then her sister Elizabeth. She began when the sisters were young women, on the day that Charles Bingley and his fascinating friend Mr. Darcy were about to enter the picture. Conceivably, Austen could have begun with scenes of family life as the elder Bennet girls learned their manners and gradually reached a marriageable age. But if she had dithered around in the backstory that way, Austen would not be one of the most beloved novelists of all time.

The Hunger Games begins with a short section establishing 16-year-old Katniss Everdeen's daily life: her skill with a bow developed by hunting with her friend, Gale; her love for her younger sister, Primrose; her anger toward her depressed mother who is mourning the loss of Katniss's father. The first scenes make it clear that Katniss lives a straitened existence under an oppressive regime. Then the story moves rapidly to the moment when Katniss volunteers to take Prim's place in the Hunger Games, precipitating a confluence of dangers. If Suzanne Collins had drawn out her beginning to include the gradual intensification of hardships endured by the people in her dystopian world, it would have taken too long to get her protagonist into the arena of the games.

Scrutinize your own opening chapter. Maybe you've spent time tweaking and retweaking every sentence. But now it's time to ask yourself if your beginning is actually the point where your main character's life is about to change dramatically.

Sometimes it helps to try pretending that your book starts with Chapter 2. Would Chapter 1 really be missed? Might it be boiled down to a sentence that fits into Chapter 2? If so, you *must get rid of* the existing Chapter 1.

Writers have trouble with this, becoming quite attached to the beginning that's already there. Throwing out a whole chapter (or two or three) can even feel so traumatic that authors have referred to it as "killing your darlings." Real tears are shed over this. But hanging on to a first chapter that doesn't belong in your book would be like . . . well, carrying around the placenta after a child is born. Your initial beginning may have taken you—the writer—into your novel, but will it do the same for your readers? What gets *you* started is almost never the same as what gets the *story* started. Learning to recognize the difference is critical to your success as a writer. I can't tell you how many times I've seen writers confuse their own entry point with the true beginning of their novel. Why do so many make this mistake? My theory: Writing an entire novel is such a big deal, if we didn't start with something familiar and friendly, we'd be too intimidated to begin at all.

When you write your beginning, maybe you feel more secure starting with a description of your protagonist's dinner table, or a meandering road, or a bird building a nest. And if writing about your hero's breakfast gets you going and takes you all the way to Chapter 2, great! Go ahead and write about crisp crumbs falling from a toasted muffin, and blackberry jam dripping artfully onto a plate. But unless it's really integral to *in media res*, the chapter that opens the way for you *as a writer* must be tossed.

Bits and Pieces

If you can't bring yourself to get rid of those delicious words you've written, here's another important tip: *highlight and move*. Or, if you prefer: *cut and paste*. Here's how it's done: Start a new document and save it as "bits and pieces of (fill in the name of your novel)." Determine exactly how much of the first chapter (or second and possibly third chapters) is getting in the way of a strong opening. Highlight those sections, then use the cut and paste feature to place them into the bits and pieces document. Voila! You have solved the problem. You don't have to slaughter your beloved sentences; all you need to do is move them. (Hint: This method can be used anywhere in your book.)

It *is* possible that you'll use a few lines from that bits and pieces file somewhere else. Maybe, as your protagonist confronts onerous complications, she has a moment remembering the simple delights of breakfast back home. If so, your details about blackberry jam will create verisimilitude. Fine. It's all good, so long as you don't add something that doesn't belong just because it's well written.

Turning Points

In your opening chapter, you'll establish what life is like for your protagonist right before the turning point that launches your story. What is a turning point? It's a point of decision, a crossroads where the protagonist must face something that makes it impossible to continue in the same direction and also impossible to go back. These turning points happen throughout a novel, but there will be a significant turning point somewhere close to the start, and it's known as the *inciting incident*. In *Pride and Prejudice*, Elizabeth Bennet meets Mr. Darcy on page 15, and his pride ignites her prejudice. This incident sets off everything that follows. At the end of Chapter 1 of *The Hunger Games*, Primrose Everdeen's name is picked to be a tribute. Katniss then volunteers to take her sister's place, which puts the rest of the main action into motion.

In the YA genre today, it's best if the inciting incident occurs within the first 10–15 pages. Any later than that, and you've probably earned yourself a rejection slip. If your story allows, it's even better to get to the inciting incident by page 5.

You'll create a series of greater and lesser turning points as your story gets off the ground and your characters establish who they are. Mr. Bingley is smitten with Jane Bennet. Mr. Wickham appears and charms the young ladies. Katniss leaves for the Capitol and meets her stylist and the people she'll be fighting.

Difference Between a Chapter and a Scene

What is the difference between a chapter and a scene? A scene is part of a story with a particular focus and mood. It has a beginning, middle, and end, usually in a single location. A chapter may consist of multiple scenes or only one, depending on the way the author structures his or her novel. Chapters usually end at a turning point, which can be either big or small.

In *Pride and Prejudice*, the first chapter consists of a single scene, a conversation between Mr. and Mrs. Bennet. But the first chapter of *The Hunger Games* has several short scenes, and each of them contributes to the understanding of Katniss's daily life before Prim's name is drawn and everything changes.

In general, scenes in YA novels are shorter than scenes in books written for adults. Chapters may be long or short depending on the individual writer. The idea is to keep the pace moving.

Pacing

What does pacing really mean when writing YA? Pacing refers to what happens to whom and how fast. It's also about what you leave out and what you put in.

If you leave out too much, your story will become lifeless or too confusing to follow. How and why does Mrs. Bennet speak to her husband about Mr. Bingley? This is important. What are the rules of the Hunger Games lottery? Give your readers what they need to know, but don't give them too much. Too many details will bog down your book. We don't need to know every last ruffle on the gowns that Elizabeth Bennet wears in the presence of Mr. Darcy. We don't need a painstaking description of each bowstring Katniss Everdeen might draw.

Beginnings and Endings Are Connected

Another thing to consider about your beginning: It has a close relationship with your ending. So until you know the ending, you don't really know where your book truly starts. The endings for *Pride and Prejudice* and *The Hunger Games* are completely connected to their beginnings. The Bennet sisters get married. Katniss survives the grueling games.

plotting

"How do you come up with a plot?" is one of the most frequent questions I've been asked. Plenty of writers struggle with plotting, so don't feel alone if you're one of them.

Germinal Ideas

Book ideas come about in mysterious ways. Sometimes, they seem to arise fully formed. More often, there's only a vague notion to start with.

In the quest for ideas, many writers find it useful to ask "What if?" (What if a fashion disaster changed a teenager's life? What if a tyrant succeeded in controlling technology? What if a teenage girl met Sherlock Holmes when he was 54?) By marinating in the imaginative space between waking and sleeping, the unconscious mind may deliver enticing scraps of dreams. (What if a princess could see any future but her own?) It can also be fun to brainstorm with friends. (What would Jane Austen say if she met you and me?) Whatever your personal creative style may be, it's worth exploring.

Cause and Effect

Cause and effect is a vital concept when building a plot. In fiction, when characters change, the reasons are clear. Scenes build on each other in a way that readers can follow. Dots are connected. Coincidences are to be avoided, especially if they resolve sticky plot points.

"But," people say, "that's not always true in reality." And yes, in daily life, coincidences are everywhere; things happen even when the dots cannot be connected or the dots are invisible. But not so in fiction. Actions taken in one part of the story lead to actions taken in another. Action, reaction. Cause and effect. This principle is integral to creating a convincing plot.

Important as the concept of cause and effect may be, it doesn't account for a strong plot all by itself. There is also the underlying structure of the story to consider. The best book I've found on the subject of story structure is *The Seven Basic Plots* by Christopher Booker (2004). This impressive and scholarly work lays out the structure of seven plots and uses numerous examples to explore the permutations of each. It deserves careful reading from start to finish.

Overview of the Seven Plots

To give you a taste of what you'll find in *The Seven Basic Plots*, I've paraphrased and consolidated each one. As you look through them, keep an eye out for which of the seven fit(s) your own novel.

1. Overcoming the Monster (*Dracula, Harry Potter*)
   - Protagonist hears of a monster, which may be human or nonhuman.
   - Protagonist experiences initial success and thinks the monster can be overcome.
   - Setbacks! The monster proves to be worse than the protagonist knew.
   - Ordeal: The monster shows itself—and it's bad! Protagonist is nearly defeated.
   - Escape for the protagonist, death of the monster. Protagonist overcomes monster.

2. Rags to Riches (*Ugly Duckling, The Light of the Oracle*)
   - Protagonist starts out poor and/or obscure.
   - Protagonist is wretchedly mistreated and scorned.
   - Everything goes wrong for the protagonist.
   - Through self-discovery, the protagonist develops inner strength and confronts what holds him or her back.
   - Fulfillment: The protagonist ends up rich and famous or at least greatly appreciated due to inner qualities that have been developed or revealed.

3. The Quest (*Lord of the Rings, Watership Down*)
   - The protagonist hears of treasure or a promised land far away.
   - Protagonist decides to make a journey to gain the treasure or the promised land.
   - Companions are chosen or possibly fated to go along.
   - Long journey for protagonist and companions follows, during which dangers mount.
   - Protagonist and companions find valuable help or advice.
   - Intense ordeal makes treasure or promised land seem impossible to attain.

➤ Tested to the fullest, the protagonist survives, proving worthy.

➤ Success: The protagonist wins the princess/prince and establishes a new kingdom, new world, or new way of life.

4. Voyage and Return (*The Secret to Lying, The Wizard of Oz*)

➤ Protagonist's ordinary world is shattered, throwing him or her into a different world.

➤ Protagonist explores the new world. Despite wonders, doesn't feel at home.

➤ Shadow appears, bringing hardship and frustration.

➤ Shadow almost takes over.

➤ Death-defying escape for the protagonist.

➤ Protagonist returns home wiser.

5. Comedy (*Pride and Prejudice, The Seer and the Sword*) This one needs a short intro because we are conditioned to associate the word "comedy" with something funny, even silly. However, in this context, to be funny is not the defining feature of the plotline.

➤ One or more characters are trapped in a life situation that's bleak or frustrating.

➤ The true nature of one or more characters is hidden.

➤ Lovers are separated by misunderstandings, or families/ friends are divided.

➤ Characters experience a change of heart.

➤ True natures are revealed.

➤ Misunderstandings clear up, bringing happiness and union.

➤ Lovers/families/friends are united or restored.

6. Tragedy (*Romeo and Juliet, Candor*)

➤ Protagonist casts about cluelessly and then focuses on something he or she wants.

➤ Protagonist commits to action.

➤ Things go wrong.

➤ Things get worse.

➤ Despair sets in.

➤ Protagonist is destroyed—by death or other forces.

7. Rebirth (*A Christmas Carol, The Hunger Games*)

➤ Protagonist falls under oppressive force or threat.

> ➤ For a while this threat seems to be contained or neutralized.
> ➤ The threat worsens.
> ➤ Protagonist experiences a living hell.
> ➤ The oppressive force seems to triumph.
> ➤ Something occurs that allows the protagonist to see the light.
> ➤ Protagonist is redeemed or set free or brought into a better existence.
>
> By examining the steps in each of these plots, you can discover useful clues about structuring your own novel. Which of the seven plots applies to your book? Where does the story begin and end? And what is the central conflict?

conflict

Every teen who has navigated through adolescence into adulthood has known days when conflict seemed overpowering.

Yay!

What?

Well, stories need conflict—like a car needs an engine. When's the last time you were riveted by a book about a sweet guy who met a darling girl and everything went wonderfully well for them and then got even smoother?

Writing conflict isn't just about adding a little tension here and there. It's about a clash of forces or values or personalities, something that escalates and doesn't go away until it's finally resolved.

Central Conflict

Your beginning will introduce the central conflict that drives your book. That central conflict will pose a question to the reader. Often, this question will never be stated outright, and yet it will inform every scene.

All of the action taking place in the story will revolve around that central question. For example, the central conflict in *Pride and Prejudice* is implied by the title: Pride and prejudice oppose true love. Readers ask themselves: *Will Darcy and Elizabeth win true love, or will their pride and prejudice keep them apart?*

Subplots each have a conflict as well, a conflict *related* to the central conflict, that also generates questions in the reader's mind. In *Pride and Prejudice*, Elizabeth's sister Jane is separated from her true love, Charles Bingley, by the conniving deceit of his friends and family members who desire him to marry someone with more elevated social status than Jane possesses. The reader wonders: *Will true love overcome interference, deceit, and social snobbery?* There are numerous subplots in Austen's masterpiece, but all are related to true love or its lack. If these subplots veered off into a different area of conflict—such as life or death in the face of dire physical danger, confronting the way magical powers can corrupt the human soul, or questioning the ramifications of free will—the novel would become absurd.

The central conflict in *The Hunger Games* is also implied in the title: Cruelty and terrible danger can break the human spirit. Readers ask: *Will Katniss Everdeen be broken?* And there are various subplots asking various questions, all related to the central conflict: *If Katniss survives, what will her survival cost her? Will Peeta continue to love her? Will her sister Primrose be safe?*

Conflict Seeks Resolution

Conflict seeks resolution, so characters in conflict are compelled to act. And action fueled by conflict is much more interesting than action with no conflict behind it.

In the cruel lottery of the Hunger Games, Katniss is not chosen: Primrose, her beloved younger sister, is picked. Katniss feels so much pain at the thought of Prim perishing in the games that she volunteers to take her place. Her love for her sister intensifies her hatred for the oppressive regime that forces young people to participate in the games. She must act.

Internal and External Conflict

If you've read any writing books, you've come across a mention of the differences between internal and external conflict, so I'll just give them a cursory glance here.

Internal conflict. Internal conflict is between the character and himself or herself. Characters may be at odds with their personal past, struggling with faults or addictions, wrestling with contradictory beliefs or ethical dilemmas, grieving a loss, or caught in any powerful emotion.

Elizabeth Bennet filters everything through a prejudice she quickly forms against Mr. Darcy, and he, in turn, looks at life through a lens of personal pride. Their flaws get in the way of their love, and drive them to take actions they regret.

Katniss is gripped by feelings of love and of hate; she longs for peace and also desires vengeance. These emotions are a potent brew that drives her to take extreme risks.

External conflict. External conflict is between a character and something or someone outside himself or herself. External antagonists are most often humans but occasionally are animals or fantasy creatures. Antagonists can also take the form of nature—storms, mountains, deserts—or they can be machines. Situational conflicts such as poverty, war, and societal oppression can also oppose a character's goals and wishes.

Elizabeth Bennet contends with foolish and angry relatives, false friends, and unhelpful parents. She must rise to the occasion or lose out on love. Katniss Everdeen encounters numerous external conflicts during the course of the games, from thirst to fireballs to venomous insects, all of which can be lethal. She must defeat them or die.

Combine internal and external conflict. By combining internal and external conflict, you ramp up the tension driving your story. If Elizabeth Bennet had only her own prejudice to deal with, *Pride and Prejudice* would not be such a great book. But Austen layers her story with other problems. If Katniss Everdeen had only external dangers to fight, her story would not be one tenth as captivating. But Collins forces her character to combat panic, self-doubt, and hallucinations, combining internal and external conflict throughout *The Hunger Games*.

Pace Your Conflict

If you give your characters short periods of relief from their struggles, you provide contrast and context. A book that is one long battle would be just as boring as a book showing nothing but peace and joy. Without light, shadows cannot be thrown.

Conflict will be expressed differently depending on where you are in your book. The beginning introduces the central conflict. The middle adds twists and turns with additional complications. The ending resolves the central conflict. (More about middles and ends in Chapter 3.)

Complications

Circumstances conspire to add complications to existing conflict, making it worse. Elizabeth Bennet attends Bingley's ball, hoping to enjoy herself, but she is pursued by Mr. Collins, the absurdly pretentious cousin who hopes to marry her. Mr. Collins treads on her toes and makes the wrong moves during dancing. Not only that, but her new crush, George Wickham, doesn't show for the ball, and she blames Mr. Darcy. Complications. Her parents and younger sisters parade their foibles, alarming Darcy so much that he intervenes to separate his friend Bingley from Jane. More complications. Elizabeth's prejudices are confirmed; Darcy's pride dictates his actions.

The rules of the Hunger Games require Katniss to fight other "tributes" to the death. One of those tributes is someone from her own district: Peeta the baker's boy, whom she knows to be a kind-hearted person. How can she kill him? And the territory of the games is unknowable because it constantly changes. These complications add pressure to a situation that's already unbearable. Will Katniss be broken?

Complications are a big part of novel writing. Believable complications heighten the central conflict and stoke the tension so long as they fit the characters and the plot. If Jane Austen had added a complication from *The Hunger Games,* such as forcing her protagonist to spend the night in a tree to escape death, that complication would not fit the character or the story being told. If Suzanne Collins had added a complication from *Pride and Prejudice,* such as a mother who couldn't open her mouth without being hopelessly silly, that complication wouldn't fit either. Examine the complications in your own novel. Do they fit the characters and the plot? Are there enough of them?

In the section on characters, we'll address the importance of stakes for each character. Suffice it to say here: Character stakes are crucial to the conflict.

Conflict Must Feel Real

To resonate with your readers, the conflict driving your story must feel actual and real. When you, the writer, truly feel the conflict you're writing about, it's easier to communicate it to your readers.

Every adversity, challenge, or hardship you've ever faced can help fuel your fiction. It's all there to be tapped—not only your own conflict, but also what you've observed in other people, and the troubles you've been told. And if there's one thing you don't want to do when writing YA, it's to skimp on the conflict.

Writing Exercise—Finding Conflict

1. Write something you've wanted to say but never said. Don't hold back—this is for you and you alone. No one else will see it, and after you look at what you've written you can shred or delete it.

2. Before shredding or deleting, look at what you've written. Ask yourself whether you held back. (Most writers will find that they've held back in some way.)

3. If you did hold back, do you know why you did, or for whom?

4. What does this tell you about conflicts you could utilize in your writing?

5. Jot down a few ideas you have for stories. Look at the element of conflict in each. Which idea is the most compelling? Which conflict is the most gripping? See the relationship?

Conflict and Story Arc

In essence, the arc of a story is about the rise of the central conflict, which becomes increasingly intense until it demands resolution. Not all resolutions are happy and bring about redemption or success for the protagonist. But one way or another, the central conflict is concluded, and the central question is answered. Elizabeth and Darcy find true love. Katniss survives, at great cost.

Conflict in YA

Intertwine the central conflict in your YA novel with the theme of coming-of-age. Naturally, when writing YA, your protagonist will not be a seasoned veteran facing the winter of life. He or she will be a young person encountering the difficulties of growing up.

message

Your message is intimately connected to your central conflict: It arises from your resolution. We're all familiar with messages that have been beloved by storytellers for centuries: love conquers all, good triumphs over evil, the soul is eternal. What about *your* book?

Many people use the term "premise" instead of "message." I like using message because the word doesn't invite confusion. "Premise" is often used to refer to the underpinnings of a particular world or milieu. By that definition, the premise of *The Hunger Games* is that North America turns into Panem, a repressive regime where the Capitol feeds off the labor of 12 districts, each of which supply it with different commodities. These underpinnings are not the same as what I mean by a message.

What Is the Message?

The main message I derive from *Pride and Prejudice* is "True love overcomes pride and prejudice, leading to happy marriage." And in the centuries since Jane Austen wrote her book, this message has been discussed by many thousands of readers. Some agree with that message, and some do not. Whether readers agree or they don't, Austen's message is flawlessly portrayed in her novel.

To me, the main message in *The Hunger Games* is "Courage must fight oppression, whatever the costs—and the costs will be high."

It's important to note that the central message in any given novel can be anything the author chooses to make it. The message doesn't need to hold true for all of the world, but it must hold true for that particular novel. If Elizabeth Bennet had found true love without ever having to confront her prejudice, the message of *Pride and Prejudice* would not have been able to stand. If Katniss Everdeen had been broken, the message in *The Hunger Games* would have changed to become "Even the brave are completely broken by oppression."

Your Message Is a Unifying Principle

Is it necessary to know your message before you begin writing? No, although the message is such an important unifying principle within your novel that if you know what it is while you're writing, you're likely to save yourself some time. And when you self-edit, you definitely want to know it.

Scenes that do not support your message do not belong in your book. This bears repeating: *Scenes that do not support your message do not belong in your book.* By support, I mean that when the scene is broken down, it is related to the central question posed by the conflict, and it serves to build toward the conclusion. If even one scene veers off course from the message, your novel will be weakened.

Subplot Messages

Can there be more than one message in your book? Yes and no. The main message will give rise to others, and these will be found in subplots. In *Pride and Prejudice*, Elizabeth's friend Charlotte enters a loveless marriage. The irritations of her situation only highlight the happiness of the couples who find true love. The message of Charlotte's subplot, "Marriage without true love cannot lead to happiness," is closely related to the main message. In another subplot, Elizabeth's flighty and conceited younger sister, Lydia, gets married, but her husband is a worthless con artist who is apparently incapable of true love. This subplot says "Without true love, pride and prejudice are not overcome," bringing us back to the main message by being its mirror image.

Themes

The subject of themes can be confusing, because people often use the word "theme" interchangeably with "message" and with "premise." This is understandable, because such usage is consistent with dictionary.com's definition of theme—"a unifying or dominant idea, motif, etc., as in a work of art." However, I would like to define theme a little differently when discussing novel writing, as "a feature that runs through a novel."

In *Pride and Prejudice*, family is a prominent theme. Family relationships are portrayed as a very mixed bag. Both Elizabeth and Mr. Darcy have relatives who epitomize obnoxiousness, although in different ways. The antics of these people provide high entertainment value along with escalating complications. But the good points of family are not overlooked: Elizabeth experiences the full blessings of family in her sister Jane and her Aunt Gardiner, while Darcy dotes on his sister Georgiana. Another theme is the repeated appearance of characters who think far too well of themselves, such as Lydia, Mr. Wickham, Mr. Collins, and Lady Catherine. And of course, the theme of marriage itself is found in many guises in Austen's novel: Marriage relationships range from miserably incompatible to delightfully harmonious. Without these themes, the message of true love could still hold, but Austen chose themes of family, ridiculous conceit, and marriage to tell her story.

The Hunger Games relies on themes of friendship and alliance. Katniss forges friendships with people who become her allies, from her friend Gale back in District 12, to her stylist in the Capitol, to her drunken mentor Haymitch, to other contestants in the Games. Katniss could have fought alone and the novel could still have retained its main message, but Suzanne Collins chose themes of friendship and alliance to advance her story.

Both novels are also infused with the overarching theme so important to the YA genre: coming of age. Loss of innocence and growing maturity create context for all of the actions taken by the main characters and some of the secondary characters as well.

To summarize: Themes are woven throughout a novel, but they are not the same as its message. They are features. And when you choose the features for your own book, pick a few and play them up. Too many themes will make the reader feel disoriented, but a few clear and consistent themes create a believable sense of continuity and help with characterization.

Edit Your Content

Scenes or themes that are alien to the basic message in a novel do not create interesting complexity: They merely clutter the meaning and reduce its impact on the reader. So as you self-edit, check to be sure each scene supports the main message and that the themes you have chosen fit your novel and your genre. Then give those themes continuous play.

setting

The setting is the environment where your story takes place. It "sets" the tone. Katniss travels from place to place in *The Hunger Games*: She starts out in District 12, and then moves onto the train for the Capitol. Once she reaches the Capitol, she resides in the luxurious quarters for tributes, where she is fluffed and buffed by her style team as well as spending time in the training center. When she gets to the arena for the games, more settings come into play: the lake and cornucopia, the forest, specific trees, a pool, stream, and cave. Each setting contains separate scenes; each contributes to the mood and action happening in those scenes.

Elizabeth Bennet experiences various locales in *Pride and Prejudice* and these varieties of setting help move the plot, but by today's standards, Austen's descriptions of setting are rather limited because they lack sensory details.

Physical settings have an emotional impact that can greatly enhance your story. Imagine yourself, right now, sitting on the edge of the Grand Canyon while reading this paragraph. Then imagine that you're sitting at a sidewalk café in Paris. Notice the change in feeling? As you pick your settings, maximize the ability of place to create mood.

Watch for Clichés

When writing your first draft, you may have thrown your characters into settings that were a bit humdrum and cliché. Maybe you overused a coffee shop for scenes where a friendship develops or a school hallway for telling secrets. I'm not saying there's no place for coffee shops or school hallways—especially in contemporary YA novels. But if you can come up with unique settings, your story will thank you. A friendship developed during the hustle and bustle of a tournament, or a deep secret exchanged in a stadium, will be more intriguing because the action is unexpected for the setting. A fight in a coffee shop would also be interesting, for the same reason—because a coffee shop conjures a feeling of warmth and conversation among friends.

Describe Settings Through the Senses

To make the most of your settings, describe them through the senses. This doesn't mean going on and on: A scattering of sentences every few pages is usually plenty in a YA novel: More than that, and you'll slow the pace too much. But vision, hearing, touch, taste, and smell each offer something to bring readers right into the story you're telling. Most of us tend to focus on one or two senses and forget about the rest. Personally, I often forget smell and taste, and I have to remind myself to sprinkle some of those details in later.

Author Laura Resau incorporates four senses to describe the Plaza de Ponchos, a Guatemalan marketplace, in this excerpt from her 2009 YA novel, *The Indigo Notebook*:

> I weave through the tunnels of stalls that smell of wool fresh off llamas and sheep and alpaca, an earthy animal smell mixing with the exhaust of passing cars. Tourists are chatting with vendors, reaching out to test the itchiness level of a poncho. Or holding up a brown sweater beside a gray sweater to decide which color

looks best. Meanwhile, the vendors are cajoling in singsong voices, a mix of Spanish and heavily accented English. (p. 18)

By mixing scents, textures, voices, and colors, Resau quickly conveys a vivid sense of place.

Use Setting to Reveal Character Emotion and Perspective

The way characters view items in a setting is a great way to offer insight into their emotions, adding dimension to characters' personalities for the reader. Here's a description of a portfolio by the viewpoint character, Catherine de' Medici, in Carolyn Meyer's (2007) historical novel, *Duchessina*:

On a high shelf reached by a ladder, I discovered a portfolio containing a number of drawings of an elephant; some were in red chalk on gray paper, others were pen and ink sketches on parchment. According to notes in the portfolio, the elephant, named Hanno, had been a gift from the king of Portugal to Leo. Pope Leo had kept Hanno in an enclosure within the Vatican walls. I felt I had something in common with Hanno—the poor elephant must have been lonely, too. (p. 145)

Time

Setting is not just about place—it's also about time. To orient your reader, make it plain how time is unfolding. Is it morning, afternoon, evening? What is the time of year? How many days have passed since Lydia ran off with Wickham? How long has it been since another tribute was killed in the Hunger Games arena? Don't make your readers guess.

If it's night and your characters are outside, remember to account for the darkness when describing visual objects. If you've just finished detailing an overpowering odor of rotten fish, don't immediately have your protagonist pick up a whiff of something subtle such as saffron (unless he or she has special doglike abilities). If 10 car alarms are rupturing the air, don't ask your characters to carry on a conversation in whispers at the same time. You get the idea.

Flashbacks. A flashback acquaints the reader with a previous time in a novel's fictional world, a time before page 1 that explains something crucial about the present. Memories will naturally arise in the minds of characters, and that's fine *if those memories contribute something of value* to the story, especially if they're confined to the occasional sentence or two. Full scenes in flashback mode are sometimes necessary too, *if they explain a key plot point.* But flashbacks slow your pace, so keep your characters in the present as much as possible; use flashbacks sparingly, and when you do, trim them as much as you can.

Here's a line of flashback from my romantic fantasy, *The Seer and the Sword* (Hanley, 2000). It was originally a longer memory, but I trimmed it into one line in a sentence: "Landen consciously slowed his breathing as he approached Emid, reminding himself what his father had taught him: *The moment is vast*" (p. 30).

Era. Time also adds the crucial concept of *era*, another aspect of setting. The era in which your book happens will shape your characters and have a big influence on the actions they take.

In *Pride and Prejudice,* the social and moral views of 19th-century England provide texture for the plot. Charlotte marries Mr. Collins—a man she must exert herself to tolerate—simply to avoid being a lifelong spinster dependent on family members. Sixteen-year-old Lydia's actions reflect directly on all of her family members—and she does not get a second chance to find true love. "The poor" are referred to as a collective unit rather than individual people with lives, while being rich is a striking qualification for seeking a wife. Social status and social protocol regulate the possibilities of almost every situation.

The era of *The Hunger Games* is a sharply divided futuristic society. In the districts, conditions are primitive for residents, most of whom do without luxuries of any sort and eke out a precarious existence only by being strong, cunning, and hardworking. Starvation is commonplace, and so are lethal injuries. But in the Capitol, high levels of technology are utilized by the citizens, who are well-fed and steeped in luxury. These people are also conditioned to view the Hunger Games, a brutal and deathly competition that takes place every year, as sheer entertainment, something to place bets on, a pageant to either heckle or applaud.

The era of your story has many components. How do your characters dress? What sorts of dwellings do they have? What is the climate—not only the weather, but also the social climate? How important is social hierarchy, and where do your characters fit within that hierarchy? What has taken place in recent history? What about ancient history—how is it perceived?

Even if ancient history is mentioned only once in your novel—or never mentioned—it's still important for you, the author, to know about it, because it has played a role in creating the culture that surrounds your characters.

Culture

Speaking of culture, which values are embedded in your story's civilization? What do people cherish and revile? How are young people treated, and what is their traditional place in society? How much education do your characters have? How do people talk?

dialogue

Characters reveal themselves through the actions they take and the words they speak. Used well, dialogue is your best shot at showing character relationships and personalities and providing context for character actions.

Jane Austen's gift for writing dialogue is a big part of why her stories capture the hearts of readers—and filmmakers—even after centuries have passed. Although she wrote her books 200 or more years ago, we can still learn from her. One of the many things she did right was to give Elizabeth Bennet an extra helping of spunk. This excerpt from early in *Pride and Prejudice* showcases Lizzy's spirit. Her mother has been talking about Jane Bennet's beauty and how when Jane was 15 a gentleman wrote her some verses:

"And so ended his affection," said Elizabeth, impatiently. "There has been many a one, I fancy, overcome in the same way. I wonder who first discovered the efficacy of poetry in driving away love!"

"I have been used to consider poetry as the food of love," said Darcy.

"Of a fine, stout, healthy love it may. Everything nourishes what is strong already. But if it be only a slight, thin sort of inclination, I am convinced that one good sonnet will starve it entirely away." (pp. 57–58)

When Elizabeth talks, readers want more. What about you? Have you given your characters extra-large personalities? What do they reveal about themselves in what they say?

Era Matters in Dialogue

Of course, contemporary teens would be unlikely to use words like "efficacy" unless they were diehard Jane Austen fans. But it's a mistake to think that every modern young person will use only a limited vocabulary. I've met plenty of teens who love words and bemoan the banal scripts expected of them. The trick to getting teens to sound like teens is not to limit their vocabulary but to get them to speak in their own voices, saying things that ring true for their characters and era.

In Todd Mitchell's contemporary YA novel, *The Secret to Lying* (2010), the characters are attending a school for the academically gifted:

"Put a cream puff up your butt," Heinous sang, catching up to us. His most recent shtick involved making up lyrics to Eddie Murphy's classic, "Boogie in Your Butt."

"Put numchucks up your butt. Put a fluffy duck up your butt. Put an Oompa-Loompa up your butt."

"The humor in this particular saying," Dickie replied, mocking the way Mr. Funt, the sophomore class English teacher spoke, "being that, technically speaking, an Oompa-Loompa would not fit up one's buttocks, not to mention the fact that Willy Wonka would never permit such egregious treatment of his workers. Thus, the ridiculousness of the claim, which leads to laughter." (p. 33)

The tone of this exchange is modern; when read aloud it's easy to believe that teenagers are talking. And the subtext tells readers that Heinous and Dickie are intelligent and creative, and also that they're adolescent boys who are trying to make up for being bored. It's so much more effective to communicate this by giving the characters genuine voices of their own than it would be through narration. That's the beauty of dialogue.

More About Subtext

Subtext in dialogue can communicate volumes to a reader. Let's examine a short passage from *The Hunger Games*. Katniss is about to leave for the Capitol, and this is her good-bye conversation with her best friend, Gale.

> "Katniss, it's just hunting. You're the best hunter I know," says Gale.
> "It's not just hunting. They're armed. They think," I say.
> "So do you. And you've had more practice. Real practice," he says. "You know how to kill."
> "Not people," I say.
> "How different can it be, really?" says Gale grimly. (p. 40)

If that particular section of dialogue had been written with the subtext out in the open, it would have been much less interesting:

> "Katniss, I've seen you hunt, and you're a great hunter. You have a chance to succeed if you can get your head around killing people."
> "Gale, because you're my hunting partner and I trust you, I can tell you what I won't tell anyone else: I'm afraid of going up against people who are armed and trying to kill me, people who could outthink my strategies."
> "What matters now is that you know how to kill."
> "I don't want to kill people."
> "The idea of killing people doesn't bother me, and it shouldn't bother you, either."

Isn't it appalling how dense and stilted dialogue becomes when subtext is brought to the surface? The only thing worse would be if the meaning in the subtext were converted into narrative prose, as in this hypothetical example: Gale knew that Katniss was a great hunter. He thought she had a chance to succeed in the Hunger Games if she could only get her head around the idea of killing people. After all, she'd killed many animals. But Katniss was afraid of going up against people who were armed and trying to kill her, people capable of anticipating her hunting strategies.

Gah! See what I mean? This might work for a first draft that was written just for the writer. But if all of the subtext in a novel is brought out and explained, the book quickly loses texture and interest.

Check your dialogue for subtext. If you don't find any, chances are good that your dialogue exchanges are too lengthy and transparent. Look for ways to be more oblique, and trim what you can. Often, less is more. Distill your words. Ask each word of dialogue two questions: Are you believable? Are you necessary? If you don't get a yes to both answers, change your approach.

Dialogue Sets Up Action

In this excerpt from Joan Bauer's (2008) humorous contemporary YA, *Peeled*, the dialogue sets up the action that will take place in the next scene:

"Hildy's not afraid," Lev assured him.

"That's touching, Radner. You go with her."

"The thing is," Lev muttered, "I . . ."

"I'll go," Zack said quietly.

Baker looked at me with something close to confidence. "Show him how we play the game here."

"Okay." I waited for more detail on how we play the game. There wasn't any.

I guess we were making it up as we went along. (pp. 162–163)

Dialogue Mixed With Action

When dialogue is mixed with action, it drives the plot forward like nothing else, as in Amy Kathleen Ryan's (2011) sci-fi YA, *Glow*. This excerpt is from the point of view of Waverly, the female protagonist:

> She tried to make sense of it: Men holding guns in a room full of children. A part of her considered that she ought to feel afraid.
>
> "Don't worry," the man with the scar said. "This is a rescue mission."
>
> "Then why do you need that?" Waverly pointed at the gun.
>
> "In case something goes wrong," he said in a lilting way, as though he were talking to a girl much younger than Waverly.
>
> "What would go wrong?" she asked.
>
> His smile was thin. "I'm glad we understand each other."
>
> He jerked his gun at her, gesturing for her to enter the room. The way he turned his back on her showed that he did not expect, would not tolerate, disobedience.
>
> Her breath laboring, she looked down at Serafina, took hold of her small sweaty hand, and obeyed. (p. 29)

Ryan has created an unbearable feeling of menace by combining dialogue and action.

Slang

To slang or not to slang? Well, as I mentioned in Chapter 1, slang terms rise and fall. Some move in and out so fast that between the time you write your book and get it published, a favorite word will have left the building. If you're writing historical fiction, you have an easy out because you can research what used to be said in the period when your novel takes place. If your story is held in the future, you can make up whatever words you like and give them any cachet you wish—or take existing words and give them an added slang meaning. Here's an example from M.T. Anderson's (2002) dystopian satire, *Feed*:

> I was like trying to sleep for the last few minutes of the flight because there was nothing to see except broken things in space,

and when we're going hard I get real sleepy real easy, and I didn't want to be null for the unettes on the moon, at the hotel, if any of them were youch. (p. 5)

Anderson's placement of *null* gives it a slangy slant, while *unettes* and *youch* add credibility to the future he created.

Whether you're writing sci-fi, fantasy, or a contemporary novel, you can come up with slang that belongs to your particular group of characters.

Internal Dialogue

Especially when writing in third person, internal dialogue can be a useful tool to reveal a character's thoughts. The format for internal dialogue in prose is italics without quotation marks, as in this example from Donita K. Paul's (2004) YA Christian fantasy, *Dragonspell*:

Kale closed her eyes against the sight, hoping to protect her stomach. The repulsive smell of the grawligs could not be shut out so easily. To distract herself, she searched her memory for tales of the mountain ogres.

What's true and what's fable?

In the stories, they eat anything they catch. Lucky for me, it looks like they prefer roasted venison to roasted o'rant. (p. 7)

You'll notice that internal dialogue is written in present tense, just like spoken dialogue.

Graphic Novels Rely on Both External and Internal Dialogue

Dialogue, both internal and external, carries a large share of the story in graphic novels, as in the image from *Freshman: Tales of 9th Grade Obsessions, Revelations, and Other Nonsense* by Corinne Mucha (2011), shown on page 54.

wild ink

From *Freshman: Tales of 9th Grade Obsessions, Revelations, and Other Nonsense* by C. Mucha, 2011, p. 14, San Francisco, CA: Zest Books. Copyright 2011 Zest Books. Reprinted with permission.

Give Each Character a Distinct Voice

Not only do you want characters to communicate who they are when they talk, but also to communicate a distinct voice. If all of the characters in a novel talk in a similar way, they begin to run together and you miss out on the outstanding opportunity dialogue provides for separating character natures, motives, and goals.

characters

A discussion of all of the elements that go into fictional characters could fill pages and pages. Because space is limited and there's so much to cover, I'm going to narrow the focus to the way conflict plays into your characters' goals, motivation, and stakes.

Goals and Motivations

The difference between goals and motivations gives stories interesting depth. Most often, goals are stated and motives are hidden; goals are direct and motives are indirect. And yet motives frequently provide as much or more drive than goals.

When Katniss Everdeen enters the arena of the Hunger Games, her goal is to get hold of a bow and survive. Survival implies killing, and Katniss talks tough. But her hidden motive is to love and be loved. Love leads her to volunteer for the games. Love drives her to befriend Rue, the young contestant who reminds her of her sister, Prim. Love pushes her to help Peeta when he's wounded, even though doing so will slow her down. Her goals are in opposition to her motives, and the internal pressure this creates feeds into the central conflict. Because she won't acknowledge her own motives, Katniss comes across as clueless and blind in her interpretations of Peeta. To the reader, it's obvious he loves her, but Katniss insists on telling herself he's just acting a part.

Characters tend to be aware of their goals and unaware of their motives until the time is right within the story for those motives to become conscious. By including contrasting goals and motives, you give readers extra satisfaction. Take a moment to consider your own favorite YA books. What are the goals and motives driving the characters? How do those goals and motives oppose each other, and how do they relate to the central conflict?

Stakes

Simply put, stakes are all about what a character has to lose. Goals, motives, and situations are all put into the mix when stakes are considered. The more there is to lose, the more the stakes go up. The higher the stakes, the more potential there is for excitement. But just putting someone's life at risk doesn't guarantee a story full of interesting tension. Compelling tension is created by weaving together the central conflict, goals, and motives, and then raising the stakes in consonance with the main message.

The stakes for Elizabeth and Darcy in *Pride and Prejudice* are nothing less than true love and happiness. Jane Austen doesn't just toss out this concept casually. She clearly demonstrates that marriage without love is a miserable state. And through dialogue and action, she allows readers to get to know Elizabeth Bennet and care about her. She also manages to make Mr. Darcy very appealing despite his pride. Readers want these two to get together!

For Katniss Everdeen in *The Hunger Games*, the stakes start with physical survival and then escalate to include the possibility of mental and emotional breakdown. Suzanne Collins doesn't just tell readers to worry about Katniss, she puts her protagonist in one dire circumstance after another. Nor does she confine the hazards Katniss must face to physical challenges; she adds mind-bending venom and heart-wrenching situations, all of which are tailored to aggravate the central conflict.

Character Arc

The term "character arc" just means that characters grow and change. Motivation, goals, and stakes drive characters to take actions that result in a slew of experiences. Characters respond to these experiences. The result is growth and change.

Some characters change very little through the course of a novel, and that in itself says something about them. Others go through rapid and profound changes. Whatever happens, finding out who does what and how and why is part of what keeps readers engaged.

Chapter 3

Getting Your Book In Shape:
Novel Writing, Part 2

You finish a book several times over.
—Amy Kathleen Ryan

voice

When it comes to YA novels, that special quality known as *a fresh voice* is what every agent and editor is seeking from a new writer. So, what is this voice thing all about?

Some experts say that voice is contained in language patterns, which bring about the tone conveyed by an author's style. Others point to the author's message and how it relates to the writer's roots, background, and personality. I agree that such factors are certainly part of voice, but those definitions are unsatisfactory and incomplete, a little like saying that great singing voices can be understood by knowing the singers' temperament, upbringing, and the many muscular contractions that vibrate their vocal chords.

Voice is more than that. For singers, it's about infusing their spirit into the music. For writers, voice is about *you* infusing your spirit into what you write.

Your Inner Teen Exercise

Getting to know your adolescent self again can be a valuable touchstone. You want that inner teen by your side as you write your YA book. He or she will help you more than anyone else.

This list of questions brings up the emotions of teenhood. I suggest making notes to yourself as you go through the list. You might be surprised at which questions strike you more than others. Don't be concerned if the answers to some of the questions happened during times in your life that fell before or after ages 13–19. Remember, the spirit of youth can move us at any time. The important thing is to get a feeling for how that spirit has affected you personally.

➤ What is your clearest memory of feeling alienated? Misunderstood? Betrayed?

➤ What is the most unfair thing that has happened to you? What did you do?

➤ In what way did your upbringing seem utterly different from that of your peers?

➤ When have you gone against peer pressure to follow your conscience?

- How do you react to authority? What's an example of authority being wrong? Right?
- What has been your moment of greatest rebellion? How about your greatest dream of rebellion?
- What's the greatest risk you've taken? How did it work out?
- Have you done something impulsive that had a long-lasting effect on your life?
- Have you been disbelieved when you were telling the truth? Have you feared the truth enough to lie? Has someone lied to you about something important?
- What is the most traumatic historical event you have lived through? How close were you to the actual events of that history?
- Have you grown apart from a dear friend? If so, was it gradual or sudden?
- Have you ever been so embarrassed you wanted to sink through the floor?
- What's the most unconventional thing you've done? The most thoughtless?
- What's the biggest mistake you've ever made?
- Have you been in a situation from which there seemed to be no way out? What did you do?
- When was the loneliest time in your life? How did you deal with it?
- When did you first fall in love? What happened?
- Has someone important to you rejected you?
- Have you ever lost control completely or done something so wild you surprised yourself?
- Have you laughed so hard you cried? Cried so hard you laughed?
- Have you ever suddenly changed your appearance dramatically?
- What has been your most euphoric moment? How did it change you?
- What have you longed to do but never done?
- What have you yearned to find but never found?
- What and whom would you die for?

Now that you've finished answering these questions, do you have a sense of a teen voice inside you, one with something to say? If so, without stopping to analyze, write a paragraph or two in that voice. *Hint:* You can apply this inner teen exercise to any of the characters in your novel, asking them the same series of questions.

point of view

You have lots of tools for expressing character voice—among them dialogue and action—but point of view (POV) is key. The point of view you choose will set up the way readers experience the story you're telling.

First Person

First person is conducive to the intimate, confiding style that puts readers right in the middle of a young protagonist's head. Will your story be enhanced by offering readers details about your narrator's inner life? Do you feel close enough to your viewpoint character to be able to write convincingly *as* him or her? If so, then first person is your ideal POV.

Every writer who uses first person will treat it a little differently. Some write as if the protagonist is opening up to a diary, including thoughts and feelings as much as action and dialogue. Others spend less time on introspection. Either way, first person makes it easy to transition seamlessly from writing action to revealing a narrator's thoughts, as in this example from Chris Crutcher's (2001) *Whale Talk*:

> I stand, shoving my chair back hard enough to send it crashing to the floor—bringing us into focus as objects of attention from five tables in every direction—then step forward. [. . .] I think I've spent a record number of days out of school for letting the heat that starts in my gut rise all the way, and I do my best to keep that under control, but the day I take Barbour out will be worth finishing the year homeschooled. (p. 26)

Although I don't have formal data on the number of YA books written in first person, it's safe to say that the percentage is high. The reason for this isn't hard to figure out: In first person, protagonists have free rein to express their personalities.

Drawback to writing first person. There is a drawback to writing in first person: Action taking place "offscreen" for the protagonist must either be reported in dialogue by other characters or else deduced by the protagonist. Ideally then, the protagonist is present for any scenes central to the story. This requirement also places limits on the plot, because the protagonist can't be everywhere at once. So if you've written a number of subplots involving other characters who take actions that aren't witnessed by the protagonist, it can be challenging to present your story in first person without cutting the action or making the book "too talkie."

An advantage of first person. One of the most delightful attributes of first person is the ease with which other characters can be portrayed through the voice of the narrator. This excerpt from Stephanie Perkins's (2010) debut novel, *Anna and the French Kiss*, shows how first person can reveal traits of both the narrator and her father:

> My father isn't cultured. But he is rich.
>
> It wasn't always like this. When my parents were still married, we were strictly lower middle class. It was around the time of the divorce that all traces of decency vanished, and his dream of being the next great Southern writer was replaced by his desire to be the next *published* writer. So he started writing these novels set in Small Town Georgia about folks with Good American values who Fall in Love and then contract Life-Threatening Diseases and Die.
>
> I'm serious.
>
> And it totally depresses me, but the ladies eat it up. They love my father's books and they love his cable-knit sweaters and they love his bleached smile and orangey tan. And they have turned him into a bestseller and a total dick. (pp. 4–5)

Anna's opinion of her father is clear. And because this is early in the novel and Anna doesn't hold anything back, readers can expect that they'll get all of the juicy details of her romantic life in Paris.

First person style. Here's another first person excerpt, this one from Laurie R. King's bestselling crossover YA novel set during World War I, *The Beekeeper's Apprentice* (1994). The narrator is young Mary Russell.

I felt like the proverbial drowned rat when I reached the lodgings house. Stopping in the portico I peeled off several outer layers and left them on a nail, dripping morosely onto the stones. I could then dig an almost dry handkerchief from a pocket to clean my spectacles while I let myself into the porter's lodge. (p. 177)

I can't resist making a note here, about style and voice. In the examples above, both Perkins and King break rules of writing. (Hard and fast rules are a bit silly, aren't they?) For example, a stickler for rules might say that the word *and* appears too many times here: "They love my father's books and they love his cable-knit sweaters and they love his bleached smile and orangey tan. And they have turned him into a bestseller and a total dick." But really the sentences are splendidly structured to showcase character voice. Also note Laurie R. King's use of the modifying adverbs *morosely* and *almost*. Some writing instructors are vehemently opposed to using modifying adverbs. Ever. And yet, when it comes to character voice, it's more effective to say "dripping morosely onto the stones" than to say "dripping onto the stones." The same is true of the "almost dry" handkerchief, which in this case is far better than "damp."

So here's a new rule: *Character voice transcends rules.* Don't be afraid to ignore rules when your character's voice calls for something different!

Past tense versus present tense. Once a rarity, present tense has been gaining popularity in YA novels. Past tense and present tense carry different flavors, of course, and we'll take a closer look at those differences a little later in this chapter. For now, here are several more examples of both, to give you a sense of the differences.

Examples of first person present tense. In Allen Zadoff's (2009) *Food, Girls, and Other Things I Can't Have*, his protagonist, a guy in high school, is 100 pounds overweight. (Zadoff lost 100 pounds after high school himself, and every word of his book rings true.)

At first people call me Tighty Whitey, Fat Ass, or the Destroyer. But none of those really catch on. Then, a few days later in History class, Justin calls me Jurassic Pork.

That catches on pretty fast.

Now instead of just being some unknown fat kid, I'm JP, Jurassic Pork, the fat dinosaur who steps on people and crushes them. (p. 53)

Lauren Myracle (2005) deftly reveals her narrator's personality in *the fashion disaster that changed my life*:

I think I need those nose strip thingies I saw on a commercial, where the girl puts one on her nose, and when she pulls it off, it's covered with little stalactites of dirt. I think whoever invented those strips is very smart. It's like, did I know I was walking through life under a crust of gunk? (p. 29)

Examples of first person past tense. Here's how David Lubar (2002) opens his book *Dunk*:

His voice ripped the air like a chain saw. The harsh cry sliced straight through my guts the first time I heard it. The sound cut deep, but the words cut deeper. He shredded any fool who wandered near the cage. He drove people wild. He drove them crazy. Best of all, he drove them to blow wads of cash for a chance to plunge his sorry butt into a tank of slimy water. (p. 1)

Denise Vega (2008) conveys emotion and action in *Fact of Life #31*:

I wondered if Abra even noticed I was gone, had slunk out like a cat who'd just knocked over the sugar.

I covered my ears with my hands. I wanted to run. Down the stairs and out the door, and keep running until my lungs burst open. But my butt was superglued to the floor. (p. 12)

Nancy Garden (2006) shows her narrator's family relationships in *Endgame*:

> Mom took me to buy school clothes toward the end of the week. She let Pete buy his by himself, but me she had to take. I don't care a whole lot about clothes, but there ought to be a school to teach mothers how to buy clothes for their kids, at least when their kids are boys. (p. 25)

First person multiple. Can you have more than one first-person narrator in the same novel? Yes. Basically, you can do whatever you like when writing a novel, as long as you make it work. If your story is best told from inside the head of more than one narrator, then that's how you should write it. But be sure to bring out a distinct character voice for each narrator.

Second Person

Second person presents the narrator as "you." Few YA books are written this way, just as few are written for adults. As a style, second person is difficult to sustain for page after page of prose: It's more suited to short bursts of conversation in the lunchroom, as in, "You don't really know what you're dealing with until it hits you in the face." Even people who sometimes speak in second person don't refer to themselves as "you" each and every time, so it's quite challenging to keep up the "you" POV for the duration of a novel. However, that hasn't prevented some authors from carrying it out. Here's a YA example from Chris Barton's (2011) *Can I See Your I.D.?: True Stories of False Identities*:

> You're not stealing the train—anymore than someone can steal an escalator. It's going to come right back to where you got it, isn't it? At least, that's how you see it when you walk out on the platform with your bag containing a motor man's two main tools—a brake handle and a reverser key—along with a Day-Glo orange safety vest. (p. 3)

As you can see, in the right hands, second person has its charms. It's immediate and informal, and it creates an unusual connection with readers.

Reader as protagonist. The *Choose Your Own Adventure* (CYOA) series by R. A. Montgomery, which is written in second person and targets readers 10–14, has had an extremely successful run. CYOA stories are structured to literally address the *reader* as "you," turning him or her into the protagonist.

Second Person Writing Exercise

Oddly enough, I have found that temporarily switching to second person when writing a first draft can be a powerful leveraging tool for busting through writer's block. If any of your characters are being elusive or uncooperative, sometimes writing those characters in second person will get them talking. Try pouring out a few paragraphs and see what happens.

Third Person

Though not as prevalent as first person, third person POV is also represented in YA books. Unlike first person, where every word must be dedicated in part to showing character voice, the third person narrator can be a more objective reporter, one step removed. This is an advantage when the author wants to focus on the events of the novel without giving quite as much attention to the personal perspective and voice of the narrator.

There are many ways to write in third person. The narrative can dip into the viewpoint of several characters or stick with one. Let's take a quick look at several of the options.

Third person limited. Third person limited follows only one character's consciousness, so just like first person, reporting actions that take place "offscreen" for the viewpoint character is not permitted except through dialogue. Here's an example from Dia Calhoun's (2000) YA novel *Aria of the Sea*:

> Cerinthe struggled with the hooks on her dancing tunic; it felt tight and small. After she yanked the last hook, the tunic slipped from her shoulders, and the white muslin crumpled around her feet. She wanted to kick it across the room. Plain old muslin! Why hadn't Tonea told her to wear a fancy costume? She had danced in muslin among girls dressed like princesses in satin, silk, and lace. (p. 12)

Third person multiple. Third person multiple presents more than one viewpoint character. Sometimes there are two, and sometimes more. Scenes are limited to what the viewpoint character for that particular scene can perceive. This POV works well when the plot is complex.

In Amy Kathleen Ryan's (2011) *Glow*, the action-packed plot demands two viewpoint characters: the girl, Waverly, and the boy, Kieran, who are separated from each other early in the book.

Hilari Bell's (2003) novel, *Goblin Wood*, also follows two viewpoint characters, Makenna and Tobin.

> **Makenna's POV:** Tears crept down her face again, and she wiped them away, sniffling. She'd have thought there'd be no tears left in her, but they kept coming. Well, let them come. They didn't matter. Nothing mattered anymore except to lift the gate and cut the screw. (p. 4)
>
> **Tobin's POV:** He banged through the door and slammed it, startling the nearest horses, who snorted and stamped. He took a second to drop the latch and pull the string so it couldn't be opened from the other side, then he ran along the corridor. (p. 78)

Character voice in third person. Sometimes authors writing in third person use voice to communicate personality, more like first person. Scenes are viewed through various characters, but rather than staying in the narrator-as-reporter mode, word choice differs for each viewpoint. My book *The Light of the Oracle* (2005) uses third person multiple with an emphasis on character voice. For example, here are three (out of eight) characters who get viewpoint scenes.

Bryn's POV: Clea had called the vulture the most respected bird. Why would a vulture be well respected? Bryn had seen vultures—great, ugly, staring things, feeding on carcasses. (p. 26)

Kiran's POV: As he trudged the grounds, he listened for Jack's silent language. People thought animal speech was heard like human words. How foolish. Only humans contrived words and sentences and disturbed the truth with layers and shades. Only humans lied; animals didn't know how. (pp. 126–127)

Selid's POV: From the moment the troubadours appeared, Selid knew she shouldn't have come. She saw a glow around them, an ethereal glow that had nothing to do with the sunshine. (p. 222)

Omniscient POV

The omniscient view is all-knowing, and it can therefore describe any character (and his or her thoughts and feelings) in any setting, anywhere, anytime. The choice the author must make is how much to reveal and when and about whom. For this reason, omniscient is also known as *unlimited.*

Omniscient or unlimited view, once the standard for novels, has become more unusual; it's rare to find it in YA books published today. One example, by author Anna Godberson, is the *Luxe* historical romance series, which is rated for ages 14 and up. In *Envy* (2009), one of the books in the series, most chapters start out in a clearly omniscient voice and then follow one of the characters more closely for the rest of the chapter, as in this excerpt:

> The hotel's guests were eating second suppers or howling in laughter or dancing far closer than they would have dreamed of doing in New York or Philadelphia or Washington, with partners they might not have considered in their regular lives . . .
> . . . Diana saw his intentions in a flash, and moved just aside of his approaching kiss. (p. 227)

Occasional omniscience. Sometimes, the occasional foray into omniscience strengthens a novel that is otherwise seen through viewpoint characters. For example, although the bulk of each *Harry Potter* book is through Harry Potter's viewpoint, author J. K. Rowling (2007) doesn't hesitate to use the omniscient view when her story calls for it, as in this example from *Harry Potter and the Deathly Hallows*:

> Many miles away the chilly mist that had pressed against the Prime Minister's windows drifted over a dirty river that wound between overgrown, rubbish-strewn banks. An immense chimney, relic of a disused mill, reared up, shadowy and ominous. There was no sound apart from the whisper of the black water and no sign of life apart from a scrawny fox that had slunk down the bank to nose hopefully at some old fish-and-chip wrappings in the tall grass. (p. 19)

Taking occasional flights of omniscience is convenient for books with lots of action taking place in various locations involving several characters.

Omniscience as applied to graphic novels. The view in graphic novels is omniscient, but because of the economy of words called for by the genre, omniscience functions differently. It's still the author's decision whom to include, and when and where, and which thoughts to reveal. But every line of illustration will convey hundreds of words of narrative. All dialogue, internal and external, is supremely distilled. And when narrative is utilized, it's carefully written to tell as much as possible with the least number of words, augmenting the illustrations.

Passive Voice

Steer clear of passive voice wherever possible when writing YA.

Passive voice: The difference between active and passive voice was studied by the writer.

Active voice: The writer studied the difference between active and passive voice.

---

present tense
and past tense

Now that we've seen some examples of both past and present tense, let's delve a little more deeply into tenses and how they play out in a novel. When it suits the story, present tense helps pick up the pace and give a sense of immediacy to the action. But it doesn't always suit the story. To illustrate, here are examples of past tense converted to present tense and vice versa.

Past Tense Into Present

T. A. Barron's (1999) YA novel *The Mirror of Merlin* is part of series in which the protagonist, Merlin, looks back on his life.

> Tilting my head back, I peered up into the vaulting branches and drew a deep breath of air, poignant with the sweetness of cedar and pine. And something else, I realized: a slight odor of something rancid, or rotting, that lurked just beneath the sweetness. Nonetheless, I drank in the aromas, for as much as I disliked being lost, I always savored being in a forest. (p. 27)

Could this passage be converted into present tense? Yes, technically it could:

> Tilting my head back, I peer up into the vaulting branches and draw a deep breath of air, poignant with the sweetness of cedar and pine. And something else, I realize: a slight odor of something rancid, or rotting, that lurks just beneath the sweetness.

But putting it in present tense doesn't fit, because the story is written as reminiscent from a wise man looking back over many years. Converting this book into present tense would destroy the credibility of the narrator.

Present Tense Converted to Past

In *8th Grade Superzero* by Olugbemisola Rhuday-Perkovich (2010), the young voice of the narrator is a perfect fit for present tense:

> "Hey, Pukey, got a pen?" Hector Vega jabs me in the back. He does this every day. Mostly so he can write "The Villain Vega"—his future pro wrestling name—all over his notebooks. I hand a blue ballpoint over my shoulder without looking, then Hector taps me so I can turn around and see him stick the pen down his throat and fake gag. (p. 3)

When the same passage is rewritten in past tense, some of its vitality is immediately lost:

> "Hey, Pukey, got a pen?" Hector Vega jabbed me in the back. He did this every day. Mostly so he could write "The Villain Vega"—his future pro wrestling name—all over his notebooks. I handed a blue ballpoint over my shoulder without looking, then Hector tapped me so I could turn around and see him stick the pen down his throat and fake gag.

Process Notes on Present Tense

When writing in present tense, flashbacks or recollections of the past use simple past tense rather than past perfect. In this excerpt from Pam Bachorz's (2009) *Candor*, note how the tense moves from present to past in the last paragraph:

> A Message drip-drops onto my brain. *Always obey your parents.*
> Asking questions will only make him suspicious. That's not the kind of thing good Candor kids do. So I go to the garage.
> The box is right where he said it would be. It's rusty. Fingerprints make polka dots in the thick dust on top. One of the latches is missing.
> It's not how it used to be. Not even close.
> The tackle box was my grandfather's. He gave it to Dad. (p. 65)

But if *Candor* had been written in past tense rather than present, here's how the recollection would need to be written:

> The box was right where he said it would be. It was rusty. Fingerprints made polka dots in the thick dust on top. One of the latches was missing.
>
> It wasn't how it used to be. Not even close.
>
> The tackle box had been my grandfather's. He had given it to Dad.

know when to show and when to tell

The motto "show, don't tell" is very big in writing instruction. And while there's good reason for this, it can be overdone.

Is it important to show rather than tell? Yes it is, *most of the time.* But every great writer mixes showing and telling. I'm even ready to make the claim that an author's unique way of combining the two is a large part of what makes up writerly voice. We'll get into this in more depth in a moment. Before we do, here's my brief definition of the difference between showing and telling.

➤ **Showing:** When showing, a writer sets forth precisely what is said and done by the characters, and what is seen, heard, smelled, tasted, and touched. Showing uses dialogue, action, and sensory description.

➤ **Telling:** When telling, a writer evaluates or interprets for the reader, informs the reader of what a character thinks or feels, or inserts what is known from a previous time. Telling uses narrative.

Sometimes, Telling Says It Best

If an author feels burdened by the need to keep every last thing in "show" mode, the story can get needlessly complicated. Sometimes it's best to just come right out and tell the reader what's up. Here's an example of straight telling from *The Hunger Games*:

> Say you are poor and starving as we were. You can opt to add your name more times in exchange for tesserae. Each tessera is worth a meager year's supply of grain and oil for one person. You may do this for each of your family members as well. So, at the age of twelve, I had my name entered four times. Once, because I had to, and three times for tesserae for grain and oil for myself, Prim, and my mother. In fact, every year I have needed to do this. And the entries are cumulative. So now, at the age of sixteen, my name will be in the reaping twenty times. (p. 13)

If Collins had been constrained by the notion that telling should never be used, she would not have been able to cleanly lay out the rules that apply to District 12 teens. The particular rule about the tesserae is not the focal point of the novel, but it is relevant. By imparting this crucial piece of information simply and directly, Collins saves the reader from unnecessary scenes. She can then focus on giving the appropriate weight to important actions such as Katniss volunteering in her sister's place.

Another example from Lynda Sandoval's (2006) *Chicks Ahoy* demonstrates how telling can do a good job of revealing character and situation.

> Most of the students are filthy rich and perfect and drive nicer cars than either of my parents. The rest of us—mostly the offspring of local academics—huddle in the shadows of this glowing social nucleus, sort of trying to bask in the feeble rays reflecting off of their veneered teeth and Tiffany bling-bling. (p. 5)

If Sandoval stayed away from telling, she would need to contrive situations to indicate that most of the students in her character's private school are rich and drive nice cars. This would stall the story, where being one of only a few middle class kids in a school full of rich kids needs to be established early on.

When Telling Becomes Showing

In the example from *The Hunger Games* above, what is *told* also *shows* a lot, through subtext. By telling the reader that she has entered her name four times each year instead of one, Katniss shows how much her family means to her: that she's willing to increase the risks on her life to get extra grain and oil for her sister and mother.

Blending Showing and Telling

In this excerpt from *Chasing Tail Lights* by Patrick Jones (2007), section *a* is in telling mode and section *b* is in showing mode. The POV is first person present tense with a female narrator named Christy, and in the book the excerpt is continuous from a to b.

a) Ryan's room is down in the damp basement, in what used to be a storage room. The walls are cracked, and it still stinks from when it flooded a few years ago, even though we ripped up all the carpet. That stinky carpet is in a pile in the backyard, along with the other junk from our lives we can't get rid of for some reason. Ryan throws his dirty clothes for me to wash in a basket in front of his door because I can't bring myself to go in there without gagging. He doesn't spend much time at home anymore, although even one second is too much by my clock.

b) I hear the front door open, and even from the distance, there's a distinctive sour smell attacking my senses. His big always-new shoes are loud on the creaky, warped wood floors.

'Where's some dinner?' I hear Ryan shout, and I feel the acid in my stomach churn. (p. 31)

When Christy tells the reader about the basement, she also communicates more about herself and Ryan: The subtext shows that she's sensitive; that the family doesn't know how to get rid of things in their lives that weigh them down; that Ryan lives in an uninhabitable part of the house; that Christy does his laundry and doesn't like it when he's around.

Don't Tell What You've Already Shown

There *is* an area where telling should be absolutely off limits. Please do not tell what you've already shown. Here's a hypothetical example, with the offending *tell* in italics:

> The mirror shows me too pale, too blond, too blotchy. My mouth tastes like a car battery. *I'm feeling really sick, and I don't like the way I look right now.*

Showing has already established how the character feels. Reiterating with telling only ruins a good segment.

middles

The middle section of your book occupies approximately 50% of the length, between the first 25% and the final 25%. Lot of writers start to flounder when they get to the middle of a novel, and wonder what comes next. This is where complications and turning points provide a sense of direction and ratchet up the pace.

Turning points in the middle of your book happen because your characters are driven to make changes. Responding to the events and people around them, they select new courses of action that reveal their growth, development, and adaptation to circumstances.

Think of the major turning points in your own life. What drove you to change? And consider your favorite books. When did dramatic turning points become inevitable for the characters? If your plot is sagging, add complications. Then add more. Create situations that *demand* change. Those situations will bring about big turning points.

Toward the end of the middle, a turning point is reached that resolves an aspect of the central conflict, *even while adding* a new dimension to that same conflict. For example, after listening to Elizabeth's angry spiel about why he's the last man in the world she would ever marry, Darcy writes her a letter of explanation. Just before this, his pride reaches a peak. And just before she reads his letter, Elizabeth's prejudice peaks.

Darcy learns to question his unbending pride, and he reforms. After reading his letter, Elizabeth realizes that her prejudice has led her completely wrong. She changes. The letter represents a major turning point for both characters. The conflict that resided in their *feelings* of pride and of prejudice is removed. However, the conflict arising from the *consequences* of their pride and prejudice doesn't drop away: It escalates.

endings

The ending of your book consists of the climax and denouement. These sections together will occupy the last 25% of your novel.

Climax

During the middle portion, you intensified the central conflict through a series of complications and turning points. At the climax, all that tension you've developed during previous scenes will explode. Bam!

Just as Elizabeth recognizes how much Darcy means to her, Lydia runs away with Wickham and disgraces the family name. Katniss must confront the last warriors left in the games—while trying to save Peeta's life.

From the beginning of your novel, you've made unspoken promises to your reader that the conflict will rise and get more complicated, and that you'll stay with it until it's resolved. You've promised that your protagonist will change, and that the climax will fit the rest of the action you've laid out.

Follow through. Do not cheat your reader with easy outs. Big crescendo. Deliver the payoff!

Denouement

The aftermath of the climax is the resolution and the wrap. How will you resolve your central conflict? The resolution depends on your plotline. Elizabeth and Darcy's central conflict is resolved by finding true love and getting married; Katniss's central conflict is resolved by surviving the games. Other plotlines call for different resolutions.

For the wrap, give your readers a glimpse of important secondary characters, too. Keep it short and snappy. Leave them wanting more.

revisions

Here we are at last. Revisions!

Revising is a lot of work, but it makes all the difference. Without it, your book will resemble an uncooked pancake. You've gone to all of the trouble of gathering top-notch ingredients. Now, it's time to mix the batter, fire up the griddle, and line up the plates.

I realize I might seem to be overly enthusiastic about this part of the process. I admit, I adore revising. The hard work of completing that first draft is finally done. Now for the fun part! I get to don my editor's toque and scrutinize every sentence. However, I know that some of you will not respond to the thrill of revisions. Forgive my mixed metaphors as I switch from spatulas to combs, but if you cringe at the very thought of dragging a fine-toothed comb through the tangles of your first draft, it's time to give yourself a pep talk. You've come so far! If you can't do revisions for yourself, then do them for the sake of your book. It deserves your best now, just as it deserved your best all along. Keep going.

Steps to Revising a Manuscript

When revising, I advise taking the process in steps. To be more exact, I divide my revision process into 14 distinct steps, described in the sections that follow.

Step 1. Let your manuscript sit. Don't even look at it for at least 6 weeks. Six months is even better if you can afford the time. (If you're writing on a deadline, you won't have the luxury of 6 months, let alone 6 weeks. You'll be lucky if you get a few days. But for your first book, this step is muy importante.)

Step 2. Print and read aloud. Hard copy reads differently than words on the screen. (Don't ask me why.) So print your manuscript and read it over in one sitting if you can. Out loud. As you read, pretend you've never heard any of it before. Better yet, enlist a friend, family member, or theatre student to read aloud while you listen.

You'll be amazed by what you find that escaped you before. We writers tend to fill in the gaps in our prose with unwritten words, not realizing that those words are actually missing from the pages. Or sometimes, we have the opposite problem: We've skipped over redundancies as if they don't exist. Luckily, it's not as easy to overlook either of these writing sins once you get some distance from your manuscript.

Personally, my first drafts suffer from both glaring gaps *and* unnecessary repetition. This means that when I revise, I add thousands of words and cut even more. But perhaps you are prone to overwrite without leaving gaps, or you could be someone whose first drafts are quite skeletal, with no redundancies. In any case, as you revise you can trim or add—or both.

If you allow your manuscript to sit untouched for long enough, and if the first thing you do after taking it out again is to read it aloud, you're likely to spot much of what needs to be revised.

I think it's important to suspend your analytical mind during this first read after taking a break from your story. Stay in touch with your gut. *Listen* to it. You won't get a chance to experience your book with this degree of freshness again for a while, so don't waste the opportunity. Don't stop to rewrite. Allow yourself only abbreviated notes. (I write things like *MORE SETTING* or *FLESH OUT* or *REDUNDANT.*) Keep going straight through to the end so you can get a sense of the overall story.

Complete rewrite? I don't want to scare you, but I should probably mention that sometimes, after your initial read-through, you'll realize that the entire book needs to be redone. Maybe it needs a different point of view. Maybe it's cluttered with too many messages. Maybe a secondary character who has stolen every possible scene is really the protagonist. The ending might be the real beginning. There can be any number of very big problems.

Well, if you need to start over, you need to start over. Writing really does resemble cooking in some ways. Once in a while, a cook realizes that no amount of tweaking will save that pot of soup: It's scorched or it has too much salt or the rice was rancid. The only remedy is to toss it out and begin again. As a writer, I've come to similar conclusions while cooking up novels. Sometimes it's just the beginning that needs to be redone, or the ending, or most of the middle. But sometimes, it's the whole freakin' book.

Is it tough to begin again? Yup. But it's better to start page 1 with a new perspective than to hold on to 325 pages that just aren't quite "it." And the need to start over does not make you a bad writer. In fact, the ability to recognize what needs to be cut—and then cut it—is an essential part of success. So if you know in your gut that you've got a complete do-over in front of you, all I have to say is: Good going! You're a pro, and I mean that.

As usual, this writing thing is not perfectly linear, so here's an important caveat: Before giving up on your book, especially if it's the first one you've ever written, you might want to get the opinion of a perceptive reader who knows how to dish out honest and helpful feedback. Why? Because it's possible that you're wrong. Maybe it isn't really scorched or too salty or rancid. It's possible that you've let your critical mind crash your read-aloud party and bring in the harsh comments too early in the process. You wouldn't want to throw out something that just needs a dash of pepper or something.

No writing time is wasted. Even if you toss an entire book, you did not waste your time. It isn't love's labor lost, because all of the writing you do improves all of the writing you do. This bears repeating: *All of the writing you do improves all of the writing you do.* Just like strength training improves an athlete's running speed, or playing scales over and over improves a musician's ability to play hot riffs, all of the words you ever put together will improve your style.

Step 3. Read aloud again, with attention to specific elements of fiction. Okay, assuming you've got a draft you can revise, you're ready for Step 3, which is to read it again. Out loud. This time, invite your critical-thinking brain to sit up front and take a close and careful look at the specific elements of fiction, making notes on each one.

> ➤ Beginning: Is the beginning really the beginning? When does the inciting incident occur? ☐

> ➤ Message: What is the main message? What are the themes? Does everything, including all action and any subplots or symbolism, support the message and themes? ☐ ☐

> ➤ Conflict: Is it effective and related to the message and themes? ☐

> ➤ Continuity: Do all parts of the book (e.g., hair color, eye color, terrain, timeline of events) agree? ☐

> ➤ Cause and Effect: Is cause and effect demonstrated for each turning point? Have redundant scenes been cut? ☐ ☐

> ➤ Characters: Is anything done or said that's out of character? Are the character motivations and goals well illustrated? ☐ ☐

> ➤ Dialogue: Is each character voice believable and distinct? Does each exchange reveal character and advance the plot? ☐ ☐

> ➤ Show and Tell: Are showing and telling used in the right amounts to showcase voice? ☐ ☐

> ➤ Point of View: Is it consistent? Is anything included that's "offscreen" for a point of view character? ☐ ☐

> ➤ Setting: Are there sensory details? Is there a clear era and culture? ☐ ☐

> ➤ Ending: Does it fit? Do you deliver on your implied promises? ☐ ☐

Step 4. First full rewrite. Enter your initial changes. Making full use of your notes, go ahead and add, subtract, multiply, and divide your words. This is your first full rewrite. Fill in gaps, remove redundancies, and remedy all of the other issues you've caught. This step takes a while, and it pays to give it the time that it needs.

Killing your darlings. As I mentioned in the part about beginnings, just because something is well-written doesn't mean it belongs in your book. Alas, some of your best writing will need to be cut. Every writer experiences this strange phenomenon. Ask yourself, "If I were to cut this scene (or word, sentence, paragraph), would readers miss it?" Because if they wouldn't, it needs to go. Padded prose is not welcome in the YA genre.

Step 5. Make an outline. Once you've entered your initial changes, you're ready to make an outline. Yes, outline. Even if you, like me, hate outlines, this is the stage where outlining will definitely help you by providing another overview of your novel. At first glance, this might seem like a recap of Step 3. Trust me, by creating an actual outline, you'll find things that you missed before.

Outlining

When I'm outlining a completed draft, I get a stack of big note cards and assign one card to each chapter. I use plus and minus signs for shorthand, and make notes on these elements:

> ➤ Setting (when and where) ☐
> ➤ Characters (true to character?) ☐
> ➤ Action (what happens) ☐
> ➤ Conflict (within the scenes) ☐
> ➤ Dialogue (believable and necessary?) ☐
> ➤ Point of view (consistent?) ☐
> ➤ General notes ☐

My outlining style doesn't exactly follow a standard format. But that doesn't matter, because I'm not turning it in for inspection; I just want to get another angle on my story. You can design your outline any way you want and include whatever you think will help you find more things that need work.

Step 6. Analyze the action sequence. The section in your outline that describes the action is crucial to gaining an overall sense of *what happens.* Now that you've outlined each chapter, you can lay your note cards on the floor. Take a look at the sequence of the action. Is it the best sequence to build the central conflict? If not, do some shuffling. Use the plot outlines from the section on plotting to help guide you. For example, if your story is one of rags to riches, does the protagonist have believable experiences of self-discovery? If not, you're missing a chapter or two or three.

When considering my outline cards, I often find that I've written a scene that duplicates something I've already established in another scene elsewhere. Then I have to ask myself which of those scenes does a better job and which needs to be axed. I may also notice that there are too many flashbacks; some of them need to be shortened or cut out completely. And sometimes, I've introduced several secondary characters that could be rolled into a single more convincing character. If so, I need to decide who stays and who goes.

Just as every scene must contribute something to the entirety of the plot, just about every scene needs an element of conflict, either in the background or foreground. Surely, I rambled on long enough when discussing the subject of conflict to convince you of its importance.

As you question and shuffle and talk to yourself, you'll make additional notes on what you find. When you're finished, you're ready for the next round of changes.

Step 7. Rewrite again. Looking at all of your revision notes can be a little like contemplating how to turn a pile of squiggling worms into a good meal. Don't panic—or if you're panicking already, you're normal. Yes, there's plenty to do, but if you've made it this far, you can finish. Go through each page with your trusty notes by your side as you rewrite again. This step takes time, because each bit that is added or dropped will require adjustments in more than one place—and every adjustment will lead to others.

Step 8. Get feedback from perceptive readers. By now, you may be truly sick of your story. It's very common at this stage to have no earthly idea whether it's the worst piece of drivel ever conceived or if it's a marvel that's driven by genius. You may feel as if it's hopeless and needs to be put out of its misery. But don't trash it yet. (If your gut allowed it through Step 1, your wailing despair now is probably just overwrought nerves and exhaustion.) You may also feel as if your book is worthy of taking the literary world by storm. But don't submit it yet, however much you may wish to do so. You still have at least five more steps, and the next one is to regain perspective.

Run it past perceptive readers. Notice I didn't just say readers; I said perceptive readers. If ever you needed helpful critique, it's now. And if ever an unhelpful critique could be horribly damaging, it's now. (For definitions of helpful and unhelpful critique, see Chapter 7.) So hopefully, you've lined up trusted and perceptive readers who will go through your book and make notes of their own.

Step 9. Apply insights. Apply the insights gained from your perceptive readers to make another round of changes.

Step 10. Read aloud and make notes. Read the whole book through again. Aloud. Make notes.

Step 11. Enter changes. As you go, remember that there *is* such a thing as revising something to death. The trick is to get finished without obsessing too much over every little detail. (I've known people to spend 25 years writing and rewriting the same YA novel.) Remind yourself—again and again—of the story you're telling. The story comes first. The story comes first. The story comes first.

Step 12. Read again, looking for flow. That's right! Read it over one more time to be sure your latest changes flow seamlessly. Correct as necessary.

Step 13. Take a breather. Give yourself a day or two so that your creative mind can mull it all over and alert you to any inconsistencies before you send off your book. Really, this is the step we all skip, and the step we all wish we hadn't skipped. It's embarrassing when I send off a novel and then 2 days later I'm doing the laundry and suddenly receive a clear, concise (and absolutely tardy) message from my creative mind, saying *the part where so and so does such and such needs to be changed to whosit getting whatsit.* Horrified, I make the change and then have to send an e-mail saying, "Oops, ignore the previous draft, here's the real one, attached." I used to think I was the only one who did that sort of thing until I started talking to other writers—and talking to agents. Trust me, it's worth taking that extra 48 hours.

Step 14. Done. You've got a stack of delicious pages, golden brown and ready to be devoured. Congratulations! Go celebrate!

Chapter 4

Writing YA Nonfiction

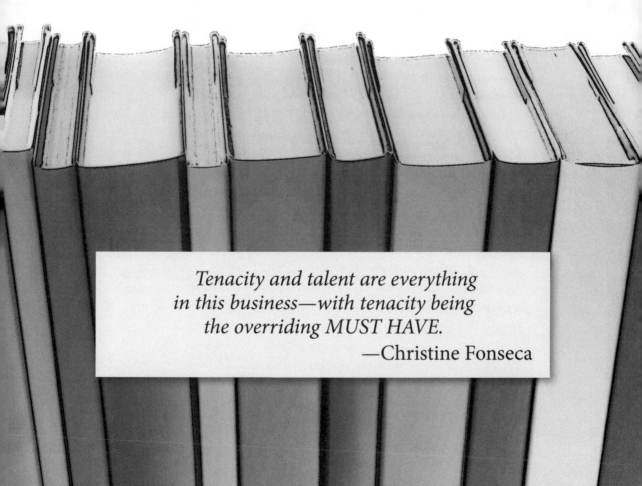

*Tenacity and talent are everything
in this business—with tenacity being
the overriding MUST HAVE.*

—Christine Fonseca

For the longest time, teens interested in reading about specific subjects were restricted to dull textbooks or else they had to find a book written for adults. Not anymore! The genre of YA nonfiction is really taking off.

Getting a book published about a topic you love is a chance to share your interest and even make a little money. But before you get started on this fulfilling endeavor, keep in mind that nonfiction writers have a different job than novelists. You must convince agents and editors of three things:

1. You're a good writer with a style that fits your audience.
2. You're an expert in your chosen subject.
3. Your subject has relevance and market appeal.

does your writing style fit the ya market?

Voice is just as important in nonfiction as it is in fiction, but many writers make the mistake of focusing strictly on information when writing nonfiction. The resulting style is about as juicy as the Great Salt Desert. Your audience is not made up of captives; they need a reason to keep reading. You won't provide that reason if you get all stark and dry with the facts and leave your voice out of your book. Here's a good example of the use of voice from Zachary Hamby's *Mythology for Teens* (2009):

> You may not be a theatre person. You may not enjoy dramas, comedies, one-acts, or musicals. Maybe you haven't even seen a staged play before, but you surely enjoy the theatre's modern-day descendants. Movies and TV owe *everything* to theatre. They're just fancier, flashier versions. And theatre? Theatre owes *everything* to the Greeks. (p. 67)

Hamby could have written something crusty and bland. He could have said: "Although you yourself might not enjoy staged theater, you probably enjoy movies and TV. The shows you like to watch are descended from Greek plays that have their roots in mythology." But Hamby didn't do that. He used juice to get his point across.

In the first edition of *Seize the Story: A Handbook for Teens Who Like to Write* (2008), I say: "Getting through a first draft feels very much like clawing my way through solid rock using only my fingernails" (p. 15). I could have said: "Writing a first draft is really difficult for me." But phrased like that, my words would hit the reader's skull and ricochet onto the floor, where they would stay. A publisher would never pick up such a book in the first place.

Emphasize Drama

If you've done much academic writing, you're probably accustomed to a style that deemphasizes drama and strives for an ultraobjective stance. For example: *Eighty one percent of novelists polled by Boring, Inc. indicated that they disliked performing the actual writing of their first drafts (Tedious Text, 2011, p. 00).* This is the style that creeps into textbooks and renders them d-u-l-l. But we are not talking about writing textbooks here; we're talking about being fascinating.

You might be the only person you know who's awestruck by earthworms, but if so, you're the perfect person to write about worm drama. Hook your readers with surprising tidbits. The longest earthworm ever found was 22 feet! And yes, to a catfish, a night crawler is super yummy! And how did earthworm burrows give rise to the sci-fi term "wormhole"?

You may have been conditioned to think that you must be dry to be accurate, but you don't: You can be perfectly accurate and still be interesting. To create interest, play up drama. It's always there. Find it, and it will help you reach your readers.

Vocabulary

When writing for teens, it isn't necessary to confine yourself to two-syllable words, but please don't be needlessly verbose. Get to the point. No room for rambling or run-on sentences! Be entertaining, but *be clear*. If your subject includes unfamiliar terms, define each term the first time it's used, support your definition with at least one example, and then create a glossary or an index.

Indexing

It's always a good idea to create an index for print books. Teens are accustomed to using search functions, and they will be annoyed if they can't easily find something they remember reading. Your publisher can help with an index. Nonfiction publishers have plenty of experience in this area.

Page Content and Graphics

Sprinkle colorful examples throughout your chapters, and include activities that involve the reader. As you write, be aware that you'll want more white space than you would find in the average book written for adults. Break up your pages with bold headings, text-boxes, lists, sidebar suggestions, and other ways to create visual texture. Photos and drawings will liven up your prose. (Your publisher and book designer will have very specific criteria for how to treat graphics, so be sure to find out exactly what they are.)

Your subject matter might also be well-suited to become a graphic format (a.k.a. comic) book. For more about graphic format in YA nonfiction, read Sari Wilson and Josh Neufeld's interviews in Chapter 11.

are you an expert?

As a writer of YA nonfiction, part of your market is teens themselves. Another part of your market is parents and educators of teens. Ideally, you'll present your topic in a way that appeals to teens but also gives parents and educators a good sense of your credibility and expertise so they can be confident about buying your book.

Publishers, too, need to feel confident in your expertise. What qualifications are they seeking in authors of YA nonfiction? Well, if you're a prominent expert in a field in which you have an advanced degree, *and* you have experience working with teens, *and* you're a writer with a flair for reaching young adults, you have an irresistible combination. However, if you're not in that enviable position, there are other ways to put your expertise into the best possible light for publishing a book.

1. **Become known as an expert.** If you are a "go to" person on the cutting edge in your field, you may be able to leverage your expertise into a book deal. Publishers may even seek *you* out. So, how do you establish yourself as an expert?

   a. *Publish articles.* When you author articles on your subject in professional journals and magazines, you create a positive addition to your resume.

   b. *Build up blog appeal.* If you're consistent about blogging for at least 2 years, and your blog has a following, you have a favorable selling point.

   c. *Give presentations at national or regional conferences.* Seek out conferences related to your subject matter. Submit presentation ideas, and when you're accepted, put together a scintillating talk. Publishers interested in doing a book on your topic may have scouts in attendance at conferences.

   d. *Offer to review books for publishers.* If particular publishers have impressed you with the quality of their line of books, offer to review titles for them. Become a reliable partner so the publisher knows you're someone to be trusted. You might be surprised by how many people will promise something and then fail to deliver it on time. Publishers need writers who will not flake out. Reviewing books is a chance to participate in a mutually beneficial service while cultivating professional relationships.

   e. *Conduct workshops for teens.* By conducting workshops for teens, you'll get a sense of how to present your topic in a way that's relatable for your audience.

2. **Emphasize experience.** Perhaps you do not have an advanced degree in the subject you're interested in writing about. Whereas it's advantageous to have a doctorate or master's degree, it isn't always necessary, especially if your book is a "how-to" on a particular craft. If you have a successful business that offers products

appealing to teens, you could turn your mojo for money into a book on starting a business even if you haven't attained a graduate degree in finance or business administration. If you've grown up in a bakery, you could write an outstanding manual on cake decorating without going to art school.

3. **Get involved in your community.** If you're a good writer active in your community, your level of experience may trump a formal education. For example, if you've run a community garden for an inner-city teen camp, you're a better bet for a YA book about gardening than someone with a recent Ph.D. in horticulture who hasn't talked to a 15-year-old since 10th grade. When I pitched the idea for *Seize the Story*, although I didn't have a master's degree in creative writing, I had led writing workshops for thousands of teens in schools and libraries for more than 7 years. I was also a YA novelist published in dozens of countries. In addition, I reached out to other YA authors through my community and asked for interviews to give more dimension to my book.

4. **Get endorsements and vetting from experts.** If you do not have a formal educational background that relates to your topic, it's wise to seek out endorsements from experts. If your subject is technical or scientific at all, find at least one person with an advanced degree who promises to vet your work.

   a. *Be mindful and professional when approaching experts.* Carefully research the qualifications of those you plan to contact. In your initial e-mail to any expert, be as clear as possible about exactly what you're hoping to receive. Request a fee schedule to show that you expect to pay a consulting fee for the expert's time and training. (To ask for vetting as a favor is unprofessional and will probably be turned down.) Be prepared to alter your text if the expert finds inaccuracies or gaps in your presentation. And remember that experts are often extremely busy. If someone turns down your project, it isn't personal.

Coauthoring

If you're primarily a writer rather than an expert, perhaps a collaboration will work for you. Maybe you have always been intrigued by gardening, but you don't know all that much about it beyond your own small plot of flowers and veggies. However, you have superb writing skills, and you think there's a market for a YA book on gardening. Then you cross paths with someone who has a Ph.D. in horticulture, an enthusiastic and knowledgeable gardener who doesn't have a background in nonacademic writing. This may be an opportunity to collaborate on a book.

Coauthoring can take many forms, with many possible divisions of duties. Sometimes, one person will provide all of the writing and the other all of the expertise. Sometimes, both people share equally in expertise, writing, and everything in between. No matter how collaborations happen, they demand excellent rapport between the coauthors, with the ability to share work and credit. If you're considering coauthoring, I recommend *The Writer's Legal Companion* by Brad Bunnin and Peter Beren, in particular the chapter on collaborations and how to set them up legally.

Fact Checking

If your book presents facts, those facts will need to be checked. Normally, your publisher will not have the resources to do this. As part of your standard contract, you will sign a document saying you have correctly represented the facts. Cite your sources, and be sure you've used direct sources rather than secondhand information. If you're unsure about your research methods, your local library is an excellent resource. Media specialists are trained to help you research anything in the world. As you research, keep close track of your references, including authors, titles, publishers, editions, dates, and page numbers so you can create a comprehensive reference list. Your publisher will have guidelines for which format it prefers for this.

Draw clear distinctions between opinions and facts so you don't confuse your readers or land in legal hot water. And if there's any doubt in your mind—or even if there isn't—about the information you're presenting, get a highly educated person on board to check your work. All of this will make your book more credible and valuable.

is your subject relevant and does it have market appeal?

Sadly, it doesn't matter how knowledgeable and passionate you are about creating tie-dyed shoes if only one in a million teens will care. If you're an authority on Tolstoy, you're out of luck in the marketplace, because it's a rare teen who reads Tolstoy by choice. And if you're an artist who practices glass-blowing, your craft is too dangerous and expensive for the average teenager.

To clarify whether your expertise will fit with YA, you might try making a list of what young people could gain by learning what you know. When you've finished, convert the items on your list into questions and then poll the teenagers in your life.

For example, if your expertise is landscaping, here's a possible list.

Young people who learn to landscape would gain:
a)   A sense of being closer to nature.
b)   Self-esteem and accomplishment from tending plants.
c)   Seeds of confidence for future homeownership.

Your related questions for teens:
a)   Would you like to feel closer to nature?
b)   Do you think tending plants would boost your self-esteem?
c)   Would you look forward to being a homeowner someday if you knew more about landscaping?

The teens you talk to might say "no" to your questions. If they do, it doesn't mean it's time to abandon your book idea yet; it means it's time to rethink your approach.

> **New list with different benefits:**
> a) Possible source of income working in yards during the summer.
> b) Learn about varieties of trees, shrubs, flowers, and stones and how they fit into the artistic aspect of landscape design.
> c) Get eco-friendly by learning about nonpoisonous pest control, electric mowers, organic fertilizers, and xeriscape methods for conserving water.
>
> **New questions:**
> a) Would you enjoy having a summer income while being your own boss?
> b) Would you like to know more about the creative aspect of landscape design, including color palettes?
> c) Are you interested in eco-friendly choices for landscaping and how to put them into practice?

This time, you might get a "yes" to every question from all of the teens you ask. If so, you know your angle. The all-important "What's in it for them?" question has been answered. You're ready to generate an outline.

A jazzy outline is great, but it's not the only thing you'll need when presenting your subject. Remember, when publishing companies take on a new book, they're investing time, energy, and money. They need to believe there's a possibility of getting a return on that investment. (For more on publisher costs, see p. 146 in Chapter 8.)

In general, nonfiction publishers are leery of being the first company to bring out a book on a subject no one has focused on before. There's already plenty of risk inherent in the publishing business, and they don't like to just throw something into the marketplace cold. Often, the reason no one has yet published a book about a certain topic is because the market for that topic doesn't exist.

You may be convinced there's a market for something no one else has recognized, but it's up to you to persuade a publisher. If you're right, both you and the publisher will win big. It's lovely to be the first to identify a niche market with sizable buying power. But if you're wrong, nobody gets nothin'. Publishers are quite familiar with "blue sky"—where a writer promises the moon and delivers a patch of mud. They will not be impressed with big dreams of success if you don't present them with a viable launch pad.

When I first pitched *Seize the Story*, my editor didn't think there would be enough interest from teens to justify developing such a book. Her company usually published titles that primarily served English teachers rather than teens themselves. At the time, there weren't any other titles visible in the marketplace that did what I wanted to do: teach all of the elements of fiction in a book designed for ambitious teen writers. I planned to cover techniques for how to write dialogue, characters, setting, conflict, plot, and point of view.

In the process of persuading my editor to give it a try, I didn't promise her the moon. I told her about my experiences leading writing workshops for teens. During every workshop, the kids wanted more, more, more. I believed that they—and their parents—would love to have a handbook about creative writing.

No doubt it helped my cause that this editor had a soft spot for young writers. She decided to take a chance. At any rate, my tale has a happy ending. Today, *Seize the Story* is in its second edition—and other books have followed in its footsteps.

Improve Your Chances With Publishers

It might take some doing to gather what you need to make your subject desirable to a publisher. I suggest mixing a pragmatic approach with enthusiasm.

When writing your proposal, never assume that a publisher is already excited about your subject. Gather practical selling points to back up your personal enthusiasm. And always be professional. Provide your list of benefits in an eloquent but *concise* manner. A few enticing bullet points will be more persuasive than a long list of details.

submission policies for nonfiction

Submission policies for nonfiction books differ from those that govern fiction. Rather than writing your whole book before you begin to submit (which is a must for novelists!), you'll create a resume, an outline, and a couple of sample chapters. This is because instead of selling a great story, you're selling your expertise and your subject matter along with your ideas on how to present it. An agent or editor will want to see not only that you can write but also how you intend to approach your subject as a whole. Along these lines, some of the publishers you approach may require additional pieces of information as part of your total proposal such as identifying your target market, researching competitive titles, and doing market analysis in advance.

The Role of Agents in Submitting Nonfiction YA

If you have an agent, and if you have a topic with such broad market appeal that you could conceivably attract a large publisher, your agent will submit your proposal for you. But many nonfiction books—and nonfiction publishers—cater to smaller niche markets. These markets don't have enough potential buyers to draw in a large publisher. If your book is designed for a niche market, instead of involving your agent in submissions, you will need to find a home for your project yourself. Once you have an offer from a publisher, your agent can get involved in the contract.

Interacting With Editors

Whether you end up dealing with a large or small press, if an editor takes an interest in your proposal and likes your writing style, he or she will want to discuss your outline. You'll receive suggestions or demands about what to include (or exclude), and these will take your outline in new directions. So unless you just adore writing for its own sake, it's a waste of time to complete a nonfiction book before you have those crucial discussions about content. You'll end up scrapping a lot of what you've written in favor of fresh ideas. (If you intend to self-publish, then you have a different situation. See Chapter 10.)

Publishing company editors do not get hired by accident. They are selected from a large pool of candidates and picked because they have talent, dedication, and skill. These professionals have their eyes on the big picture, a picture you may not be able to see from your vantage point. It's in your interest to carefully consider what they have to say: They know what the market is doing. Besides, writers who can't or won't adjust their approach are not a good risk for publishers.

Imagine you're a cook with a Ph.D. in nutritional science who has worked with a number of teens on how to make healthy food choices. You submit a proposal for a book that will cover how to avoid or even treat Type 2 diabetes with good nutrition. An editor loves your writing style but suggests a different emphasis: the role that healthy food can play in teen dating and get-togethers. The editor thinks your original idea should be streamlined and occupy only two chapters, one on basic nutrition and one on steering clear of Type 2 diabetes. The other chapters will cover having fun on dates that involve healthy food, who pays for what and when, how to host a party, peer pressure to eat junk food and what to do about it, and a section with recipes such as making your own pizza.

You could moan about how the editor doesn't understand your subject. Or you could jump at the chance to expand. If you settle for moaning, you'll also stamp yourself as an amateur—and you won't get a book contract. But if you can work together with an editor to reorganize your chapters and come up with a new outline, you'll have fun and end up with a wonderful book. The best editor-author relationships incorporate listening on both sides.

Sometimes you may get an offer that really doesn't fit the message you have for your readers. For example, an editor wants to turn your nutrition book into a weight-loss manual that zeroes in on body image and caters to fast-food sponsors. In such a case, to agree would compromise your integrity as an author. Then, of course, you're better off saying no.

Your Outline

Your outline is meant to support your sample chapters and give an idea of how you intend to treat your subject. But again, realize that the content could change significantly by the time you've completed discussions with an editor, so don't get bogged down with too much detail.

If you have ideas for illustrations, photos, or other graphic elements, including them can be a selling point, but only if you present them as suggestions rather than hard-and-fast requirements. Publishers have teams of designers with a track record they trust. Their designers will always have the final say on layout and visual elements.

Your Sample Chapters

Your opening chapter will introduce your subject and give an overview. Other chapters will break down elements of that overview. For your sample chapters, write your opening chapter and one other. Showcase your savvy and your voice. Before approaching an agent or editor, get these two chapters in the best shape you can.

Your Resume

The information you include about yourself is an essential part of selling your proposal. Why are *you* the right person to enter the market with a book on your chosen topic?

When listing your qualifications, be thorough but brief. This might sound like an oxymoron, but it isn't. Weed out any information that doesn't apply to the topic you're writing about. If you want to write about earthworms and you once contributed two lines in an obscure magazine on an unrelated subject, please do not include it as a writing credit. If you worked window-washing skyscrapers, that experience doesn't pertain to earthworms. But if you've led workshops on how to start your own night crawler farm, you have a selling point.

Rather than expounding on the facts, let them speak for themselves. Organize your education and experience into neat, succinct bullets. Editors are *extremely* busy; they need to be able to browse your resume and pick out the relevant details with ease.

To help you streamline, create two resumes, one long and one short. Cut the short one to half a page that hits the highlights. An asterisk can mention that a longer version is available on request. Busy editors will appreciate your thoughtfulness.

It's worth keeping in mind that publishers like to invest not only in specific subjects but also in particular authors who may continue to provide good books over time. Your resume and query letter is your first impression. (For tips on writing query letters, see p. 130.) If you hope for a long relationship, be courteous and forthcoming, but keep to the essentials.

nonfiction and money

As mentioned, many publishers of YA nonfiction are smallish companies that cater to niche markets. This has a number of implications for your wallet.

Advances and Royalties

If you're working with a small publisher, you can expect your advance to range from zip to negligible. However, you have a better chance of collecting royalties year after year with nonfiction than with fiction, unless your subject goes out of date. The majority of fiction books go out of print within a year or two of publication, while nonfiction books are designed for a more enduring market. Also, nonfiction can always be revised and expanded to add muscle to its marketplace physique.

Flat-Fee Contracts

Sometimes nonfiction writers are paid a flat fee to create a specific project for a publisher. Such projects usually have tight deadlines, and they are more common for writers who have proven themselves reliable. Let's say a publisher has noticed a gap in the marketplace for a manual on how to maximize the space in college dorm rooms. After negotiating with several universities, the publisher has received a large purchase order for a booklet called *Making the Most of Your Dorm Room Space*. The universities plan to give out this booklet or offer it as a free download to matriculating freshmen.

The publisher may then approach a writer and offer a contract for a flat fee to research and write up this booklet within 2 months. The publisher will furnish an approximate word count and a broad outline at the outset. Now, it's up to the author to decide if he or she wants the job. If so, a portion of the flat fee will be advanced to get things rolling, and then when the writer meets his or her deadline, the rest of the payment is made. Whether the resulting product goes on to sell a few more copies or a million, the author will not receive royalties. However, the publisher might have another job for that same writer.

Trends

If you're aiming to capitalize on a sizzling trend before it disappears, make it clear in your proposal that you're uniquely positioned to write about it. Maybe there's a sudden fad among teens involving DIY armbands made from vintage buttons and beads. It so happens that *you* have been making jewelry in your basement out of these items for the past 2 years. You know all of the tips and tricks for creating attractive designs that don't fall apart, as well as how to shop for buttons and beads. Your proposal will include a description of the fad with supporting facts, along with your qualifications and a reference to the time-sensitive nature of your book. Normally, it takes 18 months to 3 years to publish, but every now and again a publisher will move a title into rotation quickly to grab sales. Trendy topics work out better for big publishers; they can maneuver publicity to dovetail with a rising fad. In this scenario, you'd get an advance to encourage speedy writing.

nonfiction and you

You can make a real and positive difference in the lives of young people by transmitting your love of your subject, whether it's cooking, nutrition, landscaping, designing—or earthworms. Hundreds of topics are waiting to be discovered by enterprising and curious readers. So go ahead, throw your topic in the ring!

Chapter 5

Obstacles and Demons

There is no telling how many miles you will have to run while chasing a dream.
—Author Unknown

> ### The Lamppost
>
> Late night, no moon, stars hidden by cloud cover, rain slashing down. A man on foot hurries home through dark streets, wishing he'd remembered to bring an umbrella. Businesses have closed. An outage has interrupted power to the streetlights. With his head down against driving wind, the man crashes straight into a lamppost. He stumbles back a few steps, rubs his eyes, turns and keeps walking. This time he bashes into the lamppost with his left shoulder. He staggers around, winds himself up and moves forward, only to run smack into the lamppost, hitting it with his right shoulder. Afraid and disoriented, he flings himself away, striking the lamppost with his back.
>
> "Oh no," he laments. "I'm surrounded by demons!"

obstacles and demons

When writing a book from start to finish, writers often have close encounters with lampposts—and I'm not talking about the sort of lamppost found in Narnia. This chapter examines some of the obstacles you may run into as you work to finish your book. If you have no trouble finishing, you won't need this section. But if you're anything like me or my writing buddies and you get stalled when a big heavy post seems to hit you upside the head, keep reading.

I know what it's like to wobble and wander and wend my way among unlit lampposts. I also know what it's like to finish a book—whether a novel or a book of nonfiction. And when all is said and done—or written and done—there's nothing like the feeling of holding that book in your hand or viewing it in beautiful layout on an e-reader.

So how do you get from page one to the end? There's more to it than chugging away with a good idea. Often, you'll wrestle hefty demons— demons such as doubt, fear, and rejection. I confess it took me a while to get past those demons. Not only do they have steel ribs, they also have faithful cheering sections, endlessly chanting.

Give me a D, give me an O, give me a U, B, T. What's that spell?

I'd never claim to be graceful about the way I deal with doubt and fear when they are looming large. But it doesn't really matter whether I'm graceful or not, so long as I keep writing. And it doesn't matter if you're graceful, either. What's important is to move ahead.

Your Dream

I'm going on the assumption that you dream of writing a book in the YA genre. Chances are you've had this dream for a while. If you're reading this chapter, your personal demons have probably knocked you off course more than once.

Maybe you've heard too many tales of overnight success, and you've talked yourself into doom and gloom, believing your dream is located in a permanent blackout zone. It's easy to forget that the "overnight" part of a success story is hardly ever true. We don't hear how well a dream is going until that dream is actualized. We don't receive reports on a triumph before it's accomplished. Only afterward.

Going for a dream involves uncomfortable quantities of risk. So much work must be done without any assurance from the future. But we all take plenty of risks every day, whether riding the light rail to work, investing in real estate, or eating sushi. You might as well take some risks on behalf of the writing that matters to you.

Best Writing Advice

I'm about to give you the best writing advice I ever received. Interestingly enough, the advice came from a teenager. I was writing *The Healer's Keep*. As usual, I was in the throes of doubt, wondering whether the book was frightful rubbish or had the potential, perhaps, to be a good read.

My daughter Rose, an avid reader, has never minced words. I knew I could count on her to tell me what she honestly thought, so I gave her the unfinished manuscript. Rose was about 14 at the time. She disappeared into her room for a couple of hours. When she came out, she went straight into the kitchen and started fixing herself a snack without saying anything to me. In fact, she was acting miffed. She handled the bread with more force than necessary and slammed the lever on the toaster with a loud clack.

Heart sinking, I asked, "Did you read my chapters?"

"Yeah," she said. Typical teenage brevity.

"So do you have any suggestions for me?"

"Yeah," she replied, reaching for the butter knife. "Finish it!"

Finish it. When Rose urged me to finish, I had one of those "aha" moments. I realized not only that she'd liked the story well enough to be upset when it stopped midway, but also that she was giving me the best advice I'd ever receive: Finish it!

It can be easier to hope than to act, easier to imagine a large book deal than face a rejection letter, easier to daydream while doing the dishes than to invest the time needed to write down a story. But if we look closely at pressures and obstacles, we stand a better chance of getting past them.

Here's a list of some common obstacles (cleverly disguised as lampposts) that writers tend to stumble into.

obstacle #1: lack of time

Lack of time seems to be the top complaint of people trying to complete a book. What takes away our time? Jobs, family, friends in crisis, health problems, community involvement, need for sleep, chores that have to be done, closets that need to be cleaned . . . fill in the blank.

It took me 5 years to write my first book, by the way. I didn't really know what I was doing and had to grope my way through. Never a morning person, I began to get up early to write before the day's routine began. Doing so messed with my biorhythms for a while, but then I fell in love with the quiet magic of predawn. Time took on a quality like taffy. When my spirit was clenched in some way, time resembled hard taffy—unyielding and tough, seemingly impossible to work with. Yet when my spirit was open and light, time turned soft and malleable. It stretched a long way, much farther than I would have guessed it could, with flowing strands, flexible and sweet. And I finished that book.

I know that your life and mine are different, but we're all issued 24 hours a day. Look for chinks in your schedule. When you find them, use a crowbar if you have to, but widen those crevices. Seize the opening. Write the book! One usable page a day yields a 365-page book in a year. A hundred words a day (a couple of light paragraphs) yields a 75,000 word book in 2 years.

Maybe you, like me, do not churn out pages quickly. I used to think it was a fatal flaw to be slow. Then one day I looked at my garden. Different seeds sown on the same day germinate at different rates. But I don't berate the cucumber seeds or accuse them of being lazy if they're slower to grow than the carrots.

How long does it take to write 100 words? Well, naturally, it depends on you and what you're writing. But if you type 50 words per minute, that's only 2 minutes. Add in a lot of pondering and rewriting and throwing away. It's not unreasonable to say you could write 100 usable words in an hour.

It's all about finding your own pace within the schedule you have, and then making the most of it. Do you get time away from your job during lunch? Instead of going out, pack a sandwich and bring a notebook. Can't think creatively in the middle of your workday? Try getting up early to write when the day is fresh. If short bursts aren't your style, schedule a block of time during your weekend, evening, or morning. Do you watch TV or surf the net? How many hours? Cut back, and watch your manuscript grow.

Don't wait. Life is too short for waiting.

obstacle #2: rejection

The girl doesn't, it seems to me, have a special perception or feeling which would lift that book above the "curiosity" level.
—From a rejection slip for *Anne Frank: Diary of a Young Girl*

I haven't come across anyone who deals really well with rejection. Rejection feels terrible. Knowing you're in good company is small consolation.

But, oh, the company you're in!

Dr. Seuss's first book was rejected 28 times before being published. His books went on to sell more than 200 million copies. J. K. Rowling's first *Harry Potter* book was rejected 12 times. We all know the next chapter in that story. Jack London received more than 250 rejections before first getting published, and he was the J. K. Rowling of his time, his books selling millions of copies. Those are just a few of many examples.

Books are rejected for many reasons. They may be poorly written or lack marketability. The publisher may have recently signed a similar project. But sometimes it's just a matter of differing tastes.

You probably remember the first time a friend raved about a book that left you shrugging your shoulders. Likewise, you might have a favorite story that doesn't move your friend one bit. Your contrasting opinions won't make either of you sob into a pillow, I presume. Yet somehow, if something *we've* written fails to pass someone else's taste test, it's harder to accept. Fiasco! Defeat. Blood-curdling agony.

Take a deep breath. It's okay. I know, that's easier to say than to feel. But as one who has occasionally flung herself into the pit of despair over rejection, I recommend humor as a more effective way to cope. Try running a copy of your rejection letter through a paper shredder, creating confetti. Hold a party in your honor. Serve chocolate. Laugh it up. You're doing something right. At the very least, you can't get rejected if you're not putting yourself out there.

Some writers have used their rejection slips like wallpaper—which seems to me like pretty awful feng shui. Some make their rejection letters into paper airplanes and fly them into a fireplace. One way or another, we all find a way to deal.

How many rejections should you expect to receive? As many as you do. Sorry to be flippant, but unlike my fictional character, I'm not a seer. The average number of rejections for published authors is supposedly 10, but I don't know how anyone could tabulate the numbers.

All in all, rejection is not, in and of itself, an accurate assessment of worth. Plenty of writers have felt the sting of rejection and then persisted to build wonderful careers. So think of rejection as an initiation rite of sorts, an entrance requirement to the author's club.

And always remember—you're in good company.

obstacle #3: doubt and fear

Who has not felt squashed by self-doubt?

I don't know what form your self-doubt takes. For some, it's a vague paralysis that creeps over the mind. For others it may be articulated in nauseating detail. Whatever the form, self-doubt is usually a variation of "I can't do this" or "There's no point."

Where do all those doubts come from? Well, feeling doubt while you're in the process of creating makes a peculiar kind of sense. After all, knowledge brings confidence, but creativity is all about touching the unknown. Knowledge asserts "what's so." Imagination, on the other hand (according to dictionary.com), is "the act or power of forming mental images of what is not present; the act or power of creating new ideas."

The act or power of creating. That sounds good.

Images of what is not present. A bit more iffy.

And it's within that iffy zone that we find opportunities to create. In that same zone, doubt thumps its chest and utters convincing challenges. It's the nature of the beast, I'm afraid.

Navigating Darkness

When I was 17, I went to college in Santa Fe, NM. I had lived the previous 6 years in humid Wisconsin, at sea level. Santa Fe sits at 7,000 feet, and the desert dust makes sunsets that fill the sky, not only in the west but around the compass.

Behind the college was a small mountain named Monte Sol, part of the Sangre de Cristo range. It was uninhabited. I wasn't the only one dazzled by the New Mexico sunsets. A group of us decided it would be a great experience to see the sunset from the summit of Monte Sol. One bright afternoon, several classmates and I set out, climbing the steep makeshift trail to the top.

The sunset was even more resplendent than we'd imagined it would be—a blend of red, orange, and gold. As the last rays grew dim,

---

it suddenly occurred to us that after sunset, night falls! We still needed to get down the mountain. And we had not a flashlight among us.

In fading twilight, we found the dirt path. This was not Wisconsin dirt, which holds together well; this was dry, sandy dirt, which slips away, especially when the path is steep. We scrambled along, clutching at scrubby piñon trees, while night thickened. Soon we couldn't see the trail at all, couldn't even see our own feet in the darkness. After a long, bumbling trek and many scratches and scrapes, we made it back to the college grounds.

To me, that journey up and down the mountain is analogous to what happens when undertaking a new writing venture. Imagination inspires us, and we act. It's easy, in the beginning, to be so struck by a glowing vision that the thought of darkness is forgotten. We begin boldly, climbing high on the strength of the vision. Then we encounter darkness, and we must stumble through it.

As artists, we wouldn't want to miss out on the darkness altogether, any more than we would want to skip the light of day. Louis Armstrong, child of poverty and prostitution, wrote "What a Wonderful World." He sang of the "bright blessed day." He also sang of "the dark, sacred night." Why did Armstrong call the dark sacred? Maybe he was referring to the way that heartache and hard times can deepen creative urges. Or maybe he was talking about the unknown.

That unknown is mysterious. It resists control, cannot be contained by formulae, refuses to be ruled. By its nature, it does not engender confidence. But it also bestows the sort of wisdom that guides our footsteps when knowledge cannot help.

Imagination isn't limited by what is present, leading the way instead to what is not. This has profound implications for writers, who get to go into the unknown whenever we start a new book.

I don't have anything against knowledge. But when knowledge takes over, we run the risk of getting set in our ways, trapped in the territory we have already explored.

When stumbling through darkness, unable to see, it's tempting to try to use knowledge when imagination is what's called for. It's especially tempting when the darkness is deep. At that point it's hard to believe that what we don't yet know will help us the most.

Anyone who takes excursions through the unknown is likely to encounter the uglies of doubt, fear, isolation, frustration, and more. Sometimes they rise up with great fervor and make things very difficult. This is natural, normal, and to be expected.

obstacle #4: meant to be

There's a lot of talk floating around about "fulfilling your dreams" and "following your path." Sometimes the implication seems to be that if you're following your path to fulfill your dreams, obstacles will melt, or the whole experience will be so joyous, any drudgery will transform into bliss. Along those lines, I can't tell you how many times I've heard, "I was planning to write a book, but I guess it wasn't meant to be."

Huh? Eh? What? If it's meant to be, will the book write itself?

How many people do you know who will go that extra mile for their job and be amazingly patient with all the bumps in the road on the job—and then tell themselves a dream should just fall into place or it isn't meant to be?

Art does not have a special exemption from sweat. Images of writers as artists whose work flows effortlessly or not at all are false. Equally untrue is the idea that artists must live for a while in the gutter dressed in elegant black, and then when they've suffered enough, their difficulties will magically resolve.

If you were first starting out at a gym and someone told you, "Getting in shape is going to feel fabulous from the get-go. Burning fat is going to be a blast every day," you'd probably know that was a lie. Certainly after soreness kicked in, you'd know—or when you were huffing and puffing while building up an oxygen debt.

Plumbing the depths of your adolescent self, coming up with a story that really hangs together, writing that awful first draft, going over it all again and again—takes work. Intensive, sweaty work. It ain't easy!

So if you're struggling to get your book written, there's nothing inherently wrong with you. Go to it, sweat it out, huff and puff. Keep going.

obstacle #5:
waiting for inspiration

Every writer loves the days when inspiration thrums in the air, when the words are flowing like babbling brooks, when the pages of deathless prose are piling up.

I can count on one hand how many times those days have come along for me. And in each case, sad to say, by the next morning it became clear that what I'd written was in desperate need of revision.

Everyone's different. Maybe you're the sort of writer who can afford to wait until you feel wildly inspired before you get going. Me, I find it helpful to approach writing the way I approach exercise.

The more often I exercise, the easier it is to exercise again. Then I can depend on my body for energy when I need it, and if there are sudden, unexpected demands in my life, I have more reserves available to deal with them—reserves built up by regular exercise. In a similar way, the more often I write, the easier it is to write again. It's a level of writing fitness, exercising my dream body.

Dream body? Imagine the dream inside you as a body—a body that's visible to your soul. When your dream body is neglected it gets out of shape—puny and flabby and the whole bit. Undernourished. Sometimes it might even seem to be dead. But it isn't, and if you start taking care of it, it will get stronger.

It wouldn't be smart to load up on the heaviest weights your first day in the gym. And you can't expect your dream body to lift your entire dream immediately. Give it time, attention, nourishment, and exercise so it gets stronger. And as with any fitness program, there's a lot to be said for making yourself accountable when exercising your dream body. Set a few goals. Realistic goals. Start with a paragraph a day if you have to. Make a daily appointment with yourself. Then keep your appointment!

When you set a time or clear a space to write, inspiration will feel invited. Like a dear friend, it will pay you a visit. Do your friends like to call first before coming over? Do you like to have coffee, tea, and muffins ready? But what if you believed the sign of a true friend was to beat down your door at unexpected times and insist on barging in?

Treat inspiration like a friend, and it will be a friend to you. Don't wait for it to beat down your door. You might wait a lifetime.

lampposts for light

So there you have it—a list of lampposts you may bang into as you write your book. You may have encountered one or two—or all—of the above. My hope is that by naming and facing them, the lampposts lining your way will start shedding light to guide your direction.

Chapter 6

Resources for Writers

. . . the process of writing is precious and beautiful and humbling and uncomfortable and shattering and edifying, no matter what.
—Olugbemisola Rhuday-Perkovich

Your creative mind is begging you to write. You've got a book haunting you. You're ready to go. You put words on a page, and then more words. You read it over. But the words you've written aren't communicating what you want them to say. Instead of soaring like your imagination, your words seem lifeless, like birds afflicted with West Nile virus. Now what?

It's time to learn more about the craft of writing.

No one expects a painter to magically understand how to mix colors or master brush strokes without study and practice. Actors and dancers don't hope to be great without ever taking a class in theater or movement. Musicians know they must put in years before their instrument can speak with eloquence. The same goes for writing.

If you want to improve as a writer, resources abound to save you time and trouble on your writing journey.

recommended books

Dozens and dozens of books are devoted to the art of writing and the business of publishing, and the right book at the right time is worth far more than its cover price. Here, for your review, is a list of exceptional titles. No, I haven't read them all, but I've asked for recommendations, and each is somebody's favorite. All of these books, and others you'll discover, can help you immensely.

Unfortunately, you may have to dig a little to find some of these titles, because books—even excellent books—go in and out of print all the time. So if you find one you like, you might want to buy it.

Books to Inspire

➤ *Bird by Bird* by Anne Lamott
➤ *On Writing: A Memoir of the Craft* by Stephen King
➤ *A Circle of Quiet* by Madeleine L'Engle
➤ *The Triggering Town: Lectures and Essays on Poetry and Writing* by Richard Hugo

➤ *Exploding the Myths: The Truth About Teenagers and Reading* by Marc Aronson
➤ *Wild Mind: Living the Writer's Life* by Natalie Goldberg
➤ *The Word: Black Writers Talk About the Transformative Power of Reading and Writing* by Marita Golden

Books About Submitting and Pitching

➤ *Writer's Market,* edited by Robert Lee Brewer
➤ *Writing the Fiction Synopsis* by Pam McCutcheon
➤ *Get Known Before the Book Deal* by Christina Katz
➤ *Making the Perfect Pitch: How to Catch a Literary Agent's Eye* by Katharine Sands
➤ *The Renegade Writer's Query Letters That Rock* by Diana Burrell and Linda Formichelli

Craft Books for Fiction Writers

➤ *The Seven Basic Plots* by Christopher Booker
➤ *Unjournaling* by Dawn DiPrince and Cheryl Miller Thurston
➤ *From Where You Dream* by Robert Olen Butler
➤ *Writing the Breakout Novel* by Donald Maass
➤ *The Fire in Fiction: Passion, Purpose and Techniques to Make Your Novel Great* by Donald Maass
➤ *The Complete Handbook of Novel Writing* by Writer's Digest Editors
➤ *Elements of Fiction Writing: Characters & Viewpoint* by Orson Scott Card
➤ *Maps of the Imagination: The Writer as Cartographer* by Peter Turchi
➤ *Elements of Fiction Writing: Beginnings, Middles & Ends* by Nancy Kress
➤ *Story: Substance, Structure, Style and the Principles of Screenwriting* by Robert McKee
➤ *Save the Cat! The Last Book on Screenwriting You'll Ever Need* by Blake Snyder
➤ *The Elements of Style* by E. B. White and William Strunk, Jr.

- *Spunk and Bite: A Writer's Guide to Bold, Contemporary Style* by Arthur Plotnik
- *Get That Novel Written! From Initial Idea to Final Edit* by Donna Levin
- *Sin and Syntax: How to Craft Wickedly Effective Prose* by Constance Hale
- *How Fiction Works* by James Wood
- *Reading Like a Writer: A Guide for People Who Love Books and for Those Who Want to Write Them* by Francine Prose

Craft Books for Nonfiction Writers

- *Keys to Great Writing* by Stephen Wilbers
- *On Writing Well* by William Zinsser
- *Write Tight* by William Brohaugh
- *Grammatically Correct: The Essential Guide to Spelling, Style, Usage, Grammar, and Punctuation* by Anne Stilman

Graphic Format Resources

- *Understanding Comics: The Invisible Art* by Scott McCloud
- *Making Comics: Storytelling Secrets of Comics, Manga and Graphic Novels* by Scott McCloud
- *Drawing Words and Writing Pictures* by Jessica Abel and Matt Madden
- *Adventures in Cartooning: How to Turn Your Doodles Into Comics* by James Sturm, Alexis Frederick-Frost, and Andrew Arnold

Christian Market Resources

- *The Christian Writer's Manual of Style: Updated and Expanded Edition* by Robert Hudson
- *A Novel Idea: Best Advice on Writing Inspirational Fiction* by various Christian writers
- *The Rock That Is Higher: Story as Truth* by Madeleine L'Engle

Self-Publishing Resources

- ➤ *The Self-Publishing Manual* by Dan Poynter
- ➤ *The Complete Guide to Self-Publishing: Everything You Need to Know to Write, Publish, Promote and Sell Your Own Book* by Marilyn Ross and Sue Collier
- ➤ *Dan Poynter's Self-Publishing Manual, Volume 2: How to Write, Print and Sell Your Own Book* by Dan Poynter
- ➤ *The Fine Print of Self-Publishing: Everything You Need to Know About the Costs, Contracts, and Process of Self-Publishing* (4th ed.) by Mark Levine

More Books About Writing YA

Wild Ink is not the only title out there about writing YA, and it's always good to get other perspectives on the genre and how to break in.

- ➤ *Writing Great Books for Young Adults: Everything You Need to Know, from Crafting the Idea to Landing a Publishing Deal* by Regina Brooks
- ➤ *Writing And Selling The Young Adult Novel* by K. L. Going
- ➤ *Writing Young Adult Fiction For Dummies* by Deborah Halverson
- ➤ *The Complete Idiot's Guide to Writing for Young Adults* by Deborah Perlberg

Yay for books! And that's not all that's available to you.

other resources for writers

Writing Classes

Most community learning centers, colleges, and universities offer classes in creative writing. So do writing organizations, both brick and mortar and online. If you're short on discipline, class assignments can motivate you to complete essays, short stories, or even longer projects.

Writers' Conferences

Writers' conferences include workshops on the writing craft, marketing your work, and staying inspired. The good ones include opportunities to get a critique on a page or two of your manuscript and make a pitch to a working editor or agent. Some of these conferences have well-regarded writing contests for unpublished writers. Choices abound, and conferences can be excellent opportunities to hear firsthand from industry hotshots. Many of the bigger, more credible conferences are attached to professional organizations.

Professional Organizations

Writers' organizations give you the opportunity to meet kindred spirits, learn more about writing and publishing, and generally connect with the writing community. For example, the Society of Children's Book Writers and Illustrators (SCBWI) is an organization with a worldwide membership (see http://www.scbwi.org). Local chapters provide members with gatherings, classes, and support. When you join, you'll gain access to information about writing and publishing in the children's market, of which young adult fiction is a part.

There are also professional organizations dedicated to genres of adult fiction. Mystery Writers of America, Romance Writers of America, and Science Fiction and Fantasy Writers of America all have regional chapters. (To date, a Young Adult Writers of America does not exist.) Depending on the YA subgenre you're interested in, you could gain a lot of knowledge and support from attending conferences sponsored by these organizations.

Groups spring up to serve writers within a particular region as well. In Colorado, where I live, there are organizations such as Colorado Authors' League, Rocky Mountain Fiction Writers, Rocky Mountain Chapter of SCBWI, Northern Colorado Writers, Lighthouse Writers Workshop, and others. All offer classes and writing contests. Try doing a search for writing organizations in your area.

Other organizations are devoted specifically to increasing literacy among teens. The Young Adult Library Services Association (YALSA) is the fastest growing group in the American Library Association (ALA)—and the ALA has a long history of connecting media specialists throughout the United States. The International Reading Association (IRA) is another effective organization dedicated to literacy. Both YALSA and IRA have outreach programs directed at young adults themselves. ALAN (Assembly on Literature for Adolescents of the National Council of Teachers of English) links teachers who work with teens nationwide. Authors can join any or all of these organizations, and membership fees are reasonable. *Voice of Youth Advocates* (VOYA) magazine is focused on teens and literacy. Authors can subscribe.

Receiving Critique

At what point do you show your writing to other people? That's a big question. When I was writing my first novel, I didn't show it to anyone but my children, my husband, my sisters, and one friend. This runs counter to the advice you'll get from other sources who say that feedback from close family members and friends has no value. In my case, feedback from people who were close to me, particularly my children, was of great value. Both my kids have a knack for spotting discrepancies and plot holes. They were the perfect teenagers to tell me what they thought.

Back then I didn't know about critique groups, and if I had known, I probably wouldn't have joined one. I still believe that if you show what you've written to the wrong person at the wrong time, you risk sending your artistic self into hiding. When sharing your writing with other people, you lay yourself open to their reactions. Some of those reactions will be kind. Some will be mean. Some will be helpful and others completely off base. The main point: Once you put your writing out there, you can't take it back. And there's a delicacy to writing, especially at first. When you write a story, you're exposing your innermost thoughts and feelings—your view of life. This makes you vulnerable.

Sometimes, not showing what you've written is the best way to strengthen the relationship between you and the writer within. You don't dig up an apple seed to see how it's growing. You let it germinate and send shoots into the air and light. You water it. You wait until it's a good strong sapling before you hang anything on its branches—and you don't get angry if the tree doesn't bear fruit immediately.

However, it's also true that no one can read his or her own work for the first time. Good readers who will spot plot holes, cardboard characters, or stilted dialogue can be immensely helpful. When you get criticism from people who know what they're talking about and also care about helping you, it's worth more than you could ever pay. So just as showing your writing to the wrong person at the wrong time can hurt you, showing the right person at the right time gives you a chance to grow much more and much faster than you could on your own.

My first rule when receiving criticism: Consider the source. And in my experience, there are three categories of critique: constructive, destructive, and useless.

Constructive critique. Constructive critique comes from knowledgeable people who want to help you write better. They look over what you've written and make suggestions that tighten the structure, streamline the flow, highlight the characters, and help the plot stay on track.

Keep in mind that sometimes an excellent critique may be delivered bluntly. Just because the delivery is blunt doesn't mean your work is not respected or the person giving the critique has nothing valuable to offer. Some of the best advice I've received has seemed harsh at first.

When you're ready for constructive criticism, you'll crave honest feedback like a marathon runner craves water. You'll seek out people with a knack for editing and beg them to tear your manuscript apart. You'll want to hear what's wrong with your story just as much as you want to hear what's right. After listening to forthright comments about flaws and weaknesses, you'll even overflow with gratitude. That's how valuable constructive critique can be.

Destructive critique. How do you spot destructive critique? The critique will be expressed in generalities that give you nothing to work with, statements like "This is the worst thing I've ever read," or "You have nothing to say," or "What made you think you could write a story?"

When listening to critique, look for useful specifics. "I like the way this begins, but in paragraph 7 on page 2, I started to lose interest. It seemed repetitive." Or "The part where Donovan ditches Cheronne is well written, but why does she forgive him so easily?" Or "This chapter starts out at a fast pace with Ava getting close to Kira's secret, but it starts to fizzle on page 5 when Thelonius just sits around." Or even "This first chapter leaves me cold. I really start getting involved with your topic in the second chapter."

Destructive critique would say, "This is a bad story." Or "Cheronne's an idiot." Or "Thelonius? What a stupid name." Or "Your topic is boring."

The best way to handle destructive critique? I'm not sure, but deep, slow breathing is a start. Remind yourself it's just one person's opinion. You don't have to listen. If you can laugh, you're home free.

Something else that deserves mention: If you always react to critique with knee-jerk defensiveness, that's a different problem. You may be responding to constructive critique as if it were destructive. If you've received specific feedback, think it over before automatically rejecting it. Is it relevant to your book? If so, you've just been given a precious gift. But if you feel too hurt to consider the merits of the advice, you're not ready to receive critique. (You may want to go shopping for a rhinoceros hide, because you're going to need it in the writing business.) It's perfectly all right to back off and wait until you're stronger. And it's always a good idea to be selective about whom you invite to criticize your work.

Useless critique. One more category of critique is the useless variety—critique from well-meaning people who don't know what they're talking about. Either everything will be generalized in a glaze of positive comments such as, "This is the best thing I've ever read," or the advice will come out of left field, making ridiculous objections like, "I don't think your characters should tell the truth because people don't like to hear the truth," or "I think you should take out the part where Samantha knocks on Kareem's door"—when actually that particular part is central to the plot. Imagine if J. R. R. Tolkien, author of *Lord of the Rings*, had been told, "Your book is good except for the Hobbits. Why not just tell a normal story?" Or if someone gave Harper Lee, author of *To Kill A Mockingbird*, a critique saying, "You give children too much credit—you should write from the point of view of adults." Useless critique is maddening, confusing, and, well . . . useless. It misses the mark.

Sometimes useless comments are so biased in your favor it's like talking to a doting mother who says, "What zit? I don't see any zits on your face," when it's obvious there are three big ones right in the center of your forehead. Something inside you will feel restless and dissatisfied when you get a useless critique, even if it's positive.

It's important to trust your intuition. If you're not being defensive, you'll be able to recognize helpful critique. You'll light up when you're given insights that show you how to take your story from good to excellent.

And in the end, the most important critique you'll ever get will come from yourself. After all, you're the one who knows the most about what you're writing.

Critique Groups

Writing groups are designed to provide regular critique for the members. In an ideal group, laughter overflows as insights roll. Incisive comments are handed out with respect, gratefully received, and weighed within each writer's sense of purpose. Individual strengths are honored, and a context of trust and enjoyment propels the members forward. Supportive synergy surges through the group, leading individuals to create more and write better. Writers who are part of a functional group can grow exponentially, and fast. Well-founded critique is the absolute best way to improve.

But not every group will work out. Sometimes members will give you destructive or useless critique. Sometimes personalities clash. After all, there isn't a "writer" personality. You don't automatically share traits, values, or visions with someone just because you're both interested in writing.

You could get wildly inconsistent feedback. Member A thinks your wording is purple, Member B says it's too stark, Member C has no idea what you're trying to say, Member D is sure you've spelled everything out too plainly . . . You're left dazed and confused.

Finding the group that's right for you is a little like dating. Start with pieces of writing that don't matter much while you get a feeling for who you're dealing with. It's hard to know in advance who will be capable of giving perceptive critique. Even if every member of a group is well-read, a well-read person is not necessarily a good writer any more than a movie buff is a good actor. To further complicate matters, not every good writer has a flair for critique.

Critique groups, like families, have different sets of rules. Some groups operate well within a highly defined structure. For example, a particular format is followed every time. The person receiving a critique may not be allowed to speak. The critique itself must be worded with something positive first, something less positive second, and something more positive to finish up. (This is a good idea, especially for new writers who aren't used to criticism.) Other groups are loose and free-flowing and yet get a lot accomplished. Members who've been together a long time may leap straight to the heart of the critique, allowing the writer to enter the discussion.

Some groups are genre specific, seeking members with similar writing goals. This makes it harder to find enough members. More important than individual focus is group synergy, compatibility, and trust.

Trust is a big factor in effective group dynamics, and different people have different criteria for bestowing trust. For me, the big three requirements are honest criticism, respect, and confidentiality. I want to know my fellow writers will lay it on the line and won't be offended when I do the same. I want to be sure we'll all refrain from blabbing outside the group about what is discussed inside. It goes without saying that each writer makes the call on what to keep and what to throw away, including criticism.

Generating momentum. Working with writing buddies in a critique group is a fantastic way to keep momentum going. For one thing, if I know my buddies are preparing new chapters, I'm not going to let them down by procrastinating, getting distracted, or backpedaling. And I look forward to reading their work, hearing about their week, and listening to their insightful wisecracks as we keep each other accountable to the goals we've set.

Critique groups can be organized in dozens upon dozens of ways. As I see it, so long as members find help to write better and keep going, the format is secondary. Keep looking until you find a place where you fit. Professional organizations such as the Society of Children's Book Writers and Illustrators can put you in touch with existing groups looking for new members or with other writers looking for community.

dead ends

One of the things a good critique group can help identify is whether a book is heading for a dead end—meaning it has a fatal flaw. Unlike fatal flaws in characters (which can add interest), fatal flaws in the style or storyline of a book lead nowhere. I wouldn't be doing my job if I didn't point out a few easily avoidable dead ends that show up for YA writers of both nonfiction and fiction.

Dead Ends for Nonfiction Writers

Writers of nonfiction YA can dead end their books in several ways: (1) by removing all juice from their subject, petrifying it; (2) by treating readers as if they're 6 instead of 16; and (3) by presenting concepts in convoluted terms using very long sentences and obscure vocabulary. Just say it, and say it well, with enthusiasm.

Dead Ends for Novelists

Novelists can easily dead end their books by leaning too heavily on true stories when writing fiction or by preaching to their readers. Let me explain.

Basing a novel on real events. If you plan to write a book of fiction based closely on actual events you've experienced, you're heading for tricky territory.

I know I've said it's a good idea to delve into your own life and write about what's real to you. It *is* a good idea, but only if you follow the structure of fiction—which means you've got to have clear tension and resolution, character arc, and plot lines. If the story you're telling has really happened, you may feel compelled to faithfully convey the true chain of events. If you do, you're unlikely to wind up with an effective plot line.

Can an exciting book emerge from a true story? Without a doubt. We've all read examples of outstanding fiction based on true life. However, large numbers of writers trip up on this issue. They make the mistake of thinking something is automatically interesting just because it really happened.

If you decide to use actual events for the foundation of your novel, pick your details with care. Leave out the parts that don't serve. Make full use of poetic license. The story must come first. Also remember that, legally, you can get into trouble if you duplicate real people without their express permission.

Preaching. Another problem is talking down to readers. A condescending or preachy style is a big turnoff, not only to adults but also to teenagers.

As a group, teens are much maligned. "Teenager" has turned into a derogatory term, variously synonymous with troublesome, unruly, scatterbrained, and even criminal. Teens don't want to encounter this unfair stereotype when they read. They want to be respected, not patronized or lectured. Adults reading YA will not appreciate condescension either.

Does this mean you should avoid having a message? Not at all. As we explored in Chapter 3, messages are important to fiction. But don't hit the reader over the head. Embed your message into the core of the story itself.

Will the Point Be Taken?

Let's say you have strong feelings about teens ruining their future health by snarfing junk food, guzzling soft drinks, and getting only enough exercise to make it from the fridge to the computer and back again. You write a book with a character whose main activities are centered around snacks, soda, and surfing the net. Primary interactions with that character consist of some people warning him about consequences while others incite him to practice unhealthy habits. You write scenes of his ensuing battle with diabetes and end with obvious conclusions about how his lifestyle has resulted in disease.

Your motivation is to make a point and get your readers to change bad habits. But will the point be taken? For a better result, you could write about a teen with a driving ambition to design world-class gaming software. Night after night he works late on his dream project, falling behind in homework, propping himself up with caffeinated sugary drinks and fistfuls of French fries. After some dramatic setbacks, he enters and wins a major software contest, only to have his best ideas stolen by a rival. As he searches for the identity of the thief, he's getting blurred vision and excessive fatigue. Ignoring his failing health, he keeps pushing. At a crucial moment, he slips into a coma. A friend rushes him to the hospital, where he's diagnosed with diabetes. He gets treatment, changes his habits, identifies the thief, and wins back his credibility in software design.

> In the first story, the message is screaming at the reader from page 1. In the second story, the message is embedded for the reader to discover.

An example of an embedded message from a well-known novel comes from J. K. Rowling's *Harry Potter and the Goblet of Fire*. The story features Rita Skeeter, a journalist whose pen drips lies about Harry Potter. The message: Don't believe everything you read.

Some people worry that unless teens are bludgeoned with a blatant message, they won't receive it. Not so. Young people grasp complex ideas with ease. They're perfectly capable of adding profound perspective to any discussion. And they're certainly able to pick up messages left in the background of a book.

Another way to talk down to readers is by backing away from conflict, dancing around it, or inserting pat resolutions. Teens are ready for a more complex approach. Do not cheat on the conflict. Weak or undeveloped subplots won't cut it either. Fill your plot with twists, turns, and interesting secondary characters. And remember that young people care about more than dating, clothes, and social status. Most teens are far from shallow, and the same goes for adults reading YA.

Respect your readers, and they'll respect you back. When writing, I make it easy for myself by simply assuming my readers will be smarter, better informed, more savvy, and in all ways more brilliant than I.

honing your craft

Your story deserves your best writing, and there are loads of resources around to help you improve. All approaches are valid so long as they get you to write your book. However you learn best, whatever gets you to practice most, do it. And keep going.

Chapter 7

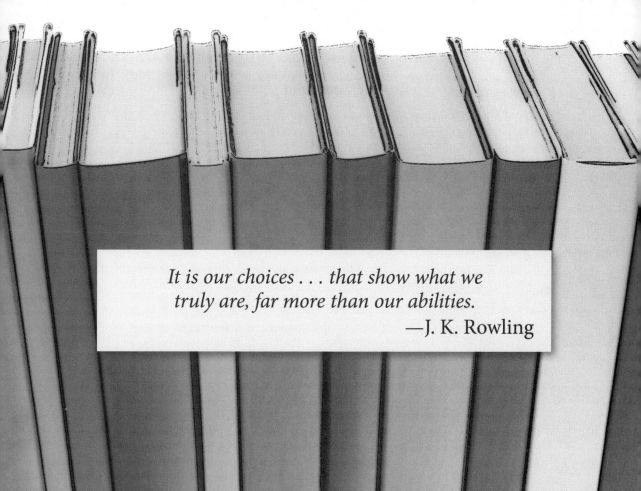

Submitting Your Manuscript

It is our choices . . . that show what we truly are, far more than our abilities.
—J. K. Rowling

Writing is to publishing as cooking in your own kitchen is to running a busy downtown restaurant, as singing in the shower is to performing in a stadium, as a small beloved pet is to a great big zoo.

Not the same.

Some writers are content to write purely for the sake of getting the story down. Publishing doesn't interest them. My grandmother was that way. She wrote wonderful stories for her children and grandchildren without a thought of offering them for publication. If you're like her, you'll miss all the entanglements of the business side of things. That's perfectly okay. You might be happier, too. But most of us want to be published and get our books out there, so this chapter outlines the process of submitting your manuscript.

agents

Editors at publishing companies are deluged with submissions. Consequently, large publishing houses have chosen to cut off access to writers who are not already represented by an agent. Thus, if you want an editor at a large publishing house to consider your book for publication, the next step after finishing your manuscript is to find a literary agent.

The difference between literary agents and editors is that literary agents represent authors, and editors represent publishing houses. Editors *acquire* manuscripts. Agents *represent* manuscripts. Literary agents sell manuscripts to publishers on your behalf. They know how to negotiate for you, because they're experienced with elements of the market you may not understand, elements such as royalty advances, foreign rights, audio and screen rights, and contracts.

Your agent is invested in you. Agents are paid a fixed percentage of an author's earnings (between 15% and 25%). An ideal agent believes in your work, is well connected in the industry, has a good idea of where your book would find a market, understands contracts and clauses, and manages time effectively. Such a person is invaluable to your career.

An agent is not required, but an agent makes the whole process easier for many reasons. Agents know the market. They know what is realistic. They're highly trained professionals, and they're in your corner.

Sometimes, though, authors meet an acquisitions editor of a publishing company, form a direct connection, and sign a contract without agent representation. If a publisher allows you to represent yourself, you'll just need to understand contracts or involve an attorney.

Approaching Agents or Editors

So how do you approach an agent or editor you hope will take an interest in your book?

Write the best book you can write. This might sound like a "duh" piece of advice, but it's first for a reason. You'll be up against hundreds, if not thousands, of other submissions in the course of a single month. You've got to write something that stands out.

Agents and editors lament the volume of submissions they receive that are riddled with grammatical errors and typos, not to mention poor plotting, weak characterization, dull dialogue, lackluster setting, ambiguous point of view, jumbled style, and incoherent voice. If your book has an obvious problem in the first chapter, no one is going to read far enough to find out your second chapter is fabulous. The majority of manuscripts are rejected based on the first page. True!

Agents' and editors' days are jam-packed with responsibilities and obligations that have nothing to do with sitting leisurely in a chair reading manuscripts. You've got to hook them with the first page—and the second, third, 12th, and last.

Write a log line. In case you haven't come across the term "log line," (a.k.a. tag line), it's a sentence or two that sums up your story in an enticing way. For example, here's a log line from aspiring YA novelist Rebecca J. Rowley's book *My Way Home*: "Fifteen and pregnant, Reagan Stiles longs to find support and acceptance from her estranged older sister before her water breaks." My log line for *The Seer and the Sword* is, "A prince born to peace and privilege loses his father, his kingdom, his sword, and his freedom. How does he rise to become the greatest warrior of his time?" The log line for *Seize the Story* is "a writing guide for teens that reads like a novel while delivering elements of fiction such as setting, characterization, dialogue, plot, and point of view."

A good log line will have an "ooh" factor. When you say it out loud to friends, they will nod and smile and say "Ooh." A lousy logline will make people blink slowly or even cringe.

Writing a pithy log line can be challenging—but take the challenge. You'll be glad you did. Then, when someone asks what your book is about, instead of staring blankly ahead with nothing but "uh" on your tongue, or launching into a rambling chapter-by-chapter description, you can bring out your log line.

Be ready to make a verbal pitch. A verbal pitch amounts to an in-person query. In a brief speech, you tell an agent or editor about your book.

Verbal pitches often take place by appointment at writers' conferences. (Occasionally they happen more spontaneously—during mixers or dinner conversations.) A scheduled pitch will typically allow writers between 5 and 15 minutes with an editor or agent. One to 5 minutes are allocated to make the pitch itself, with the rest of the time assigned for feedback and conversation.

Easy as pie.

Ha!

I've seen writers get sick over verbal pitches: sweaty palms, trembling voice, and overwhelming nausea. No wonder. How do you sum up your whole book in a couple of sentences without sounding rehearsed and wooden?

A tall order, for sure. It's natural to be nervous. But verbal pitches are definitely worth doing. If you impress an agent or editor with your personality and story ideas, you've transformed yourself from a complete unknown to a person of positive interest.

To maximize your chances, prepare a good log line, and then relax. Be friendly and professional. The agent or editor is there because he or she is looking for great manuscripts—and you're there because you have a wonderful story to offer. A perfect match.

During your verbal pitch, you may be asked about something known as your "platform." This is not about shoes with mighty big heels. It's not about your political stance. The agent or editor you're speaking with wants to know how/if your background and previous writing experience will give you credibility and help market your book.

For example, when I pitched *Wild Ink*, I mentioned that I'd led well-attended writers' conference workshops on how to write YA, and that

I'd read a lot of YA books authored by people who might (and did!) contribute interviews for my proposed book. Also, I'd hosted a radio program about writing called *The Page Turner*. Finally, I was published internationally with many awards and honors to my name. That was my platform for *Wild Ink*.

Laura Resau's books, including *What the Moon Saw, Red Glass*, and *The Indigo Notebook,* feature modern American teens visiting South America. Resau is a bilingual anthropologist. She spent 2 years in the mountainous Mixtec region of Oaxaca, Mexico. Her education and travels lend credibility to her stories—an example of a platform for fiction.

Admittedly, it's easier to build a platform for nonfiction than for fiction—and when *The Seer and the Sword* was first written, I had no platform to speak of. I'd never entered a fiction contest, never attended a writers' conference, and didn't know diddly. So if you're in a similar boat, don't worry too much. A book can still float simply because it does.

Learn how to write a synopsis. With any submission of a novel, you are going to need a synopsis. A synopsis is a summary of your book, telling all of the main points about what happens, from beginning to end. Written in present tense, the synopsis cannot include any dialogue.

Why do you need a synopsis? Because literary agents and editors will ask for one. They like to look at a synopsis to see if your story hangs together.

Many writers, myself included, find it harder to write a synopsis than an entire novel. It isn't easy to condense all of the nuance and craft you've put into your book into a brief story in present tense. It's tricky to get the feeling of the book into a page or two—and conveying the feeling is a big part of your job. I recommend Pam McCutcheon's book *Writing the Fiction Synopsis*. McCutcheon clearly presents all the information you'll need to write your own synopsis.

Study how to write query letters. Every submission you make, whether by e-mail or hard copy, requires a query letter. A query is your formal introduction to yourself and your work. Queries are deceptively difficult to write because you have to figure out how to say, "I've written a book. Would you like to read it?" in a fresh, enticing style. You have to blow your horn without sounding like you're blowing your horn. You must be pithy without being curt. Yeesh!

Writers who violate certain standards for query letters will be rejected on the basis of the query letter alone. The most common complaint I've heard from agents and editors? Query letters are too long. They want to be able to eyeball the entire letter and see only three or four short paragraphs. The whole thing should be no more than a standard 8 1/2" x 11" page when printed out.

Format for a Query

1. Establish a connection with the person you're writing—either by reminding him or her of when and how you met, or by giving a simple, *brief* explanation of why you've chosen that particular agency or editor. Do not exceed two sentences for this, and double check the spelling on the person's name.

2. In one paragraph, make your pitch about your book. Use your log line. If you're pitching a novel, bring in the voice of that novel to give a *short* glimpse of what the story is about and who's involved. If you're pitching a nonfiction book, give persuasive, *short* bullets about your topic and its relevance to the YA market. This section of your query will be no more than one paragraph or a few sentences long, including information about word count and genre.

3. List your writing credits—publications, awards and honors, and contests won—unless they're obscure or outdated. (Do not launch into an impassioned autobiography about how much writing means to you. Do not say how much your mother loves your book. This is unprofessional.) Also briefly list anything relevant to your general pitch. If you don't have any writing credits, stick to info about yourself that supports your platform. Again, this should be as concise as you can possibly make it.

4. Close with appreciation. Attach your synopsis and any sample chapters that have been requested. After your signature, clearly show your contact information.

Research submission guidelines. Literary agencies and small publishers have websites listing exactly how they want to be approached, but many writers fail to study submission guidelines and therefore take themselves out of the running.

The first thing to look for is whether the agency or publishing company deals with YA titles. If so, search more deeply to determine which subgenres are included and whether your book qualifies. Carefully read submission guidelines and then follow them—to the letter! If an agent or editor requests a single-page synopsis, don't fudge it and send 5 pages. If only two sample chapters are allowed, don't send more. If a marketing analysis is required, don't skip that part. And if e-mail queries are not welcome, print out your query letter and send it by snail mail. Do not assume all agencies or companies will be the same; whatever the agency or company asks for is what you should send.

The ultimate resource on submitting your work is *Writer's Market*, edited by Robert Lee Brewer. It defines format requirements and markets, listing where and in what form writers can sell their work. By giving the most current information available, *Writer's Market* spares writers a lot of tedious research. The whole thing is available in book form or via a digital subscription (http://www.writersmarket.com) that gives access to updates. (Updates become necessary because editors and agents change houses, submission guidelines shift, and publishers may go out of business or new ones may arise.) *Writer's Market* is divided into sections: literary agents, book publishers, consumer magazines, trade journals, contests, and awards. Agents are listed with their contact info and submission guidelines. Publishers appear alphabetically with information on the genres accepted by each press and tips on what the editors are looking for.

In your quest for an agent, you might want to pick up *Guide to Literary Agents*, edited by Chuck Sabuchino, which lists agencies, the genres they represent, style preferences, and submission guidelines or how to obtain them. Other ways to find good agents include looking on the acknowledgments page of books by writers you admire to see if they have mentioned their agent. (Please do not e-mail writers and ask for contact information for their agents. This is inappropriate and will not win you friends.) You can also search the Internet, go to writers' conferences, and hear about good agents via word of mouth.

Remember that agents and editors are not obligated to respond. When you approach an agent or editor who hasn't asked you to submit a query, you're in a category known as unsolicited submissions. Some agencies and many publishing companies do not accept unsolicited material at all. Doing your homework will help you make good use of your valuable time.

Expect a long wait. Agents and editors are overwhelmed with submissions. Depending on the agency or publishing company, expect to wait 3–12 months for an answer to your query. If you receive a positive response, you're ready for the next hurdle: If your book is a novel, you get to send the entire thing, either as an attached file or as hard copy, depending on what is preferred. After that, expect to wait another 2–6 months before you hear back from the agent about whether he or she will represent you, or from the editor about whether he or she will accept your book. (If your proposal is for nonfiction, you will go through negotiations about your outline.) Please don't call about your submission unless 6 months have gone by. Then you can make one phone call or send one polite e-mail asking about the status.

Consider submitting to more than one agent or editor at a time. If published authors are rejected an average of 10 times before being accepted and it takes up to a year to get a reply, the math is pretty obvious. Ten years is too long to wait for a "yes." Simultaneous submissions may be the way to go, but at the same time, be smart. Research individual agents and editors, and then craft your queries to reflect their individuality. Don't write a form letter query and blanket everyone you can find. A generic letter is easy to spot. It will tell the recipient you haven't done your homework. This is important.

Always be clear with those to whom you submit material. When your submission is multiple, make a note of it in your query. (Occasionally, agencies or publishers will ask for exclusive submissions. It's your choice whether to agree to this. There should be some trade-off for you such as an agreement to get back to you more quickly than normal, say within 3 months.)

If, after sending out several carefully researched query packages, you end up with more than one agent who wants to represent you, or more than one publisher asking for a contract, you have a hot property. How do you decide which one to choose? That's a problem you want to have!

Be prepared: Your manuscript will be assessed for commercial value. If marketing were not the last word in publishing, how different the world would be. Lack of marketability automatically excludes some wonderful books. But publishing is a business, and the object of the game is to make money.

The publishing industry is in the midst of change as it continues to adjust to the implications of the Internet and other e-technology. For a long time, books, newspapers, and magazines were the province of the printed word. Now the Internet is a vast storehouse of information, offering fierce—and free—competition for the publishing industry.

Publishers are not designed to be lending institutions for artistic endeavors, and the days when large houses published books solely upon literary merit without a marketing angle are fading fast. Publishers are now forced, by the nature of the game they're in, to gamble heavily on books, losing money on roughly 7 out of 10, breaking even on about 2 out of 10, and making money on only 10% of the works they publish.

To a publisher your art is a product first and foremost. It has to be.

Another way to look at it: If you belong to a writing group or class where you've had the opportunity to read unpublished writing, or if you've read fan fiction online, you know that some of it is well done. But would you pay for it? If the answer is yes, take it one step further and ask yourself if you'd invest money to print and market the work in hopes of getting a return. That's the question publishing houses must answer every day. Agents who decide to represent you must be convinced they can sell your work. They must be able to confidently ask a publishing house to gamble—on you!

Another factor is commercial viability (or lack thereof): An agent or editor may have recently signed an author who offered a project similar to yours. This is where luck enters the picture. Let's say you've submitted a brilliant book about triplets who explore string theory together once they've discovered their unusual genes give them the ability to slip in and out of other dimensions. But the agent has just worked hard to sell another series about twins who double for each other while slipping in and out of alternate realities. Though not exactly the same, the books are too similar to find a market with the same agent or publisher.

This really does happen. All of the time. It's the luck of the draw, baby! But if you get a short note saying an agent liked your writing style but has a similar project in the works, take heart. Whoever took time out of a busy schedule to write you an individualized note meant every word.

Another dragon in the publishing world is trends. As discussed in Chapter 1, you may have written an excellent historical novel during a time in publishing when historical novels for teens are considered passé. Your book might have taken the world by storm 10 years ago or 10 years hence, but right now it's not likely to get a hearing.

What happens if you receive a rejection letter with a note saying the person considering your work loved it but doesn't believe it has enough market appeal? You could rack your brain for a marketing angle and then try to persuade whoever has rejected you of the merits of your plan. The chances of succeeding with that approach hover between zero and minus one, so it's probably a waste of time. You could humbly ask if there's anything you can do to ratchet up the market value of your work—in a note, of course, not a phone call. Then listen to suggestions. Maybe revisions are in order. Perhaps if you subtract a few peaceful scenes in favor of more action—or change the ending—you might begin to see how your story could be stronger and better. Tackle revisions gratefully.

Then again, maybe an agent or editor asks you to rethink your entire message, remove your true voice, or turn your female protagonist into a male . . . Now we're getting into a tricky area. You want to be an author and get published, but at what price? At what point do reasonable requests to improve your story turn into demands to sell out? Personally, I listen very closely to everything I'm told, and then I let my soul be my pilot.

Realize that agents and editors are people, like you. Naturally, you're looking for someone simpatico with your style. Sometimes this process takes a while! Just keep your head, your heart, and your patience, if you can.

Getting the call from an agent. If an agent decides to represent you, he or she will probably call you. (Oh fabulous day!) The call will include some effusion about how delightful your book is and an offer to sign with the agency. You'll look over the agency contract before you sign.

Unlike book contracts, agency contracts are short and straightforward. (If you get one that's long and unreadable, you should be suspicious, and check with an attorney.)

Now all you have to do is sign and do the happy dance, right?

More waiting. Sorry to say, even once you have an agent, you'll go through more waiting while your agent submits to publishers on your behalf. This can take from a few weeks to a year. Once a publisher says yes, take the time to celebrate before processing the fact that you'll wait between 2 and 12 months for a contract. The contract will specify that your book will be published anywhere from 18 months to 3 years from the date of the contract. Whew! An ironic twist to an industry in which time is of the essence.

But hey, a contract in hand is a *great* feeling.

writer beware: things to watch out for

The publishing game is complex. When you're new to the game, it's possible to make some big mistakes. Here are some scams to put on your radar.

Agent Scams

A true agent will help you more than you can imagine. Unfortunately, anyone can list herself as an agent, so be careful out there. Because so many writers are trying to break into print, the publishing industry has attracted its share of unscrupulous people trying to take advantage of naïveté. Some do this by calling themselves agents when they're nothing of the sort. If an "agent" does any of the following, get out without looking back:

> ➤ The "agent" collects reading fees. In other words, you are charged money because the agent has read your book. Legitimate literary agencies do not charge for reading your work. The Association of Authors' Representatives Canon of Ethics specifically prohibits agents from collecting reading fees from clients or potential clients.

> ➤ The "agent" offers you a contract that penalizes you or charges you should the agent fail to sell your work in a specified period.

This is not a professional practice among agents. Always read contracts with care.

➤ The "agent" gets cagey about revealing other clients and makes excuses when asked for references. Established agents are proud of their clients.

➤ The "agent" asks for money up front to offset the costs of marketing your manuscript. Reputable agents do not charge up front. They make their money from a percentage of your sales. If they must buy extra copies of your book to market to foreign countries or have other extra expenses, they might charge you costs, but they will subtract those amounts from advances or royalties.

Bogus Writing Contests

Another scam is bogus writing contests. Whereas winning large-scale and well-regarded writing contests can give you something to put in your query letter, please do not get scammed into sending exorbitant entry fees to Jack the Writer's website contest. And don't ever sign away your rights to a contest.

Winning a contest given by an obscure or unknown group will not increase your chances of finding a home for your book. To be worth your while, a writing contest should be run by a large magazine, a publishing company, a college or university, a legitimate awards organization, or an established writers' conference. Entries should be judged by qualified people. This is more rare than you might think. Authors are busy, and many of us have no time to judge contests.

I've never entered a fiction writing contest. But I've read remarks from several contest judges about other entries submitted by friends. Some of these judges—unpublished themselves—have given what I consider to be appallingly bad advice. Some seemed to be interested in crushing the aspirations of the entrant into dust. So keep in mind it isn't necessary to win contests to get published. That said, it's true that if you want to add credibility to a blank writing resumé, winning a big contest can help. For example, *Writer's Digest* sponsors several annual writing contests that are nationally known. And if you were to rack up several wins at conferences with good national reputations, all the better.

Predator Publishers

Yes, there are so-called publishers who really just want to take your money. There's a bit more information about this in Chapter 10. In short, before signing with any agent or publisher, please do a search on that person or company. Before sending money to anyone who claims to be holding a writing contest, do your research. There are predators out there. Don't be any easy mark.

agents—in their own words

The agents I've interviewed are, of course, active and trustworthy agents working with YA authors. Their words follow.

Edina Imrik

Bio: Edina Imrik works for the Ed Victor Literary Agency. She does not accept unsolicited queries.

What makes a manuscript stand out for you? What characteristics—other than good writing—make you sit up and take notice?

Having a strong narrative voice is important from page 1. However, writing is such a subjective business, every person will favor different things. Even if the work is well-written it may not be picked up by the first agent who reads it, so it is worth sending it to a few people.

What are some of the most common mistakes writers make when writing YA? When sending in manuscripts?

One of the most common mistakes writers can make is not researching their intended readership enough. How could anyone write for a specific age group if they don't know what they like to read? Books, just like everything in the world, are changing all the time, and it is important to keep up with what is out there. Research is also important when submitting a manuscript to an agent. The writer needs to find out the name of the person they want to send their work to and if they are willing to consider unsolicited manuscripts. If the answer is yes, they need to find out what material the agent needs—usually three sample chapters and a synopsis. It is important also to send a stamped envelope big enough for the return of the work, or state in your letter that you do not want your work returned—this is common courtesy. Another mistake is sending random chapters, rather than the first three. Nobody should do this—random chapters don't make sense. If the first three chapters are not good enough to be sample chapters, they need to be rewritten.

How much weight do you give to a synopsis as opposed to sample chapters?

This is entirely up to personal preference. I personally read the chapters first and if they intrigue me, I like to see how the rest of the book will work before asking for the whole script. I normally never ask for more than a one-page synopsis.

If you could suggest one thing that would help writers find success, what would it be?

Write an interesting and engaging cover letter with your submission—it is the first thing the agent will see, and the more you engage them, the more likely they will read on.

Lilly Ghahremani

http://www.fullcircleliterary.com

Bio: After graduating from the UCLA School of Law, Lilly Ghahremani soon decided to "use her powers for good," representing authors across a variety of genres. She is always interested in well-paced young adult fiction, multicultural themes and characters, and explorations of the undiscovered facets of teen life. (She says that a witty and self-deprecating character will always catch her attention!) Her agency is always happy to add talented new YA authors.

What makes a manuscript stand out for you? What characteristics— other than good writing—make you sit up and take notice?

We all say the same thing—that a manuscript stands out for us when it keeps us up at night. But what does that mean? In the YA genre, the most important thing you can do is create a character we can relate to. Does your character have interesting quirks and flaws? Is she a compelling, interesting, observant person? For my own taste, I'm a huge fan of humor—there is so much in adolescence to poke fun at, and I love when authors indulge themselves. What will make me take notice is strong writing combined with a youthful voice. Sometimes we'll receive a beautifully polished manuscript, but it's clear that the (adult) author is the ventriloquist. Keep an eye out for little slips—did you accidentally use a phrase from the 1980s that our fearless protagonist would never have known (because she wasn't alive yet!)? Those sorts of slips take me right out of the moment.

For me, the beauty of the teenage years is the incredibly weird and unique worlds we create for ourselves at that age. I love to be invited into a world that wasn't my own but to be invited in a way that makes me want to stick around.

What are some of the most common mistakes writers make when writing YA? When sending in manuscripts?

As I mentioned above, writers with the best of intentions will accidentally give an adult voice to the teen genre. Don't get me wrong—our teen readers are brilliant and mature, but there are certain ways they wouldn't speak—such as the way their 55-year-old author would. It's common to see adult writers slip out of voice or write in a voice they think teen readers will relate to. The worst thing a writer can do is lose touch with their audience, to write in a cave. The best YA writers are those who are reading current YA, and paying attention to how the YA market is growing and changing. What magazines does your target reader read? Are you reading them? Are you watching their shows? Do you really "get" them or are you trying too hard to be the "cool" adult and not putting in the time?

Another mistake I see is trying to be provocative for provocation's sake. People constantly ask me if they should write edgy since "edgy sells." But with the process of publication taking as long as it can, your book may not hit shelves for a while. Write something that is timeless. If you're going to be edgy, do it because your story requires it, and because you feel deep down that that is the most sincere way to tell your tale.

I'm also iffy on dating a book. Too many Lindsay Lohan/Aaron Carter references can date a book unnecessarily.

Regarding mistakes upon submission, I'd say:

➤ Being overly eager (a.k.a. the "Red Flag" mistake). You want agents to take their time and read your submission. If you "nudge" them before the 4–6 week mark and if you consistently badger them with e-mails, you will ensure your quick relegation to the pass pile.

➤ Not checking what the agent accepts (a.k.a. the "Waste of Time" mistake). Make sure you're sending your wonderful YA manuscript to the appropriate agent. Make sure you're pursuing agents who are as excited about the YA market as you are.

➤ Not being familiar with the genre (a.k.a. the "Amateur" mistake). If you are undertaking YA authorship as a serious career, you need to devote the time and energy to getting to know your industry as much as any other profession. What books are exciting young readers? Read about them in *Publishers Weekly*, and be sure to rub elbows with local librarians and bookstore salespeople. They know what is happening on the ground, and you should, too.

Is there something about the life of an agent that you wish more writers knew about or understood?

I wish authors knew how difficult our job can be. Our job is to pick out not only what's "good," but what is so excellent that we would stake our reputation (and time) on it. We work on commission, so we have to pick up projects we feel we can be fully invested in for however long it takes to find them that right home. On the flip side, you, the author, deserve an agent who feels that same excitement you do about the potential for your work. Ultimately I wish authors knew that an agent's response isn't a reflection on their eventual success. It's a reflection of our workload and our own enthusiasm.

I often explain to my classes that our evaluation of a manuscript is exactly what you do at the bookstore—you pick it up, you read through a few pages, and if you're not really feeling invested in taking it to the counter, you don't. You want to match up with the reader who can't wait to pay and hunker down with your novel, not the person who felt pressured to buy because it was at a sale price! It's worth waiting for the perfect agent. We all work very, very hard, but you need more than just a hard worker. You need that perfect person.

Writers should also know that this is a small industry, so take deep breaths before sending "revenge" e-mails.

We're all in this industry because books mean the world to us. Agents work around the clock to be sure there are new books for our readers. You may reconnect with an agent on another project (this has certainly happened for me) or you may run into him or her along the line. Stay positive and move forward. The perfect agent is out there.

How much weight do you give to a synopsis as opposed to sample chapters?

I absolutely give sample chapters more weight. Sure, I have to be interested in the storyline, but I get a sense of that from the query already. The pages are what really count to me. Do I keep reading the submission because I can't stop myself, or am I reading because I was promised something good in the synopsis? I don't want to get stuck in that situation, so I read the book for the book and usually keep the synopsis to the side, just in case I need a refresher.

And as far as format, I honestly don't mind what format a synopsis comes in (although 20-page chapter-by-chapter synopses are a bit much, and I imagine a nightmare to draft).

If you could suggest one thing that would help writers find success, what would it be?

I think a good attitude will get you very far in this industry. It sounds cheesy, I know. But it encompasses many elements—staying open to criticism and feedback, realizing there are possibilities and that "where a window closes, a door opens" (i.e., if an agent passes on your book, it might just mean a better agent for you is yet to come!), and to stay confident. We need wonderful books for our young readers. You are doing an important—no, crucial—thing in writing them. Good deeds are rewarded.

Erin Murphy
http://emliterary.com

Bio: Erin Murphy founded Erin Murphy Literary Agency in Flagstaff, AZ, in 1999. She does not accept unsolicited queries or submissions, as she prefers to focus the bulk of her time on her client list, which includes authors and author-illustrators of picture books, middle-grade and YA fiction, and select nonfiction for children and young adults.

What is important for writers to keep in mind when approaching an agent?

Two complementary things: the agent's needs, and the author's own needs. Authors should research agents—their client lists, their style, and approach, what they are seeking and what they are not—rather than approaching agents blindly. They should also know what they themselves need and what their expectations are. You can write a perfect query that informs the agent of your accomplishments, amazing contact lists, and available manuscripts, but if you don't have a sense of what you hope to accomplish with an agent's help, you don't know what you're looking for—and the agent might not see space for herself in your future, either.

What are some of the most common mistakes writers make when writing YA?

Writing to trend. Focusing on concept over quality. Leading the characters through the action, instead of letting the characters become fully formed. Not developing an ear for realistic dialogue. Writing too young, which can also mean being afraid to go to dark/scary/edgy/realistic places. (In which case, a story can often turn out to be middle-grade instead of YA, of course; but authors often don't realize the distinction and write a middle-grade story in which, say, a girl owns and drives a car.) This can also mean the writer is simply hedging bets and writing too safe, which makes for a bland story that doesn't stand out.

Is there something about the life of an agent that you wish more writers knew about or understood?

Wow, good question! Well, I can't speak to other agents' lives, of course, but I suspect one thing we all share in common is we're way, way too busy, as are editors. I know it can be easy to wonder, "What is taking so darned long? Why haven't they gotten back to me yet?" I'm always feeling guilty about the things I haven't gotten to yet; I'm well aware that keeping a writer waiting is deferring a dream.

If you could suggest one thing that would help YA writers find success, what would it be?

Listen. Listen to your own voice. Listen to good feedback. Listen to your instincts. Listen to your characters when they won't stop talking to you.

Chapter 8

Getting Your Book Traditionally Published

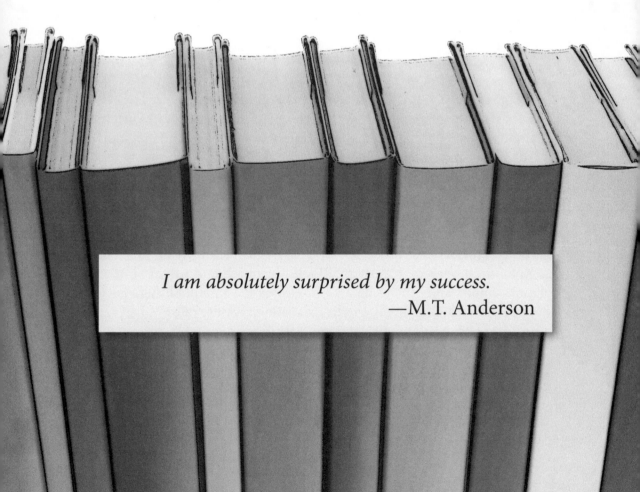

I am absolutely surprised by my success.
—M.T. Anderson

People in the publishing industry are far too busy to take each new author by the hand and educate us, yet authors are expected to know what's going on—even when we don't. When I got my first "yes" from an agent, I knew plenty about how to take a flight of fancy, but I knew zilch about the publishing business. I was so ignorant, I was afraid I'd unknowingly commit some heinous gaffe and wind up sailing alone through the empty spaces in my head, oxygen deprived and missing a parachute.

I flew by the seat of my pants and learned as I went. You, however, may appreciate a guided tour. So if you're curious about what happens after a publisher says "yes," read on. This chapter describes the weird wonders of taking your first flight as an author. We'll explore the view of contracts, taxes, editing, cover design, and working with small versus large presses. In addition, editors in the business offer their tips for writers seeking publication.

contracts and money

Your book contract will state terms for royalties, advances, and rights. Royalties are the percentage of book sales paid to the author. A variety of amounts can be designated, depending on the publisher, the edition (hardcover or paperback or digital), the publisher's market base, and so on. What used to be a standard rate for royalties isn't necessarily standard anymore, because of changes in discounting policies for retailers, eBooks, and other developments in the industry. Therefore, it's impossible to give you a certain figure for what your royalty rate will be. At the time of this writing, a *very* low-end royalty would be 4% of the retail cost of a print book or 10% of an eBook. Very high end would be 15% of a print book and 30% of an eBook. However, some publishers have stopped differentiating between print and eBook royalty rates. Whatever the royalty rate, it will be spelled out clearly in your contract.

New writers often ask why their royalties are such a small percentage of the eventual price of the book. "I wrote the book!" they protest. "Without me, the book wouldn't exist. If it sells for $6.50, shouldn't I end up with more than $0.40 a copy?"

Here's why royalties are such a small slice of the big cake. Publishers must cover all the following costs: editing, designing, cover art, printing (which can get quite expensive depending on the print run), marketing, shipping, warehousing, sales staff and book expos, distribution, and author royalties. These add up to a big investment, and the income for publishers is only 30%–60% of the retail price of the book, depending on the publisher's situation, agreements with retailers and distributors, and other costs.

Not only that, but retailers can order as many copies as they wish of a particular title from a publisher, and then if those copies don't sell, they can return the books. The retailer owes nothing for unsold copies. (When "returning" mass-market paperbacks, retailers often don't return the books themselves. Instead, they rip off the front covers and send them back without the interiors, to save shipping. The books themselves end up in landfills because it's illegal to sell a book without its cover— for obvious reasons.) Loads of books are returned. And the publisher absorbs the loss.

Advance

An advance is the amount the publisher pays you before any sales take place. (Not all publishers pay advances.) Editors arrive at this amount by guessing how many copies of your book can reasonably be expected to sell. Your advance will dovetail with the size of the initial print run planned for your title. A print run is the number of copies of your book your publisher prints at one time. (EBooks are all ordered on-demand, so there is no need for a print run, but the book must be formatted for eReaders. More about that later.)

To determine your advance, the initial print run number is basically multiplied by the projected retail price of your book. That total is then multiplied by your projected royalty rate. For example, a print run of 5,000 hardcover copies is planned. The retail price will be about $15.00. The print run multiplied by the retail price (5,000 x $15.00) is $75,000. If the royalty rate is 10% of retail on hardcovers, your advance will be in the ballpark of $7,500 (10% of $75,000).

As your books begin to sell, you will gradually earn out your advance. Once your sales have exceeded the amount of royalties covered by your advance, you'll begin to receive royalty checks. (Sadly, the majority of books never earn back their advance. However, the author is not expected to return it.)

It's customary for advances to be broken up. For example, 25% of the advance is paid upon signature of the contract, another 25% when the publisher approves the final manuscript, and 50% when the book is actually printed.

What amount should you expect? Well, offers for advances fluctuate so wildly that applying the law of averages becomes meaningless. I mean, if you stick your feet in a broiler oven and your head in a bag of ice, the average temperature will say you're comfortable—a misleading concept. A celebrity author could get a million dollar advance (extremely rare in the YA market), whereas authors who work with small presses might receive a grand or two—or no advance at all. Most nonfiction publishers do not give advances, but rely on royalties instead. That said, the "average" advance for a YA novel by a new author is between $5,000 and $15,000.

eBooks

The e-explosion has arrived. As publishers scramble to keep up with the market, you might think that every book out there would be offered as an eBook. The reason this doesn't always happen is because putting books into e-format is a painstaking process involving time and money. It's not just a matter of throwing an existing document into an e-reader; it's another investment on the part of the publisher. (For more information on what's involved, read the interview with Brian Schwartz on p. 191 in Chapter 10.)

Taxes and You

As soon as you receive money from your first book contract (or your first sales above a specified amount if you are self-published), you become a small business. As such, you are required to file a Schedule C to accompany your yearly tax return in the U.S. (or its equivalent elsewhere). This is pretty easy to do yourself with the help of a program such as TurboTax or TaxCut, but you must save your receipts for business expenses and keep a record of all of your income. I throw all of my receipts into a folder marked "expenses" and all of my income statements into a folder marked "income." Then I deal with the whole shebang at once, sometime between February 1st and April 15th. You might prefer to use an accountant. Whatever works—just don't neglect this important duty.

One of the things you'll need to keep track of is the expenses and income related to buying and selling your own books. Yes, even traditionally published authors must pay for copies of their own books. Although it's common for people to assume that authors have access to unlimited free copies, this is not the case. The publisher has footed the bill for the book, and although as the author you'll get a discount similar to that of a retail provider, your books are not free to you. Buying them is an expense; selling them is income. If you sell them, you will need to have an agreement with your publisher that lets you do so (not always allowed), and you will need to apply for a sales tax license and keep current with sales tax payments.

If you get paid for talks, you will be a subcontract or contract worker. By the end of January of the year following any payment you receive, whoever paid you must send you a Form 1099-MISC listing the amount. The same form will be sent to the IRS. You must include this money as income on your Schedule C, and you will owe estimated taxes on it.

You will be paying quarterly estimated taxes on all of your income, including federal and state income tax, as well as federal self-employment tax. You can find all of the federal forms you need at http://irs.gov. State forms will be at your official state website. Your tax is calibrated on your profit. Profit is a simple equation: Business income minus business expenses. So, it's a good idea to keep those receipts. Things like advertising, having a website, paper and ink used for writing purposes, taking writing classes, and mileage to and from paid talks can all be written off once you have income as a writer. But guidelines change, or you might run into special circumstances, so check with an accountant or the IRS to find out which of your expenses qualify as a tax write-off.

Rights

As for rights to your work, I'm not qualified to address this complex subject. I do know from experience that each time your book goes into a foreign country, you will receive a separate contract and a separate advance—unless your original publisher has bought world rights, in which case your foreign rights will be spelled out in the original contract and your foreign advance will be split with your main publisher. In some cases, as opposed to an advance, the amount will be a flat fee for licensing your title to a foreign publisher. Your agent—if you have one—will fully understand the sale of your publishing rights and will negotiate the best terms possible for your situation. I also recommend getting your own copy of *The Writer's Legal Companion* by Brad Bunnin and Peter Beren, which does a great job of covering the ins and outs of first rights, serial rights, foreign rights, copyrights, and other subjects of interest to writers.

editing

Once you have a contract, the next step along your trek to fame and fortune (or notoriety within your family and a few extra bucks in the bank) is getting your book edited. Depending on the size of your publishing company and the contract you have, you may wait a year or more before you enter the editing process. (Use the time to get started on your next book.) When it's your turn in the rotation, your book will receive your editor's concentrated attention.

First, you'll receive an e-mail or have a conversation with your editor about revisions. For example, an editor who worked on *The Seer and the Sword* sent a 2-page e-mail asking for additional exposition in a number of places. He'd noticed, for instance, that I'd left out a pivotal scene regarding the hero's capture. (Duh.) Depending on your style, you may get notes asking for expansions, deletions, or both. If you tend to be lean, even skeletal, with your prose, you'll be asked to flesh things out. If you're wordy, you'll be asked to trim. (If, despite my advice in Chapter 3, you've kept a redundant scene that you cherish because it's beautifully written, get ready to set aside your darling.)

Editors will treat your manuscript the way a good mechanic treats your car, rooting around in the heart of the engine and pointing out what needs fixing. The diagnostic reports can be devastating—like when your whole book needs to be rewritten. But editors don't get to be where they are by accident. If they tell you something's flat or too full of air, odds are good they're right.

The editors I've had are some of the most dedicated and skilled people on Earth. They've given me a big garage full of knowledge and handed me tools I didn't know existed. I've adored working with them. But I've met writers who didn't agree one bit with their editors, and thought editors were exerting too much control without understanding what the writer was trying to achieve. Sometimes personalities and styles just don't mesh. It happens, but try to make the best of it.

Think carefully before telling an editor that he or she is completely wrong. Editors are trained to spot those telltale grease marks on your manuscript that indicate engine trouble within. They have a gift for you—the gift of objectivity. And they care about your book. They've staked their company's time, money, and reputation on you—an excellent reason to listen to what they have to say.

Editors do a lot more than edit, too. They handle many aspects of the business, from acquiring manuscripts (which means reading recommended manuscripts from agents and unsolicited submissions, if accepted) to preparing marketing plans for specific books.

An editor you're fond of may leave the publishing house that owns the rights to your book. This can turn into a setback for you because the editor who acquires your manuscript is the one who guides your book from prepublication to post printing. If he or she leaves, your book is "orphaned." Much depends on the next editor assigned to it. Sometimes, the new editor has even more enthusiasm than the editor who first acquired it. Sometimes, the new editor doesn't take an interest or is too overworked on behalf of other projects. Occasionally, your book won't be published after all. (Because unforeseen things happen in publishing—things such as editors leaving or companies going out of business, your contract will have a clause saying if the book isn't published within 2–3 years, all rights revert to you and the publisher has no more obligation.)

When you've completed revisions to the satisfaction of your editor, your book is ready for the next stage of the process. This is a major turning point in your career. Most book contracts specify delivery of an "acceptable" draft of your manuscript. You now have an editor-approved draft, so you've fulfilled that clause. You're well on your way.

line editing and copyediting

After you've completed broad revisions, an editor will go through and line edit your manuscript, looking for awkward or overused phrases, inconsistencies in characters, inaccurate statements, and so on. Sometimes this is the same person who gave you recommendations for revisions. Sometimes it's the copy editor.

Copy editors are trained in the fine points of grammar, among other things. They check through your book for correct spelling, punctuation, and word usage, as well as continuity. Copy editors are extremely meticulous and may catch things your literary editor missed.

After getting the comments from the copy editor, you'll go over your whole book again and rewrite as needed. By then, you may be getting a tad sick of that book. You'll have gone over it so many times you hardly see the words anymore. In some moods, you may even feel like the copy editor is a horrible quibbling nitpicker. So what if you used the word "clamor" too often? Who cares if there's a run-on sentence on page 129? But copy editors know what they're doing. They're helping you polish your work, and they deserve a vote of thanks.

If you sincerely disagree with a copy editor who wants you to remove phrases or paragraphs that you believe contribute something important, it's your call. As the author, you have the final say. It's still your book.

cover design and layout

Meanwhile, your cover is being designed. Despite the old saying "Don't judge a book by its cover," everybody does it and everybody will keep on doing it. Covers matter, because they attract the attention of potential readers.

Editors who have been in the business for decades will tell you that when it comes to sales, a book's cover is more important than the book itself. Kind of a blow to us as writers, but all too true. You've probably come across badly written books with fabulous covers that became best sellers. Or the opposite situation: original and well-written books with dismal covers, dying an unsung death in the marketplace.

Important though the cover is, being a writer doesn't mean you have expertise in the area of artwork for book covers. To be blunt: If you have a traditional publisher, forget your ideas for the cover. The publisher chooses the artist, designer, and concept. So unless you're a renowned illustrator publishing a book on illustration or a graphic novelist doing your own illustrations, you won't be consulted about the cover art except in a "yay or nay" sort of way (if that).

Your cover represents your book to the world. Publishing companies have experts on hand who will give your book a cover designed to appeal to its audience. These people will do their best to brand your book with a look that's inviting, intriguing, and easily recognizable, a look that can be used repeatedly for future books you write.

Your novel will then be formatted for printing. A design editor will decide font, type size, and layout.

blurb writing

Part of your book design includes a blurb—that enticing little teaser on the inside or back cover designed to appeal to browsing book buyers. People glance over the blurb before deciding whether to turn to page 1.

It's a little scary to realize that a book you've labored over for years will rise or fall according to one small paragraph written by someone else. But that's how it is. Depending on the size of the publishing company you're dealing with, you may or may not get a chance to approve your blurb.

A good blurb is crucial to a book's survival, but it's not normally written by the author. Professional blurb writers (often editors or assistant editors) are trained in the art of a quick pitch, and some of them have a real flair for it.

galleys

You will receive a proof of your book, often referred to as the "galley." Galleys are pages showing your book in print format. You'll either receive a hard copy, or the pages may be sent as a digital file that accepts comments and changes. Either way, you'll read through the galleys to catch any errors.

Even if you're completely fed up with your book at this stage, it's worth the effort to read through it with close concentration one more time. Every word. This is your last chance to spot errors and get them changed.

advance reading copies (arcs)

ARCs are actual softbound books in the same format as the final book. They go out to reviewers, distributors, and sometimes book buyers. They are not for sale; they are for review. They're meant to spearhead your book, and give it a chance to have some presence in the marketplace before it's actually published.

Review copies go out 3–6 months in advance of the actual book. Sometimes ARCs have not yet been proofed and corrected. If so, they will say "uncorrected proof" right on the cover.

Positive reviews can make a big difference to your book, opening the way for schools and libraries to stock copies. This is vital for YA books. Teens and adults who like reading YA often find new titles by browsing library shelves. Friends recommend books to each other, and if those books are easy to find in a library, they stand a better chance of gathering a word-of-mouth following.

School Library Journal, *Kirkus Reviews*, and *Publishers Weekly* are nationally known publications that include reviews of new books for young adults. *Young Adult Library Services*, *Voice of Youth Advocates*, and *The ALAN Review* feature articles on how to promote teen literacy and serve the teen community. All of them have book reviews. Your publisher will try to secure reviews through such services.

Newspaper book reviews are almost a thing of the past now. But online communities and bloggers abound, many of whom gladly accept review copies for giveaways on their sites. Some offer reviews written by teens themselves. The more reviews you can get, the better.

the book

One fine day, a box will be shipped to your residence. The box will contain your author copies of your finished book. Printed. Bound inside a cover. Wow. Few things in life can equal the bliss of holding your own bouncing book in your hand and knowing it now has a life of its own.

Time to celebrate. Throw a party. Show up in style for the reading you've arranged at your local bookstore. Did you know you can order a big cake with the cover art shown in frosting on top? As you sign copies, revel in the culmination of all of your effort and hope, persistence and patience, turmoil and uncertainty. You've done it! You're published!

large presses, small presses, and you

New writers sometimes assume the experience of getting published is similar no matter what size the publishing house, but that's not the case. I can't speak for every author or publisher, but I've worked with both large and small publishers now, and I've noticed differences between them.

Large Presses

The offices for Random House, Inc. are located in a skyscraper right off of Times Square. When I scheduled a visit with them, I walked from my hotel through a bustle of crowds—and missed the entrance at first because I was craning my neck at how high the building reached.

Imposing glass doors opened into a lobby bigger than my last apartment. Behind a long counter, four employees were needed just to check appointments and issue security badges for approved visitors. After showing my ID and getting a badge, I passed through the security gates into a wide hallway. I grabbed an elevator to the 19th floor, which included children's books and YA, a place honeycombed with offices and cubicles filled with busy bees working hard to create buzz for thousands of books. Random House fills the whole building. Wow. I felt like a drop of honey inside a humongous hive.

Approaching a large press. Unless you make a one-on-one connection with a large press editor, agent representation is required when approaching a large press.

Advantages and Disadvantages of Working With a Large Press

Advantages
- ➤ Bigger budget than a small press.
- ➤ Your publisher's name is well known.
- ➤ Distribution channels are wide and well-maintained.
- ➤ Your book will be reviewed by prominent review services.

Disadvantages
- ➤ Less personal attention.
- ➤ Staff turnover can be swift.
- ➤ Your book is released at the same time as dozens of other books.
- ➤ Print rotations are scheduled far in advance; it may be years before your book is published.
- ➤ Once published, the bar for sales is so high that most books rapidly go out of print.

Small Presses

When I visited the small press that published the first edition of *Wild Ink*, I felt like I had entered Mary Poppins' bag. From the outside, the building didn't look big enough to hold more than one desk, let alone a successful publishing company. But inside was an active staff of editors, a shipping center, computers, and books galore. I sat down with the editor-in-chief herself to pitch my ideas. Within a short time, we had reached an understanding.

Different sales practices. Small publishers cannot afford high numbers of returned books, so they look for niche markets, markets unlikely to send orders back. Some small presses market to libraries only, some to regional interests, some to educators, some to other specific groups. And even if you're exceedingly popular within the niche of your small press, your sales are unlikely to hit the stratosphere. For one thing, a small press doesn't have the financial capability to order enormous print runs and pay for the type of marketing that creates top sellers. However much they might wish to, small press editors cannot promise you a big budget marketing plan. But you can take comfort in knowing that your book won't slip through the cracks either.

Depending on the type of book you've written, your personality, ambitions, and ideals, you may be better served by a smaller house. If you want to be a superstar, a small press won't satisfy you, but if you're looking for modest success in a friendly atmosphere, you could be very happy with a small press.

Finding a small press. To locate a small press that suits you and your work, go through *Writer's Market*, which has a section on small presses and what they're looking for. The majority of small presses publish non-fiction only, but between A and D, I found five that publish YA fiction.

Approaching a small press. As of this writing, most small presses do not require agent representation before considering a manuscript. When approaching small publishers, follow the guidelines listed on their website. Assess whether your book would fit the publisher's existing catalog. If you've written a sunny tale, for instance, don't query Dark Horrors Press. If your story is contemporary YA fiction laced with profanity, don't approach a Christian publisher. And if the title of your book is *Glorien, King of the Ripcloche Elves*, don't bother sending chapters to a press that publishes only history and science.

Advantages and Disadvantages of Working With a Small Press

Advantages

➤ Your book is likely to stay in print longer.

➤ Shorter lead time between contract and publication.

➤ More access to the people connected with your book.

➤ Your book will be one of only several new titles printed in a year. (You can work closely with the marketing department to spread the word.)

➤ More attainable definition of sales success. (In a large press, sales of 20,000 copies barely register, but in a small press, sales of 20,000 are celebrated.)

Disadvantages

➤ Smaller budget than a large press.

➤ Small or nonexistent advance.

➤ Distribution channels are narrower.

➤ Not always reviewed by prominent review services.

interviews with editors

This chapter on publishing wouldn't be complete without the editor's perspective. Next are interviews with editors of both fiction and nonfiction who give their insights on what they look for from writers. Laura Backes, Jessica Clarke, Cheryl Klein, Bella Pearson, Sharyn November, and Lacy Compton answer questions about an editor's life and about common mistakes writers make when writing and submitting for the YA market.

Laura Backes

http://www.write4kids.com

Bio: Laura Backes has been part of the publishing field since 1986. She's worked at some of New York's top publishing houses in publicity (Ballantine Books) and subsidiary rights (Farrar, Straus & Giroux), as a literary agent (Goodman Associates and later with The Backes Agency), and as a freelance editor for small presses and self-published authors. Since 1990, Laura has helped educate countless aspiring authors on the craft of writing for children as publisher of "Children's Book Insider: The Newsletter for Children's Writers" (see http://www.write4kids.com for more information). Laura is also the author of *Best Books for Kids Who (Think They) Hate to Read* and articles on writing published in *Writer's Digest* and *The Writer* magazines and was the technical editor for *Writing Children's Books for Dummies.*

Is there something about the life of an editor that you wish more writers knew about or understood?

I think writers commonly have two misconceptions about editors. One, they think editors sit around their offices all day reading. And because they envision editors ensconced in armchairs, reading with a cup of tea and a scone at their side, they wonder why editors can't take the time to personally respond to every submission. Or why editors complain when people send them inappropriate submissions (fiction when the publisher only does nonfiction, picture books when the editor specifically asks for novels, etc.). In reality, editors spend their days in meetings, editing manuscripts already under contract, negotiating new contracts with authors or agents, preparing reports for the sales and marketing departments, and going to more meetings. The reading is almost always done in an editor's spare time. So it's important that authors not waste that precious time with unprofessional submissions.

Two, many authors think editors go through the slush pile looking to reject as many manuscripts as possible. But every editor I know who reads unsolicited submissions does so because she's an eternal optimist. She desperately wants to find new writers to publish. Even if an editor works with a list of famous, established authors, she still needs to constantly find new blood. And nurturing a new talent is one of the joys of the job.

What are some of the most common mistakes writers make when writing YA?

I think many writers misunderstand what makes a young adult novel these days. I've been critiquing manuscripts for writers for 18 years, and very often when someone sends me a YA novel, it's really a middle grade book with a 15-year-old protagonist. In young adult books, the main character comes face-to-face with an adult situation for the first time, and absolutely must deal with it. At the end of the book, that character is no longer a child. The protagonist has grown up either mentally, physically, spiritually, emotionally, or all of the above. He's lost a certain amount of innocence and naiveté and is better able to take on the real world. Not everything he learns is necessarily pleasant, because reality can be bittersweet, but the main character is now facing the situations from the plot with eyes that weren't completely open before the book began.

Many YA manuscripts don't have that edge to them. They're about finding a date for the prom or getting in with the popular crowd. Those situations can certainly occur in a YA novel, but they would be part of a larger, more substantial story.

Another mistake some writers make is not including any subplots. Young adult novels are as richly layered as novels for adults. The main plotline must be reinforced by related subplots that explore the protagonist's relationship with other characters or delve into connecting aspects of the protagonist's life that shed light on how to deal with the story's conflict.

If you could suggest one thing that would help writers find success, what would it be?

You'll always hear editors tell aspiring writers to read, read, read, and it's such important advice that I'm going to give it as well. That said, I think another element to success in the YA market is developing your own unique voice. In YA more than any other age group, an author can hold the reader's attention on the power of voice alone. Many novels are written in first person and center around the narrator's inner struggles. If they're created with a strong, original, convincing voice, the reader will feel like the narrator's best friend. A writer's voice takes a while to emerge, so be patient. Don't rush it. Get to know your main character and try writing short essays in her voice every day. Allow your character to be flawed as well as fabulous. Urge her to talk about anything and everything that's important to her, even if you don't plan on using the information in your book. You want to disappear into your character, and at the same time you want your character to come alive. It can be a little scary—losing yourself to your story—but that's how the best books come to be.

Jessica Clarke

Bio: Jessica Clarke started her career in publishing as a bookseller at a small independent children's bookshop before joining Puffin Books in 2008 as Editorial Assistant. She joined Random House as Editor in 2010. The explosion of the YA genre means that around 50% of the submissions she sees are YA.

Is there something about the life of an editor that you wish more writers knew about or understood?

Unfortunately, it's not all reading manuscripts! Being an editor basically means you're project manager for a vast range of titles at any given time—so your time is always incredibly stretched. It would be brilliant to be able to read and edit all day, but about two thirds of my time (at least) is taken up with admin and liaising with all the other in-house departments. Also, by the very nature of our job, we see a lot of manuscripts. Given the above point about how (relatively) little time we have to read, manuscripts that are immediately engaging will inevitably be the ones that are read to the very end.

What makes a YA manuscript stand out for you? What are the top things you look for in a new author?

All publishers always talk about finding a "voice"—that's the thing that no amount of editing can make up for. If the author truly "gets" everything about the story they're writing, are completely inside their characters' heads, and—the secret ingredient that's often missing— understands what their reader wants, then the most time-worn ideas can be turned into an exceptional story. That said, with so much of YA literature being based around similar concepts or constructs (especially in paranormal and urban fantasy), when you find something based on a unique and truly original idea, it's really exciting.

What are some of the most common mistakes writers make when writing YA?

Not getting inside the head of their characters. Remember what it's like to be a teen? You think you know everything. Inevitably, readers can tell when an adult is just pretending to get their world.

If you could suggest one thing that would help YA writers find success, what would it be?

Know the market and the competition. And only write a story that needs to be told—the one that won't leave your head.

Cheryl Klein

http://www.cherylklein.com

Bio: Cheryl Klein is a senior editor at Arthur A. Levine Books, an imprint of Scholastic, Inc.

Is there something about the life of an editor that you wish more writers knew about or understood?

I know some writers appreciate this, but not all: Editors work *a lot*. We read probably 200+ manuscripts per year, make judgments on them, write sales copy and acquisition memos, work with our designers, present the books to our sales staff and create sales strategies, attend meetings, and somewhere in there actually edit the books—all of which takes time and thought and energy. Then we want to give our books under contract (which we love) our best time and thought and energy out of that—plus we want to have personal lives and fun as well! I'm routinely here till 7:00 at night on weekdays, and I usually work on Saturdays (and often Sundays too). So if I haven't gotten back to you, it isn't personal; it's that I'm trying to keep up with my workload and yet not get burned out altogether.

What are some of the most common mistakes writers make when writing YA? When sending in manuscripts?

When writing YA: They write what the trends are rather than their own story. Every publisher has been deluged with vampire manuscripts in the wake of the success of *Twilight* (just as wizard manuscripts went through a renaissance after *Harry Potter*). But what made those books successful was not just their entertaining plots—it was the writer's ability to tap into the truth of teenage experience (forbidden love, wrestling with maturity and death) and represent that in an entertaining plot. Teens, I think, are really looking for truth more than anything else—some nugget of experience or reality that reflects their own lives or offers them guidance through the muddle of adolescence. If they find that, they'll hook into it.

When sending in manuscripts: Make sure the publisher actually publishes the kind of book you've written. I still remember the manuscript I opened as an editorial assistant, thinking it was another middle grade novel, only to discover in the first five pages that it was an adult erotic fantasy . . .

If you could suggest one thing that would help writers find success, what would it be?

Read. This is the most common advice out there, I know, but nothing is so useful in teaching good prose rhythms for your voice and familiarizing you with the genre you're working in—the better for you to put a stamp on it all your own.

Bella Pearson

Bio: Bella Pearson is a senior editor with David Fickling Books, an imprint of Random House. She has worked for David Fickling Books since 2001; previously she completed an MA in children's literature at the Roehampton Institute and worked in an independent children's bookshop in London for many years. She lives in Oxford with her family. Please note: David Fickling Books does not accept unsolicited queries.

Is there something about the life of an editor that you wish more writers knew about or understood?

There can be nothing more exciting in one's working life as an editor than a new manuscript fresh from the photocopier that on first read sends a shiver of excitement down the spine—as a result of the writing, the subject, the originality, the pure quality of the author's work—whatever the reason might be. This sense of exhilaration and the potential discovery of a new talent is the main reason I do my job (although it can be quite a rare occurrence!). So perhaps the most important thing I wish that more writers understood about the life of an editor is that we really are on the same side. There are those who do all the work on their novel—the writers—and then those who do all the searching and reading and deciphering—and sometimes the twain really do meet. The satisfaction and excitement which comes as a result of publishing a fantastic novel from an extraordinary new writer, and sending it out into the big wide world to be read by as many people as possible, is the most thrilling feeling of all, and should not be underestimated! And the more chances we have to do that as publishers, the better.

What are some of the most common mistakes writers make when writing YA? When sending in manuscripts?

Perhaps the most common mistake made by writers of children's literature as a whole is to talk down to their readership, and nowhere is this more evident than in the genre of teenage/YA fiction. This can be evident in many ways, but is particularly obvious in dialogue, where it can become apparent that the author is attempting to emulate the YA lingo of the time—or equally importantly, in subject matter, where sex, drugs, and rock and roll can sometimes come way ahead of the most important thing: story.

Just like the rest of us, young adults read around their own lives, much more so than most adults; but many writers make the mistake of believing that they are interested in just a few restrictive, hormonally based things—which results in plenty of substandard, issue-led novels. This is, of course, not to say that these issues are not essential in the lives of young adults—just that coming to terms with the adult world should not be seen as first and foremost more important than the integrity of the narrative.

On an entirely different note, in answer to the second part of this question—first impressions really do count! Something as simple as reading a manuscript with double spacing can make all the difference—there is just so much on your desk that the easier to read, the better. If I receive a manuscript that has a straightforward and brief letter of introduction, and a clearly laid out text, then I am much more open and interested when it comes to reading and responding. If the manuscript has come from someone with professionalism, who is taking writing seriously, this can only help to endear them to the recipient who is peering around wobbly piles of manuscripts taller than themself.

The bells and whistles that can come whirling through the postal service are more likely to make me think there must be something wrong with the writing itself if so much song and dance is necessary to draw attention to it. For instance, I once received a gift voucher, which of course I sent back. Bribery aside, I've gotten manuscripts accompanied by multicolored paper packaging and childlike bubble writing; photos of all the family and pets; one of the cleverest (and most dishonest!) times, someone sent in their book with a postcard claiming to be from a sales rep who knew me, proclaiming the book's popularity with readers.

If you could suggest one thing that would help writers find success, what would it be?

If we are talking about individual characteristics, determination is one that springs to mind—the life of a writer is a hard one and can be a lonely one, so a great deal of strength is needed to keep going and remain hopeful. As in everything, tastes and likes vary tremendously from editor to editor—and although I'd like to think that I and all editors are absolutely open to all sorts of material, inevitably some part of the decision-making process will be down to the sort of thing we personally enjoy. So if one individual rejects a book, this is not the kiss of doom; the ability to brush off the rejection and continue believing in your work is essential in order to find the right publisher.

Sharyn November

http://www.sharyn.org

Bio: Sharyn November is Senior Editor for Viking Children's Books and Editorial Director of Firebird Books, which is a mainly paperback (reprint) imprint publishing fantasy and science fiction for teenagers and adults. Her many authors have included John Barnes, Charles de Lint, Alison Goodman, Elizabeth Hand, Nina Kiriki Hoffman, Diana Wynne Jones, Ellen Klages, Kelly Link, Nnedi Okorafor, and the editorial team of Ellen Datlow and Terri Windling. She is one of the few children's book editors who works directly with teenagers; their love of speculative fiction was the seed of her founding Firebird Books, which launched in January 2002. She was named a 2004 and 2005 World Fantasy Award Finalist in the Professional category—in 2004 for Firebird Books, and in 2005 for editing. *Firebirds Rising* was a 2007 Finalist in the Anthology category.

Is there something about the life of an editor that you wish more writers knew about or understood?

It's like being a plate spinner on the old Ed Sullivan show. It's an involved, complicated job—lots of meetings, paperwork, brainstorming, and emotional engagement. (I consider it a vocation, rather than a job, actually.) One thing an author should always remember: Your editor is as invested in your book (and its success) as you are.

What are some of the most common mistakes writers make when writing YA? When sending in manuscripts?

When writing YA . . .

➤ Following trends rather than following your characters, story, and heart.

➤ Assuming that anything older than a picture book is YA. (Yes, really!)

➤ Not thinking about who the book is really for—who will read it. I suggest writers think about what they read as teenagers; it takes you back to your elemental self and what mattered to you then, and orients your internal compass.

When sending in manuscripts, make sure that you get the editor's name and title right, and be as professional as possible in your cover letter and presentation. I would also add that manuscripts that are sent without SASEs go straight into the garbage.

If you could suggest one thing that would help YA writers find success, what would it be?

Define what success means to you, and be honest about yourself and your writing.

Lacy Compton
http://www.prufrock.com

Bio: Lacy Compton currently serves Prufrock Press, an independent nonfiction publisher, by editing the company's trade books, managing *Creative Kids* magazine, and organizing promotions for all of Prufrock's titles.

Tell us about the life of an editor working on nonfiction books in the YA market. What is it about your job that you wish more writers knew about or understood?

My role as a nonfiction editor encompasses many other responsibilities than just reading and critiquing work. I must acquire new titles by attending professional conferences to scout out ideas, watch the trends in our section of the bookstore for potential leads, find authors by doing research online, and read prospectuses from authors and agents. Much of what we do to acquire books is proactive. We have a vision for our company, and we're very firm in our policies of having research-based and intelligent nonfiction (even in our books for teens).

I also develop contracts, set due dates, and make sure manuscripts are on track. In addition, as the primary editor for our trade division, I coordinate books' publication dates and sales materials with our distributor, Sourcebooks. I develop launch sheets and catalog information for the books, pitch the titles to the Sourcebooks sales staff, and work with our designer to develop covers.

Once a manuscript is in, the traditional editorial process takes place. Because of my work with the trade books, once one of my books is released, I move that title from my editorial process to my publicity process, finding reviewers for the book, showcasing it at conferences, and working with the author to promote the book in any way we can.

The process for nonfiction is likely similar to that of fiction, except that we require our authors to have credible sources to back up their work. As a niche publisher, we print smaller quantities than larger publishers. We only do advance copies for a few titles each year, and only a small portion (about 10–12 of the 50 titles we publish each year) end up with distribution in the retail bookstores. Our authors won't be set up for author appearances across the nation, they won't be read by millions, and they most likely won't hit the bestseller lists. But they will have a quality book that looks and reads well, a personalized editorial experience, and true and honest reviews from readers who are passionate about the subjects they are covering.

What are some of the most common mistakes writers make submitting books for consideration to an educational press?

I strongly urge writers to read a publisher's guidelines carefully before submitting, and to look over its current product line to see if your work actually fits. Many nonfiction authors tend to do the legwork themselves, and mistakes occur if you're not careful. Many people are also confused about our target audience—teachers and parents of kids who are gifted and advanced learners, along with the kids themselves. The idea of "gifted" isn't as simple as many people think, so the best advice I can give writers is that if you're submitting something to a niche publisher, do your homework first!

If you could suggest one thing that would help writers find success, what would it be?

Write every day! Don't be afraid to submit your ideas, and if asked to do so, don't be afraid to let go of something you really love about your book idea to try something else. Writers often get pigeonholed into something they want or a vision they had for a book, when it's just not marketable. Listen to those who are in the business and take their advice.

your publishing journey

Just as the old proverb says, a journey of a thousand miles begins with a single step. And when you're an author, a giant step in that journey is to learn about marketing—up next in Chapter 9.

Marketing Your Book

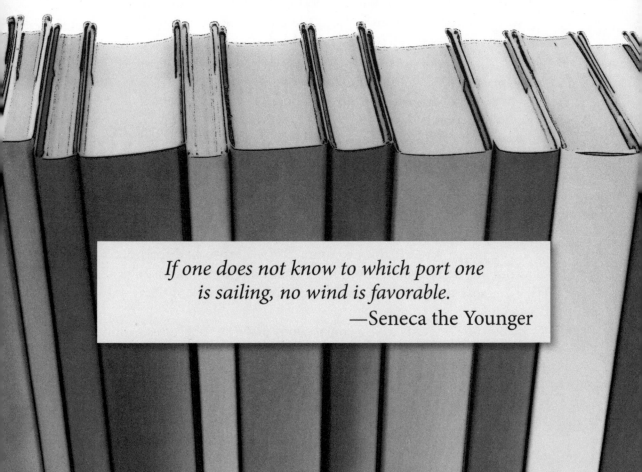

*If one does not know to which port one
is sailing, no wind is favorable.*
—Seneca the Younger

Your introduction to the Marketing Beast happened when you first crafted a query. Whether you think of that beast as a beauty or a monster or both, and whether you want to pet it, shoot it, or run from it, it's going to play a big part in your career. You want people to hear about your book. If they don't hear about it, they're unlikely to buy it and read it. You wrote it, so clearly you believe in it. Now it's time to let others know it's out there.

I grew up without a TV and saw very few movies. Books—and my own mind—were my entertainment. I loved books. Really, really loved them. But that didn't mean I had a single clue about marketing when my first book was published. At that time, I thought all books automatically appeared on bookshelves in bookstores. People bought them, and that was that. Nothing could be further from the truth. To explain, I'll share a little of my own experience getting acquainted with book marketing.

Right after *The Seer and the Sword* came out in paperback (after doing really well in hardcover), I visited the Tattered Cover in Denver—one of the biggest bookstores in the world. I went there to browse and, of course, ended up in the teen section. There I saw massive displays holding multiple copies of a few chosen books that were published by large houses. No one walking into the teen section could have missed those displays—they rose up from the floor and dominated the view.

However, I had to hunt for my own book. Eventually I found a copy tucked away, spine out, on a shelf stuffed with paperbacks by dozens of authors. I would never have found it if I had not been looking for it. And I realized right away that the catchiest cover in the world cannot reach a reader when only the spine of the book is visible on the shelf. Then I looked for a book I admired by another author. It was nowhere to be found. I asked a clerk if the store carried it. They didn't, but he offered to order it for me.

Later, I discovered that it's common for writers to find their books spine out in a bookstore. It's even more common not to find them at all. Why? Because there's only so much shelf space and only so many marketing dollars.

If your book doesn't have a conspicuous place in bookstores nationwide, does it mean you're not a good writer? Of course not. Your book can receive many honors (as mine had) and still not be very visible. Getting a good spot on retail shelves is all about a complicated mix of sales pitches, name recognition, random chance, and other ingredients that defy analysis.

your advance indicates the size of the marketing budget

How do you know whether your book has a chance of getting prominently displayed in retail outlets and online banners, with the cover facing out? One reliable indicator is the amount of your advance. A large advance—in excess of $100,000—means more risk to the publisher and thus more marketing for you. The bigger your advance, the more likely that the publisher has decided your book has a good chance of making it onto the bestseller lists.

Is it good news for you if you get a large advance? Usually. However, a big advance for a book that turns out to be a sales flop can sink your career—because if a publisher puts a boatload of money into an advance for a book that flounders, that publisher is not going to buy your next book. (Henceforth you may have to adopt a pen name.)

How do big publishers decide which authors get large advances and good media marketing campaigns? Well, prolific authors with a groundswell of word-of-mouth, authors such as J. K. Rowling, Stephenie Meyer, Sarah Dessen, M.T. Anderson, and Lauren Myracle, are good candidates. An extra boost in marketing for such an author will capitalize on the momentum of his or her sales and increase them even more.

But that doesn't mean every author who starts to develop a following will get a marketing boost. Many, many books are left to make it—or not—on their own. Why?

marketing is expensive

Publishers cannot afford to put up the cash to make a splash with every title they print. Most new authors are not aware that for a book to become a mega bestseller with sales in the millions, the publisher must order huge print runs—at considerable cost. (By the way, it's less expensive to print a million copies of one book than 100,000 copies each of 10 books.) Media campaigns are not cheap, either; they require concerted placement, lots of savvy, and plenty of dollars.

If a writer has name recognition already—by being famous outside of the world of books—a publisher can capitalize on that. Instead of working to create new name recognition, the publisher can draw attention to the fact that a celebrity has written a book. For example, when pop star Madonna entered the children's book market, her name was her passport to royal marketing. Her book had a first printing north of a million copies issued in dozens of translations. (Unknown writers who had struggled for years to hone their craft, only to find that their books would not receive much attention, weren't very thrilled to see their sales overtaken by a celebrity's book. But large publishers have made the argument that giant bestsellers keep them solvent, which is what allows them to publish unknown authors.)

To further confuse things, every once in a while authors with no sales history at all are picked for star treatment. Maybe their publisher spots a niche in the market and gambles that a particular book, by filling that niche, can justify a big-budget marketing plan. Maybe there's something about the author's life story that lends itself well to the creation of a marketing angle. And maybe the book is just such a page turner that nobody can put it down!

You might hope to be among those fortunate authors who get picked for bestseller treatment, but if you're not, remember that those authors do not necessarily have an easy time of it. The pressure to turn out top sellers is intense and can be hard to sustain.

Major marketing campaigns are no guarantee of success. Publishers must contend with the utter unpredictability of the marketplace. Sometimes a book fails to sell even after heavy publicity. Readers just aren't captivated. What should have been a superstar turns into a black hole for the publisher. Then again, a book with a $100 marketing budget can come out of nowhere and shine, shine, shine. When this happens, publishers must scramble to order a big enough print run to fulfill the public's desire for copies or lose sales. Many times, the wave is missed.

Midlist Books

What about "midlist" books—books that never make the bestseller list but have respectable sales in the tens of thousands? They often go out of print because their publishers can't justify the cost of continuing to print and warehouse them. They may be excellent, but they didn't build a following in time.

A bit of good news for novelists: Young adult novels are given a little more leeway in the marketplace than novels for adults. YA books are allowed more time to find their way with readers in libraries and schools, whereas novels for adults can live and die in the space of 3 months.

Bottom line? Unless you have a large publisher that decides to put the money and energy into hyping your book—a rare occurrence—do not expect huge displays in stores or tours paid for by the publisher. You and your word-of-mouth cheering section will be picking up the slack. Yes, if you're serious about your career as an author, you may have to pump some of your own money and brainpower into marketing.

marketing yourself

There are some basic things you can do to help your publisher sell your books. (Also true if you self-publish.) One is to get an author website. Another is public speaking. And of course, there's always networking—through blogs, social networks, and the like.

Author Websites

Author websites have become almost essential. You want to have a presence on the web. The norm for authors is to get your full name (or pen name) dot com. If the name is already taken, you can opt for dot net or dot biz. Your site should reflect your personality as a writer. It's a good idea to keep it updated, too. (I know that sounds like obvious advice, but I frequently forget to update when I get super busy with everything else.)

Public Speaking

I've found speaking to be one of the best ways to generate interest in books. You can speak at local libraries, schools, writers' conferences, and other forums. How do you let people know you're up for speaking? Network. Be available. Let connections develop. Attend gatherings of authors and readers when you can. Talk to media specialists and let them know you're available for school programs. Working with teens can be a lot of fun. By visiting high schools and middle schools, you get a chance to meet the teens in your reading audience and interact. "But," you say, "I'd rather dance with a tornado than speak in public." If you feel that way, you're not alone. Many writers are introverted by nature or have no experience with public speaking. So if you're a shy soul or you've never given a talk, you might want to start a course at Toastmasters (http://www.toastmasters.org).

Getting Known Without Making Public Appearances

If you're too intimidated by public speaking, there's always the Internet. Some schools will set up chat rooms for writers or do e-mail interviews. Blogs—if you find a niche that no one else is covering—can help you build an audience. So can interactions on social networking sites, where fans can find you and then spread the word among their friends.

Book Signings

When I throw a book release party at a local store in my own region, plenty of people show up to celebrate with me (and buy my book). But in places where I don't have a big network of friends, book signings are hit or miss—and my experience jives with those of other authors. Therefore, traveling to far-flung cities in hopes of building a following may not be the best use of your time or your marketing budget. It's much easier and more satisfying to do a blog tour.

Blog Tours

Whatever your writing niche happens to be, there will be bloggers posting about it. By guest blogging or interviewing on various blogs, you can increase exposure to the market that's waiting for you, and you can return the favor by letting your friends and fellow authors know about the blog sites you visit.

Copromotion

Sometimes, it just feels more natural for writers to talk up someone else's books than to talk up our own. And lately, simpatico authors are banding together, taking turns mentioning each other's books, cohosting interviews, holding book parties together, and just generally supporting each other.

advice from marketing experts

I'm not an expert on social media or blogging, so I got in touch with people who are, and I asked them for interviews. They kindly obliged.

Tricia Lawrence

http://www.realbrilliant.com, http://www.authorblogger.net

Bio: Tricia Lawrence is an associate agent with Erin Murphy Literary. She has worked as a book editor since 1995 and advised authors about their writing, marketing, and social media since 2005. Since 2012, she has concentrated solely on helping her author clients build successful careers. Tricia only accepts submissions by referral or if you've met her at a conference.

You work with writers on integrating social media, blogging, and other web tools to market their books. What's the most effective combination for writers of YA?

YA writers have so much opportunity to interact with their audience: readers, buyers, parents, librarians, and teachers. I often start by calming social media nerves. As a YA writer, you have put some time in to learn to write YA; thus, you will not become proficient using social media, blogging, and web tools overnight. It too takes time. But not all your time. First, set strict boundaries around your time. I recommend one hour a day to study, learn, interact, observe, blog, etc. If you want to spend more, fine. But you should be getting it down to a nice steady dose and then you stop and you go write. We are writers first of all! Second, find your passion. If you love writing about true love, or friendship, or secrets, or compassion, or you notice there's a theme in everything you love to read and write, go there. Don't try to use social networks and become a person that you aren't passionate about. Third, find authors or bloggers you resonate with and watch how they deal with social media and blogging. Do they blog once or twice a week? Do they feature other authors or talk about the writing process only? Do they discuss a theme completely unrelated to writing? What pieces of their social media, blogging, and web tool strategy could you use?

What are the most common mistakes you see YA authors make in marketing?

Freezing up because of nerves. Thinking that they are terrible at marketing, when really, the best marketing (the one that is proved over and over and over) is word of mouth. Social media marketing is simply telling people about your book, about how you wrote your book, about other authors you like to read, about themes you are fascinated by and can't stop reading or writing or thinking about. If authors simply followed their passion and did not clam up, but used every chance they could to talk about what they care the most about, marketing would be the easiest part!

What are some approaches for shy or private writers to take advantage of the web?

Nowadays, writers can do so much from the privacy of their own home office. Used to be, an author had to get up and get dressed, put on pantyhose (yeck!), and go out and visit bookstores, schools, and libraries in person. There are still opportunities for that, but these days, it can all be done via e-mail, Skype, Twitter, Facebook, Google+, YouTube (no pantyhose required!), and more. The opportunities for an introverted writer (I'm one too!) to be able to be more comfortable while still interacting with their readers are amazing. I'm so grateful I can record a video (and delete it if I am all nerves) rather than have to stand up and do it live without any additional chances to redeem myself.

Why and how do writers set up blogs? What's a good length for a typical blog post? Is it important to add graphics or pictures to each blog entry, or does it matter?

A writer can set up a free blog on Wordpress.com, Blogger, Tumblr, or LiveJournal in about 5 minutes. Those are great practice, because you can figure out if this blogging thing fits you (some writers I work with prefer to record videos—called vlogging—rather than write anything other than their manuscripts) and if you've got enough to write about to sustain a blog in the long term. However, I think a serious writer should consider adding a hosted blog (through Wordpress.org) to their website. This should not cost thousands, but it will cost. Check with your writer friends for website/blog designer referrals.

A great blog post runs around 550 words; however, you can run them shorter. What worries me are blog posts that are longer. This means you might want to edit yourself a bit more before posting. By all means include images (there are places to get images for free all over the Web; some Flickr accounts allow you to use their images provided you link back appropriately) if you care to. Images help convey information that would take a thousand words. You can blog quite successfully without them, but most readers prefer them.

Tell us about the role of guest bloggers.

A guest blogger appears on a blog (with their YA novel or as an aspiring YA writer) as a way of raising visibility online. Guest bloggers answer questions from the audience or from the host blogger, typically in written format. Sometimes, the guest blogger will appear in a video with the host blogger in the form of a Skype chat, or as Libba Bray and Maureen Johnson have done so successfully, together in the same room, volleying questions, answers, and jokes back and forth. Being a guest on someone else's blog is an honor; however, it is up to you to decide which blogs you would like to appear on. Be sure to mention it on your own blog and social media networks to drive traffic and generate comments and followers.

What is the role of a web marketing consultant? How do writers find a good one, and what can they expect from the process? What's realistic and what isn't?

A social media strategist/web marketing consultant/PR firm, publicity firm is all the same—helping a writer sell more books and become more visible. While old-school PR and publicity firms and consultants are fast coming up to speed on this new social media approach, web marketing consultants and social media strategists are often a bit more cutting edge. You can expect to pay several thousand dollars for a range of services—from banner ads to guest posts to blog tours to NPR or television appearances. The more the firm or consultant does, the more it costs you; thus, I am a big fan of bootstrapping it. Pay a consultant the initial money to learn the tools, and then use them yourself. Be present in your promotion and marketing activities; don't expect to farm it all out in the beginning. As you sell more and more books, you can hire virtual assistants or interns, but for now, figure out what you really want to do and how you can learn it yourself. You'll save yourself money in the long run.

What about e-mail newsletters? Are they helpful for unpublished writers, or just published writers? Are there any legalities YA writers need to be aware of when posting links to sign up for their newsletters?

An e-mail newsletter is a great way to further engage with your audience. Usually, these are for published writers who either have had books come out already or are waiting for their publication date. These newsletters offer a quick solution to let everyone know about upcoming appearances, promotions, book news, etc. As to legalities, YA authors will be offering newsletter signups for the gatekeepers—librarians, parents, teachers. I don't advise creating newsletters for kids. Publishers, parents, teachers, and librarians would need to be involved anyway, if kids were signing up for newsletters.

For unpublished writers, especially for those writers who have a very strong theme or passion that they write about, an e-mail newsletter on the subject of their passion—in other words, a themed newsletter—might be something to think about before selling the book. This is frequently used in nonfiction publishing and is called building a list. For nonfiction books (not usually kids books), having a list is a big part of the book proposal. This practice has not yet made it all the way over to YA writing, but you can certainly use it if it fits your subject matter.

Kerrie Flanagan

Bio: Kerrie Flanagan is the Director of Northern Colorado Writers (NCW) and a freelance writer with articles in national and regional publications. She is a frequent contributor for *WOW! Women on Writing*, and six of her essays have been published in various *Chicken Soup for the Soul* books. Through NCW she provides 200+ members and other writers with the tools, encouragement, and information needed to find success.

Why and how do writers set up blogs?

Blogging is a great way to stay connected to readers, to hone your writing skills, and if you are a nonfiction writer, a way to position yourself as an expert on your topic. I started my blog, The Writing Bug (http://www.the-writing-bug.blogspot.com), because I have a passion for supporting and encouraging other writers. With the blog, I can connect with those writers, share resources, inspire them, provide insight into the publishing industry, as well as drive traffic to my website.

The two most popular blogging platforms are Blogger and Word-Press. I chose Blogger because it's free and allows you to monetize your blog with advertisements. They also have great features and design elements at no extra cost. WordPress has different levels, so with the free version, you can't monetize your blog. They also have different features that you can pay for like extra storage, custom design, and premium themes. They are both good, so you have to decide what features are best for you.

What do you consider to be the biggest benefit of blogging? Are there any drawbacks, and if so, what are they?

Blogging provides me a platform to write and connect with a community of writers. I also get to write about what interests me. While I want to make sure my posts are well written and grammatically correct, it is a more relaxed venue. If I had a novel out, it would provide me a way to get to know my readers. The biggest drawback to blogging is the time factor. It is important to make sure it doesn't interfere with your regular writing.

What's a good length for a typical blog post? Is it important to add graphics or pictures to each blog entry, or does it matter?

When people are reading online they usually have limited time, so it's best to keep blog posts short: somewhere between 200–400 words. Paragraphs should only be a couple of sentences long, with a space in between each. (Don't indent.)

Graphics and photos will catch readers' attention and help to break up the content, so I try to add these whenever possible. Be sure to get permission before using copyrighted images.

What has blogging done for your career as a writer? Is a blog a good forum for publicizing books?

Since my goal is to help other writers on their writing journeys, most of what I publish has to do with writing. I use my blog as a platform to position myself as an expert in this field. I share my thoughts, provide resources, inspire, encourage, interact with other writers, and link to my published articles from the blog. In terms of my career, it has helped tremendously by establishing my credibility as a writer and as the Director of NCW.

For those who write books, a blog is an excellent way to publicize a novel and connect with readers. But in order for it to be effective, you need to be consistent with how many times you post each week, spend time visiting and commenting on other blogs, and interact with those who comment on your blog.

Any advice for writers about following agent/editor blogs?

Following agent and editor blogs is a good thing. It provides insight into that person and what they may or may not be looking for in queries and manuscripts. A lot of times they will share queries they liked, what type of stories they would love to see more of, pet peeves, recent acquisitions, information about their clients' books, and the list goes on. Interacting with them by leaving comments is good, but be sure to remain professional.

Chapter 10

Self-Publishing Your Book

All the risk is mine, but so is all the reward.
—Becky Clark Cornwell

I'll admit that once upon a time I was a snob about self-publishing. Back then I believed it was the ultimate hubris for self-published writers to call themselves authors. Self-published books seemed to be popping up every time I turned around, and I thought of them as wasted trees sacrificed to the egos of those unable to accept that they couldn't write well enough to find a "real" publisher.

My prejudice was not unfounded. I've seen self-published books written at the level of "roses are red, violets are blue"—only without the roses or violets. They stink. Okay, so that's the bad side.

There's another side though. Sometimes dedicated, talented, skilled writers cannot get the attention of an agent or editor, or don't want the hassles of getting published through traditional channels. For such writers, self-publishing is the way to go. More and more people are selecting this option, and there are now tens of thousands of new self-published titles every year.

Advantages and Disadvantages of Self-Publishing

Advantages

➤ You won't have to wait years until your book is available. Whereas traditional publishers have a tight rotation of books scheduled years in advance, self-publishing can happen in a matter of weeks after the book is written. If it's important to you to give your teenage son or niece or friend a book you've created—and before that person is 35—this can be quite a motivating factor.

➤ You won't have to worry about submitting and being rejected, submitting and being rejected, submitting . . .

➤ You'll be in charge of your own work from beginning to end.

➤ If your book sells well, you get to keep the profits.

Disadvantages

➤ Because the only screening process necessary for a book to be self-published is the writer's wallet, plenty of self-published books are terrible. You will, therefore, have to find a way to set your work apart if you want to create a market for it.

> ➤ You won't have the advice and guidance of a professional editor, unless you hire someone. The person you hire might not have the expertise of someone working directly with current titles in an active marketplace.
>
> ➤ Your book is unlikely to appear in retail stores. Distribution channels for self-published books are lousy. Traditional review services do not accept self-published titles.
>
> ➤ You'll have to pay for everything, and you may not recover your initial investment. This is fine if your ambition is not about cash.
>
> ➤ You'll be in charge of your own marketing plan. Without established distribution channels, this is much tougher than most people anticipate. You'll have to go out and find your audience.

As a self-publisher, you will oversee all steps of the publishing process yourself, hiring help as needed while you prepare your book for print or e-readers. There are lots of resources to help you, including manuals (some of which are listed in Chapter 6) and self-publishing associations.

print on demand

If you go with a print format, you'll need to decide on a printer and a print quantity. In the past, both traditional publishers and self-publishers had to agree to fairly large print runs in order to get a reasonably priced book. (The larger the print run, the lower the price per book.) Printing just a few copies of a book was simply not cost effective. Now, however, print on demand (POD) technology allows you to order small quantities of books as you need them. The price of a book is still higher in small quantities than in large quantities, but it's not so exorbitant that it's completely out of range.

POD has caused many changes in the world of publishing, and those changes are still taking place. Many companies provide POD services, but there are important differences between them. Just because someone sets up as a POD company doesn't meant that company knows how to put out a quality book. If your printed book has a lousy binding that falls apart after one reading, or if the ink on the pages is badly prepared, or if the cover is suboptimal, that book will send the wrong message about you as an author.

Shady PODs

Some POD companies simply provide printing services. But some try to present themselves as actual publishers and persuade writers they've landed traditional contracts when signing up. (Traditional publishing companies don't charge you a cent when they agree to publish your book.) Then these companies proceed to give you a "royalty"—which actually means that they *take* a royalty for a book that is entirely your own investment.

It is very important to research your options carefully and to know exactly what you are getting into before you sign on with a POD publisher. You may be able to find something that suits your situation perfectly, but please proceed with caution.

Copublishing

A copublisher furnishes you with editing, book design and distribution, and other services customarily provided by a publisher, but you split the costs. In other words, you foot part of the bill for developing and printing your book or formatting it for e-readers. How much of that bill you cover is negotiated by individual publishers. How much your royalty rate increases as a result of your investment is also a negotiable point.

Copublishing can be a great solution for small publishers and authors alike. But again, please do your homework here. There are many things to keep in mind, as this interview with Fiona Veitch Smith of Crafty Publishing explains.

Fiona Veitch Smith

http://www.craftypublishing.com

Bio: Fiona Veitch Smith is a writer, editor, and university lecturer based in Newcastle-upon-Tyne, UK. She runs an editorial advice service through The Crafty Writer (http://www.thecraftywriter.com) and also offers free online courses in creative fiction and nonfiction writing. She recently branched out into publishing through the Crafty Publishing imprint.

What are the defining differences between traditional publishing, self-publishing, print-on-demand services, and copublishing?

A traditional publisher will foot the whole bill and take full responsibility for the editing and production of your book. The publisher will also market and distribute your book, although you will still be expected to participate in promoting it. You will be paid royalties on the sale of a book and in most cases will receive a monetary advance on your royalty once a contract has been signed. In other words, in the first instance, *they pay you.*

If you are a self-publisher you do everything yourself. You pay for and arrange the production of the book and are fully responsible for editing the text. You also take it upon yourself to market and distribute your book to bookshops or direct to the public. Distributing the book to bookshops is the most difficult aspect of self-publishing and what makes traditional publishing, along with its quality control, the first-choice option.

A POD company is essentially a printer who has an online presence. The only difference is that most POD companies give you an option to link up with a distribution wholesaler to make it easier for you to get your books into shops. However, the onus is still on you to contact the shop and ask them to stock it. A POD company will also virtually warehouse your stock so you don't have boxes shoved under the bed and will post out copies to customers "on demand." They do not do any marketing for you beyond perhaps featuring you on their website. You foot the whole bill and are responsible for editorial quality control.

Copublishing is when you and the publisher split the costs, but all of the "traditional" functions of a publisher are provided. Splitting the costs usually takes the form of an advance stock purchase, which you can then resell to recoup your costs. In other words, you commit to buy x-amount of copies of the book. This will guarantee that the publisher can cover the basic costs. Increasingly, formerly traditional publishers are offering copublishing deals to new authors whom otherwise they feel are too big a financial risk.

How do writers distinguish between quality POD companies and vanity publishers masquerading as traditional publishers?

A POD company should be up front in what it is offering. "Big name" companies such as Lulu, Lightning Source, and Smashwords do not claim to be publishers. If you put any of these company names into a search engine, the company blurb will feature key words such as "self-publishing," "printing," and "distribution."

If you are unsure about a company, try this simple test: If you cannot tell in under 10 seconds whether or not it's a POD company or a publisher (whether reputable or not), then there's a problem; they should be that up front about it.

There are a host of online writing communities where fellow writers share their horror stories about vanity publishers. Again, do a search with the key words: "Company Name" and "vanity publishers." If you are looking for a traditional publisher rather than a POD company or copublisher, beware of anyone who advertises that they are looking for new writers. A traditional publisher does not have to do this. You should also look at the royalty percentages on offer: a traditional publisher will not offer anything beyond 15% (more likely 7%–10%).

How do writers find a good copublisher? What should they watch out for?

➤ See if the publisher also offers traditional publishing contracts. If not, this limits your career progression from copublishing into mainstream publishing. If the publisher's traditional wing is listed in one of the reputable market yearbooks (such as *Writers' & Artists' Yearbook*, *Writers' Handbook*, or *Writers' Market*), you have a better chance of getting good service, as they will have a reputation to protect.

➤ Look for evidence that they can and will distribute your book into bookshops, not just "making it available" to bookshops on request. Anyone can do that if they have a registered ISBN, and it is no more than you would do yourself as a self-publisher.

➤ Check out the publicity surrounding previous titles (again, ask your favorite search engine). If there is nothing beyond the company and author's own websites, I would question their marketing effectiveness.

➤ Consider the bottom line. How many books do they expect you to purchase? Can you honestly sell that many through your own contacts? I would think twice about anything over 700. In addition, make sure you are being offered a minimum of 35% in royalties to compensate for your financial risk.

ebooks

If you've decided to self-publish, it makes a lot of sense to put your book up for sale in online bookstores. This involves getting it professionally formatted for e-readers. There are companies out there that will charge you to do this—and then charge you a perpetual royalty rate as high as 50%, just for having done the formatting. Other companies will simply format your book for an hourly fee. (It does take time and meticulous attention to do it well.) For more information, read this interview with self-publishing expert Brian Schwartz.

Brian Schwartz

Bio: "Authorpreneur" Brian Schwartz is an award-winning author and creator of the 50 Interviews series, which has published more than 20 titles in the last 2 years. He launched ePubConversions.com in 2010 to assist other authors and publishers to take advantage of the shift in technology and get their own books published to the major eBook marketplaces.

You have self-published both print and eBooks with success. What can you tell us about the difference between print and eBooks? Is it important to offer both options?

I advise authors that an eBook should be their first priority. As small publishers without a major distributor to get us into bookstores, our eBooks outsell our print books. Although an eBook has start-up costs for layout and cover design, once those costs are earned out in sales, there is no further overhead to contend with. Print books have upfront costs of layout and design, and also require the ongoing expenses of printing. So I encourage anyone considering publishing to first get their book online as soon as they can. If they can manage to provide readers with a print option as well, they will tend to sell more of both. It's about gaining visibility in as many places as possible. Word of mouth is still the most effective form of marketing, and the more places and formats available, the better. For the print option, I recommend print-on-demand so they aren't stuck with a garage full of books.

What's the importance of a platform for e-publishers? What are some examples of a successful platform?

If you're a nonfiction author, a platform is vital, but it's a little bit of a chicken and egg situation. It's easier to build a platform on a topic once you have written a book on that topic. However, the more you can do to establish yourself as a leader in your field, even before your book comes out, the further along you'll be once the book is launched.

For a fiction author, having a platform and online presence helps you stay in front of your readers if you use that platform to give them more of what they want—your story and your characters.

There's no shortage of people who will offer to help you build your platform and will be eager to take your money. But I would caution writers that no matter how much time and money you put into building your platform, it won't matter much unless you've chosen a reachable niche that isn't already saturated.

Do you advise self-published writers to hire an editor before offering their work for sale?

Absolutely. You'll get bad reviews if you release a book that isn't well edited. Nothing will kill your sales faster than negative reviews.

What do writers need to know about formatting an eBook? What are their options, and what are the drawbacks and benefits of each?

It depends if you're still writing a book or you've already written a book and now want to get it converted to e-format. If you have used a common word processor program such as MS Word or Open Office, it'll be much easier to get it ready for the eBook formats, which are essentially straight text with some simple html coding to define the styling.

The challenge with a book that has already been published in print is that all the formatting needs to be redone for the e-reader format. This process involves stripping out the headers, footers, page numbers, and images, and making sure all the text in each paragraph is continuous so it'll reflow properly on an e-reader. When my company does this conversion, we create a hyperlinked table of contents and redo any footnotes or endnotes so they are hyperlinked as well. It's a fairly involved process, which is one of the reasons why the adoption of eBooks by publishers hasn't been faster—it's essentially the same as creating a new layout for an existing book. There are some tools that conversion specialists use to help speed up the process, but for the most part, it's still painstaking.

Anyone who has used any of the "auto-conversion" tools will tell you the end result is far from pretty and doesn't remotely resemble the print edition. When eBooks first came out, readers were willing to put up with the lack of formatting, but now they won't buy a book that is improperly formatted.

interviews with self-published writers

Still wondering whether self-publishing would suit you? Here's something else to put into the mix. Following are interviews with self-published authors of YA fiction who have agreed to share their experience and expertise with you.

Becky Clark Cornwell
http://www.beckyclark.net

Self-Published YA Book:

An UnCivil War—The Boys Who Were Left Behind

What are the advantages and rewards of self-publishing?

Speed, for one. If you're talented, you can write, edit, and produce a good book within a year. Dealing with traditional publishers, large or small, can be as slow as a turtle on Valium. Also, all the money from a book sale goes straight to my bottom line. I was at a big book signing with a famous author. He watched in amazement as I stuffed $10 bills right into my pocket (the lion's share of which was pure carnivorous profit). For every book he signed, he got only 18 cents, which he never actually saw for 6 months. (Of course, when he got his 6-month royalty statement, it had lots more money on it than what I had wadded up in my pocket over a 6-month period.) And I love the autonomy of it all. I can do whatever I want to promote or distribute my book. All the risk is mine, but so is all the reward.

What are the disadvantages and trials?

Self-publishing is like getting a Ph.D. in every aspect of book publishing while sitting on a lighted Roman candle. My biggest problem has been distribution. Grab a hankie and listen to my sad story. Three thousand copies of *An UnCivil War* were delivered to me in August 2001. Remember what happened in September? Yeah. My marketing plan was all about mailing free copies to reviewers and distributors, but no one was accepting any mail because it might be tainted with anthrax. I had to totally regroup and rethink my plan, which got scaled back to within an inch of its life.

So, I've sold those 3,000 copies in lots of weirdly fun ways, none of which I envisioned when I started. Mostly I sell books at book signings during conferences for teachers and librarians, at school visits, or at events for home educators. But I've sold books standing in line at the post office when someone asked about the 10 identical envelopes I was mailing.

The other disadvantage is that it's exhausting doing everything yourself. My humble little business venture is easy compared to many, and I have the luxury of not having to work a day job. But still, I've found that I can either write and create or I can handle business. I can't seem to do both consistently, even though I'm a fairly organized, self-disciplined gal. I find it easier—and certainly more fun—to write than to deal with book production or fulfillment or update my website.

What have you learned about marketing?

I'm one of the rare writers who loves marketing. I already had a solid foundation in it because my husband and I have owned a successful small business since 1994, and it was always my job to do the marketing and promotion. I'm a good schmoozer, I like meeting people, and I'm always happy to talk about myself and my book or writing and publishing. I read a lot of books about marketing too, especially book promotion.

What has surprised you the most about self-publishing?

I guess the most surprising thing to me was how hard it was to land distributors to get my book into bookstores and libraries. And I hear it's even harder now. Just as I was getting into the Wunnerful World of Publishing, most of the big distributors redefined their terms and wanted the publishers they dealt with to have more than a handful of titles.

Now it's easier to find distribution in nontraditional channels via the Internet, but that's an increasingly noisy and crowded marketplace. You need to create some serious buzz to get noticed.

What's the most important advice you have for people considering self-publishing?

Do your homework. Know what you're getting into. Seek out people and organizations to help you in your journey. Understand that writing is rewriting and publishing is marketing. Hire an excellent editor who will do everything from checking your commas to seeing your manuscript as a whole. Spend money for a gorgeous, eye-catching cover and spine. If you're writing for kids, know kids. Your father/mother/spouse/child/neighbor/dental hygienist is not your critique partner—find lots of people who don't love you to tell you the truth about your writing. Get an ISBN. Barcode your book. Don't let anything about your book look like you did it yourself. Solicit competitive bids for everything. Check references. Practice safe accounting. Embrace Becky's Rule of At Least Two: Do at least two marketing things every day, add at least two names to your database, and write for at least 2 hours.

Teresa R. Funke
http://www.teresafunke.com

Self-Published Books (YA and MG):
Remember Wake, Dancing in Combat Boots, Doing My Part, The No-No Boys, V for Victory

Why did you decide to self-publish?

When I decided to self-publish back in 2001, I was no stranger to publishing, having sold dozens of articles, short stories, and personal essays to literary and commercial magazines and run a freelance writing business for 10 years.

There are many reasons people decide to self-publish. For some, it's a matter of maintaining control over their work. For others, it's about timing; they need the book to be available sooner than the publishing industry's typical turnaround of 18–36 months. For others, it's because they tried the traditional houses first and were turned down so they decided to go it on their own. For still others, it's the spirit of the entrepreneur that drives them, the desire to do it all themselves. For me, it was all of those things.

I'd initially tried to submit my first book, *Remember Wake*—a historical novel—to traditional publishers. I even had an agent. But the agent had the manuscript for several months and then promptly retired from the business. A few editors had asked to see the book, but sat on it for months at a time before rejecting it. An editor once told me *Remember Wake* was so good she couldn't put it down, yet she still decided not to publish it. I found that totally perplexing.

Meanwhile, during the 2½ years that I was submitting the book, the people on whom the novel was based—people connected to Wake Island in World War II—were starting to pass away. Suddenly it became more important to me to get the book published and into the hands of the remaining survivors than it did to get that big New York contract. So I contacted a print on demand company and within a few months, I had a printed book to sell or give away.

I had assumed I would continue to submit *Remember Wake* to traditional publishers, but I never did. I got caught up by that entrepreneurial spirit and the desire to see if I could make the book a success on my own, which I accomplished. My second book, *Dancing in Combat Boots*, was also turned down by several top agents, who told me they admired the book but weren't convinced a short story collection would sell well. So I started a press with a partner and published that book myself. *Dancing in Combat Boots* went on to become a finalist for the Colorado Book Award, and I didn't stop there: I've continued with more titles for middle graders in my Home Front Heroes collection. And now when people tell me they love my books, it feels even better than if I'd had a major publisher because I did it all myself.

What are the advantages and rewards of self-publishing?

Advantages include being able to produce the books you want without having to make changes to suit a publisher's idea of the marketplace. You can make more money off the sale of each book than a traditional royalty would give. You have a say in the cover design, something most traditionally published authors are not allowed. Many authors come to self-publishing after seeing one of their traditionally published books virtually ignored by their publisher. I'm also able to roll with the changes in the market. For example, I'd written *Remember Wake* for adults, and not until later did I figure out that teenagers were finding and loving the book. Then I was able to shift some of my marketing focus to include them. I'm thrilled that they enjoy it.

What are the disadvantages and trials?

Self-publishing is most definitely not for everyone. Whereas most traditionally published writers have the luxury of spending much of their work time on their writing (and the occasional book signing or school visit, etc.), self-published writers spend countless hours on layout and design, promotion, distribution, tracking inventory, dealing with buyers, etc. It takes a special kind of person to make it big in self-publishing, someone who is interested in all aspects of the business and is willing to work very hard.

What have you learned about marketing?

I'm not gonna lie to you. Marketing self-published fiction can be an uphill battle. Whereas self-published nonfiction books can sell very well based on the credentials of their authors or on the subject matter of the book, fiction is subjective, and many people aren't willing to take a risk on a self-published novel that may or may not be good. The first thing you must do for your book is have it professionally edited. And make sure your back-of-the-book blurb is so compelling any kid picking it up will simply have to open it. If you haven't produced a well-written, well-edited book, no amount of marketing will save you.

Once your book has been edited and you've identified your target market, you're ready to take the first step on that uphill journey. When you reach an obstacle, go around it. Many book reviewers, for example, won't touch self-published fiction, so forget about them. Suggest a feature article to your newspaper instead. Many bookstores won't carry self-published fiction, so don't waste your time trying to convince them otherwise. Instead, find a way to reach your target markets directly. With teens, that often means using the Internet. Oh, and get yourself a website, especially if you're writing for teens.

The biggest challenge in self-publishing, especially with fiction, is finding ways to spread the word about your book. But if you can think of marketing as a creative endeavor, you'll be amazed at the clever ways you can come up with to promote your book.

What's the most important advice you have for people considering self-publishing?

Consider your goals for your book. If you want to see your book in every bookstore in America, if you want to try to sell 100,000 copies, then try the traditional publishers first. If they don't pick up your book, but you still feel it's worth publishing, do it yourself. If the whole concept of self-publishing appeals to you from the start, then do it and do it right. Read books on how to self-publish, attend talks and seminars, join self-publishing organizations or submit to their newsletters, and most importantly, talk to other self-pub authors. Keep your goals realistic and your hopes high. Oh, and don't order 5,000 copies on your first print run, especially with fiction. Please trust me on this one. Start with 1,000. If they sell out, great! Order more. There's nothing more depressing than a garage full of unsold books. And there's nothing more satisfying than saying, "Guess I need to do another printing."

Chapter 11

Interviews With YA Authors

*Sure, it's simple, writing for kids . . . just
as simple as bringing them up.*
                                        —Ursula K. Leguin

On the following pages are interviews with authors of young adult fiction and nonfiction who are writing and publishing today. They answer questions about what's involved with subgenres, dealing with rejection, and various approaches to finishing a book. Then they delve into the rewards of being a writer. Please note that each author's profile only includes a selection of his or her works. For more, please visit the websites provided.

Fiction Authors

Nonfiction Authors

fiction authors

M.T. Anderson
http://www.mt-anderson.com

Published Books:

Burger Wuss; *Feed*; *The Astonishing Life of Octavian Nothing, Traitor to the Nation* (Vols. I, II, and III); and others

Your books are so original, they're not easy to categorize. *Feed* is a futuristic dystopian satire that raises social issues even more relevant today than when you first wrote it. Your *Octavian Nothing* series is written in a completely different style and uses historical fiction to explore the human condition. I'm guessing that your books reach as many adults as teens. Did you have any idea when you began these books that they'd be so effective at opening discussions among readers?

I certainly hoped that would be the case! I try to write about issues that fire me up. In many ways, it's my anger or unhappiness about a thing that makes me want to write about it.

Success for writers is often hit or miss. Are you surprised by your success? Has being labeled controversial helped you reach more readers?

I am absolutely surprised by my success. I write for the kids who are like me and my friends were: the nerds, the kids who are often marginalized or too shy to speak. (I wasn't too shy to speak . . . In fact, I'd say I was too shy to STOP talking.) So I write for a small (but passionate!) audience. I never anticipated that the books would have a wider audience, and I have to admit, I'm delighted.

How many rejections have you received in the course of your writing career? How did you deal with being rejected?

I've dealt with many! It's important just to soldier on. For one thing, it makes sense to be working on one thing while submitting something else, rather than just sitting back and waiting. That way you have a little more momentum to get past the rejections when they come in. You can always tell yourself, "What I'm writing now is so much better than that old thing!" (It helps.) But also, don't forget that many writers get many, many rejections before getting published—and then the same books become perennial favorites of thousands of people.

What's your approach to finishing a book?

Even in the cases where I don't know the intricacies of a plot before I set out to write, I do know the key scenes, and I write toward them. I strain toward them.

But sometimes it can be tough to keep going! One thing I do is sometimes switch off between projects, writing something very different. For example, while writing my very dark Gothic historical novels (the Octavian Nothing books), I took vacation breaks and wrote light little middle-grade novels (my Pals in Peril series), which were as wacky as I could make it. Switching off between these projects really helped to restore me. As my editor says, "A change is as good as a rest."

Those breaks to switch off between projects also allow me to go back to a project after a month or so with a new perspective. Problems that seemed insoluble when I was in the midst of them, knee deep in construction, don't seem too intractable anymore.

What's the most important thing you've learned as a writer?

Ramen recipes.

Oh. You mean, writing related, not income related? I would say that the one dictum I've learned that sums up a lot of the hard lessons of writing is this one: The plot should embody the theme and the conflict. The theme and the conflict should arise out of the plot. That is to say, whatever the abstract emotions you want to have come out of your book, they must be concretized in actions . . . You need to have characters who are really going to play these things out. Having fake people sit around and feel a certain way is never as powerful as having them act a certain way and having their lives materially changed *because* they feel a certain way.

What is most rewarding to you about writing?

I love the moment of writing. Being in the zone, and sitting there typing away furiously, and pacing around, and sitting down again and writing more . . . being completely wrapped up in it in the moment. Then you look up, and hours have passed. And then you look down, and you've written complete garbage. But something will come out of it! And more importantly, the experience of working out your thoughts and ideas and dreams is, in itself, pleasurable, liberating.

What's your best advice for people who want to write for teens?

It's a tougher racket than it appears right now! I guess my hope for beginning writers (which is not precisely advice) is that they'll pay attention to their language, to the way they tell their stories, and that they'll do something truly different and truly astonishing to make the rest of us sit up. The teen market is glutted—glutted—with copycat fiction of all breeds. That's where a lot of beginners want to head. But what we need is something new, something transformative. So ask yourself, what are your eccentricities? How can you lean into them? How can you serve them up to us in a way that will dazzle us with the unexpected? I get excited just thinking about the personalities I don't know yet who I'll be introduced to through their books. Good luck!

Pam Bachorz
http://www.pambachorz.com

Published Books:
Candor; Drought

Your YA books are dystopian novels. What drew you to write in this genre?

I never set out to write dystopian books—in fact, I didn't even become aware of that genre until after *Candor* was sold! Instead, my goal is to write stories that ask "What if?," and that speculate about worlds that might exist right around the corner. Ten years ago they would have called that science fiction. I don't care what genre people feel my books fall into, so long as they read them!

What can you tell us about your writing process?

The hardest part of writing, for me, is just finding the time. I juggle a full-time job and a family along with writing. So I schedule at least 10 hours for writing each week and post that schedule on my study door so everyone can see it. And then I do my very best to stick to that schedule.

Once I get a chance to sit down in my chair, my first step is to outline the story I'm working on. I don't need to know every detail, but I do need to know what the major plot points will be. No doubt my outline will change between drafts, but having a direction in which to point my daily writing really helps to get my fingers moving.

After I've finished a draft, I print the whole thing out and do a brutal pen-and-paper edit. Finally, I enter the changes into my electronic manuscript and send it to a few trusted critique partners for their feedback.

Despite all my planning, I end up tossing a *lot* of what I write, and I do major restructuring during revisions. In the last major rewrite of *Drought*, I tossed about 75% of what I'd written, or 75,000 words. And I have a whole other version of *Candor* in another character's voice, minus the last few chapters. Luckily, I write fast once I'm inspired.

How many rejections have you received in the course of your writing career? How did you deal with being rejected?

When I started out, I was trying my hand at picture books and short stories for younger readers. Those were heartily and rapidly rejected by probably at least two dozen magazines and publishers. I've never stopped to count! Once I tried YA, I achieved publication relatively quickly. But even after you publish, you experience a new sort of rejection in reviews. For every reader who loves your story, there will be another who will detail all the reasons why they hate it.

I try to use rejection in two ways: as a lesson and as fuel. There's almost always something to be learned when a manuscript is rejected or a book is panned. I think it's important to stay open to what's being said. If your work is still in manuscript form, consider whether you need to make changes (likely you do). Also, rejection is the fuel that lights my competitive fire. If someone doesn't want my work, I have a sort of sick compulsion to go out there and find the person who does—or to really tear into editing the work until it's irresistible!

What's the most important thing you've learned as a writer?

Don't sit around waiting for inspiration or the impulse to write. The best writers are the ones who consistently give themselves time to simply sit and write. Half of what you come up with may be terrible, but you'll come up with some gems, too. You can always edit out the terrible later on.

What's your best advice for people who want to write YA dystopian novels?

Write about what fascinates you. *Candor* explores brainwashing, which has always interested me. *Drought* incorporates healing waters—something I have always wondered about, having grown up in an old-fashioned "spa" town. Also, read a ton. Know what's already out there in the market and consider how your voice can add something new. Study the authors who do it best. You'll learn something from every single one.

T. A. Barron
http://www.tabarron.com

Published Books:

The Great Tree of Avalon trilogy; *The Lost Years of Merlin* series; *The Adventures of Kate* trilogy; and others

Please say a few words about the YA subgenre in which you write.

I write books I would like to read. That means each story must have four essential elements—a character I care about, a magical place, a gripping dilemma, and a compelling idea. With those four elements in place, I can feel sure that the reader—and myself—will have an enjoyable journey. And so I like a story where an individual must deal with personal issues as well as overarching issues. The mythic quest—call it fantasy if you prefer—allows me to incorporate all of these qualities.

The realm of fantasy gives me a great opportunity to wrestle with some of life's biggest questions in the context of a good old-fashioned page turner. For example, telling the story of Merlin's lost years allowed me to explore the idea that all of us have a magical person hidden down inside of ourselves. Just like that unknown boy who washed ashore, each of us has the potential to reach for the stars.

Fantasy allows me to bend the rules of our existence—highlighting troubling issues of our time. In a way, this kind of story is like a bent mirror. I can write about life with more intricacy and power—bending the rules of our world—in order to emphasize certain elements and deemphasize others.

How many rejections have you received in the course of your writing career? How did you deal with being rejected?

To answer your question, dozens of publishers rejected my first manuscript, which I wrote during my years as a student at Oxford! No kidding. And it hurt: There is no such thing as a warm and fuzzy rejection letter. The book never got published, but the process taught me a great deal about the craft of writing a novel. Even more important, it made me realize my own passion for writing. So the point is: Don't ever give up. If you have the passion to create, you must follow it! Persevere!

What's your approach to finishing a book?

The key, I have found, is to find whatever ways you can to get to the end. Complete the thing, even if you're feeling discouraged about it. Then you have something whole to work with, to rewrite or reorder and make into a story that makes you feel proud. For example, sometimes it helps to start the tale, then skip right to the ending while it's fresh, and then fill in the middle. Or you could do as I do, which is to continually rewrite—front to back, front to back, as if you are polishing a sphere. In your revisions, you can always add new themes or characters that add power and originality to your tale. By the time you are done, your sphere will glow with its own unique light!

What's the most important thing you've learned as a writer?

Writing allows me to experience anything I want. It is a great way to live as fully and sensuously as possible—to drink in the richness and diversity, the mystery and terror, the surprise and beauty, of life. It is also a great way to experience many lives at once: As a writer I can find the voice of a 12-year-old girl, an ancient stone, or a young wizard. Through my characters, I can experience life in the most wondrous ways. If I'm lucky enough to find a character that has lots of richness and depth, such as Merlin, then as the character grows, so do I. And, I hope, so do readers.

What is most rewarding to you about writing?

Writing allows me to explore wherever and whatever I choose. It has taken me back in time, to a distant galaxy, to the place where the sea begins, to Merlin's magical isle—and many more places as well! Best of all, though, writing is a way to explore the biggest questions of life. Not to find the answers, perhaps, but to do some thoughtful exploring of the questions. The two most rewarding parts of the experience are first, when a word or character or place or idea comes out just right—and second, when something I've written truly touches someone else. Some of the letters I've received have been unforgettable enough to keep me up late at night working on the next book.

What's your best advice for people who want to write for teens?

Write an excellent, gripping story that will last for some time—and reach people of all ages. That's what matters most.

Sometimes, when people ask me what age group I write for, I reply: "I write for children of all ages." That is really how I see it. Too often, people who write for young people underestimate their readers. They oversimplify and write "down" to young people. That is a terrible mistake! Let's give young people more credit for intelligence, curiosity, and serious concern for the future of our planet. So I never write "down": I always treat my readers as intelligent, caring people who are my equals.

In the same vein, we also should not underestimate adults. Many adults still have inside themselves a healthy, vibrant child. Even adults who have lost touch with their inner youth often yearn to rediscover their ability to wonder, to explore, to adventure, to laugh, to feel surprise and awe and mystery. These adults, despite their mature concerns, still possess—or want to possess— the freedom and freshness and openness of youth. That is why I write for adult children, too.

Perhaps this explains why my readers are all ages and descriptions. Yes, I write about heroic young people, such as the young wizard Merlin. But I chose that age for my five books about him because I felt that was the best way to tell that particular story— not because I was aiming my story at a particular audience. The experiences of young Merlin are, I think, a metaphor that could feel true for people of all ages, a metaphor about becoming a wise and caring human being. In sum, a writer must be true to his or her own self. That means we need to listen to the story in our hearts, and then write it the very best we can. Then our story, like a small, handcrafted ship, will sail away . . . and touch shores we can't even imagine.

Joan Bauer
http:/www.joanbauer.com

Published Books:

Squashed; *Rules of the Road*; *Hope Was Here*; *Peeled*; *Close to Famous*; and others

Please say a few words about the YA subgenre in which you write.

I write contemporary YA, although my second novel, *Thwonk*, is a fantasy. I think the power of YA is that it meets kids right where they are and deals with issues that touch them now. The challenge of this for me is to write fiction that illustrates a young person's powerful place in a world filled with vast unfairness and brokenness. I use humor to illuminate as much as I can—and that isn't always easy when I'm talking about alcoholism in a family, dishonor in politics, corporate greed, or misrepresentation in the media. Those are big issues, and to bring a teen character into them while keeping his or her teen-ness intact is hard. Often in the beginning of a story, I'll start writing the main character in a voice that sounds like me. They can't sound like me; I'm 56 years old. So taking *big* issues and cutting them down to size and bringing the character into the milieu takes work. I do find it personally exciting, though, when I get that teenage voice right, because to look at big issues as a teen is encouraging, fascinating, and hopeful to me.

How many rejections have you received in the course of your writing career? How did you deal with being rejected?

Early on when I was trying to break in as a screenwriter, I had lots of rejections. I remember one guy left a message on my answering machine saying, "Got your script. Not my cup of tea." Click. Dismissive rejections like that have staying power, because after a while they begin to wear you down. I wish I could tell you that I don't take those things personally, but I do. Still, I've also learned that it's important to try to understand what someone might not like about my work, see if they are right, and try to improve. You can't please everyone—if you do, you're probably writing pablum. You also have to know when it's time to defend your work because there is a great deal of bad advice out there, so you can't be the kind of writer who bends to every suggestion and loses the vision of what you were trying to create. As a YA author, my first novel, *Squashed*, won the Delacorte Prize, so I've not had novels rejected. I do have a half-finished novel in my drawer that still calls to me late at night. I put it away 2 years ago because I couldn't finish it. I've learned that all the writing I do—the books that win awards and the ones that don't— are all equally necessary. Each story seems to have a seed of the next book in it somehow. I try to remember that. I try to write the idea that just won't let me go. The one thing you can't let rejection do is stop you from writing. Just start the next story—start it. Starting has great power.

What's your approach to finishing a book?

In later drafts, I get an exhilaration at the end, kind of like climbing a mountain and getting close to the summit. Sometimes, though, I'm pretty sick of what I've been working on, and in the later stages, I just push through. I work very long hours at the end—10–12 hours a day. But, you know, giving birth isn't easy!

What is most rewarding to you about writing?

Two things—when I know that my work has made a difference in someone's life, and I just love the part of the creative process when my characters begin to tell me what to do.

What's your best advice for people who want to write for teens?

Respect them. Appeal to their higher natures. Give them hope.

Hilari Bell
http://www.sfwa.org/members/bell

Published Books:

The Goblin Wood trilogy; the *Farsala* trilogy;
Knight and Rogue series (*The Last Night*);
Trickster's Girl; and others

Please say a few words about the YA subgenre in which you write.

I write YA SF [science fiction] and fantasy. An interviewer once asked me why writing/reading SF and fantasy were important, and I shocked her by replying that writing/reading fiction isn't important. Curing cancer is important. Ending world hunger is important. Heck, putting good brakes on a car is important. Writing fiction? Now don't get me wrong, there's nothing in my life I enjoy more than reading a good book, and I love being a writer almost as much as I love to read. Nothing serious, either! I want an exciting story with some humor, a bit of drama, good characters—and I want my happy ending too! None of this gloomy stuff.

All that said (Off topic? Who, me?), SF really is the literature of ideas—you can explore more interesting concepts in an SF setting than in any other genre. And for character development and excitement, I don't think there's anything that beats fantasy. But important? I'm an entertainer, and I adore it—but I also like to keep it in perspective.

How many rejections have you received in the course of your writing career? How did you deal with being rejected?

I've never actually counted my rejections, but since I wrote for 17 years before I finally had a novel accepted, there are lots of them! In fact, I keep hoping that someday I'll get into one of those contests they sometimes hold at writers' conferences for the largest number of rejections judged by weight. I might not win, but I bet I'd make the top 10.

How did I deal with it? Argh! To tell the truth, I think that by the time I should have quit—would have if I'd had any sense—I'd put in so much time and effort that quitting would have been an unhappy ending. I don't read tragedy—I certainly didn't want to live one! So I just kept slogging onward till I finally sold. I should add that looking back over my early novels, there's a reason why they didn't sell! You have to be good enough. And even when you're good enough, there's an appalling amount of luck involved in the process. Getting published is not an easy thing to do, and the best advice I can offer you is to go to writers' conferences as well as SF conventions. I'll also add the most true comment on the topic I've ever encountered (I heard it from a speaker at a writers' conference, by the way): "The ones who have been published are the ones who didn't quit."

What's your approach to finishing a book?

My approach to finishing a first draft is to break it down into daily tasks (for me, that's a minimum of 8 pages per day, 5 days a week) and I try not to look ahead at the looming mass of work. If I've done my daily pages, which I tackle first thing in the morning, then that's all I have to do today, and I'll worry about tomorrow when it comes. I am, however, strict about doing this 5 days a week, week in week out, till the book is done. If I'm consistent, it adds up to a finished draft pretty quickly.

What's the most important thing you've learned as a writer?

The most important thing I've learned as a writer is probably how to write. There's an incredible amount of craft involved in writing, and looking back at my earlier manuscripts, I realize how far I've come. I should probably confess that about half my published novels are "trunk books" that racked up scores of rejections when I first wrote them. But I still liked the stories, and when I hauled them out and rewrote them copiously (or took the story and wrote it all over from scratch, which in many ways was easier than rewriting), they worked just fine. It wasn't bad stories that kept my books from selling, it was bad writing. And I hope my writing continues to improve for years to come—I never want to stop improving my craft. Never.

What's your best advice for people who want to write for teens?

The best advice I can give anyone writing for teens is to write for yourself first. If you write a story "for teens" you'll probably end up talking from your maturity to their inexperience. A kid will pick up on that and reject it in a heartbeat—and small blame to them! But if you write a story that happens to have teenage characters—but is mostly just a story that you love, that you want to tell, and that you'd like to read yourself because it's the kind of book you find wonderful—that will work for any reader, of any age.

Dia Calhoun
http://www.diacalhoun .com

Published Books:

Avielle of Rhia; The Phoenix Dance; White Midnight; Aria of the Sea; Firegold

Please say a few words about the YA subgenre in which you write.

All of my books are fantasy novels. I love writing about other worlds because it truly lets my imagination take flight. Also, fantasy writers mine the subconscious, burrowing deep into vast underground caverns for their material, and I find that journey fascinating. I love the way metaphors and symbols become so very important in fantasy. In my books, magic often becomes part of the voice of the characters; in other words, there is a relationship between magic and the hero's truest self.

How many rejections have you received in the course of your writing career? How did you deal with being rejected?

It took me 5 years to sell my first novel, *Firegold*. It was rejected by six publishers. Even after having six published books, I still don't have everything I submit accepted. I deal with rejection by mourning for a while and eating a king's ransom in chocolate. But I always have some project going, so I find it easy to distract myself from the rejection, and get on with new work. My agent keeps sending work out.

What's your approach to finishing a book?

I don't have an approach! That's the problem. I worry and worry that I could make the book better. "Just one more revision," I think, and proceed to move a few "the's" around the page. Letting go and sending a book out is like leaving your baby naked on a doorstep and hoping someone kind will find it and love it and tenderly wrap it in swaddling clothes. So it's easier to do just one more revision.

What's the most important thing you've learned as a writer?

I must write about what I feel passionate about, whether it is marketable or not. Writing comes first and publishing comes second. I've learned that if I worry while I'm writing whether something is going to sell or get an award, that completely ruins the creative process for me. My best work comes when I dig deep and don't worry about outcomes.

What is most rewarding to you about writing?

I love the feeling of being a sculptor as I write, chipping away at material bit by bit until the shape of the story emerges. The "ah-ha!" moments when ideas connect with a crackle of excitement and electricity are joyous. And seeing a kid reading one of my books is rewarding, too. Also rewarding is giving back to the reading community, which is why I cofounded readergirlz, an online book community promoting teen literacy, with three other YA authors: Janet Lee Carey, Lorie Ann Grover, and Justina Chen Headley.

What's your best advice for people who want to write for teens?

Read as much YA literature as you can. Find out what teens are concerned about in their daily lives. And remember what your life was like when you were a teen. Write every day and don't give up hope. It took me 5 years to write my first novel, *Firegold*, and 5 more to sell it. Then 2 more before it was made into a book. That's 12 years. If something is rejected, revise it, or write something new. Don't ever stop writing.

Chris Crutcher
http://www.chriscrutcher.com

Published Books:

Running Loose; *Whale Talk*; *Staying Fat for Sarah Byrnes*; *Deadline*; *Angry Management*; and others

Please say a few words about the YA subgenre in which you write.

I write realistic fiction, mostly about teenagers. The challenges are exactly the same as writing realistic fiction about people of any age. I don't have to make the reader believe what I write happened, but I have to make them believe it could have. If I cared about being censored, a special problem would be writing about issues or in a language that doesn't offend people, but I don't, so it doesn't. The biggest challenge in writing realistic fiction is making it real.

How many rejections have you received in the course of your writing career? How did you deal with being rejected?

If I remember correctly, I got rejected by *Reader's Digest* one time and then once with an earlier version of *Running Loose* before I got serious. I was very lucky to find an agent with the next version, and she had one or two rejections before she sold it and was conscious enough of my delicate sensibilities not to tell me about either of them until after she'd made a deal. I was very lucky getting my material into the hands of the right people.

What's your approach to finishing a book?

Hurry. By the time I'm close to finishing it, I just want to get it done. I write very fast and then go back and slow down and add whatever else I need.

What's the most important thing you've learned as a writer?

I wouldn't begin to know how to answer that. The most important things I've learned as a human came with what I do, not what I write about. Writing is just getting down my version of what I see.

What is most rewarding to you about writing?

Truthfully, probably the advances and the royalty checks. It's a tremendously freeing thing to be able to make a living at something I love. But just behind that, it's the responses from readers and the idea that I may have added some small piece to the huge volume of American literature.

What's your best advice for people who want to write for teens?

Know your subject. Respect your subject. Don't preach to them. Tell the truth as you know it and let it fall where it falls.

Nancy Garden
http://www.nancygarden.com

Published Books:

Annie on My Mind; *Dove & Sword: A Novel of Joan of Arc*; *Good Moon Rising*; *Peace, O River*; *Endgame*; and others

Please say a few words about the YA subgenre in which you write.

I've written in a number of subgenres: fantasy, contemporary, horror, gay and lesbian, mystery, history. Each one presents its own challenges, although all require the same basic ingredients: believable, consistent characters; a credible setting; logical plot development; overall honesty.

Fantasy and horror need world creating to a greater or lesser extent depending on the specific story, and that can be very challenging; I especially admire authors who've created complex worlds unlike our own—Tolkien, of course, and Pullman. My books in those genres are far simpler, and much more closely allied to our own world.

The challenge in mystery is to weave enough red herrings into the plot to mislead the reader and at the same time plant real clues that, at the end, make the reader say "Oh, of course!"—or at least not shout, "But that's not fair—nothing was said about that!"

In historical fiction, the challenge is to reflect the period so accurately that the reader is removed from the present era—and never to jolt the reader by, for example, suddenly introducing a contemporary object—say, a fork that hasn't yet been invented—or using an expression (like "Okay!") that no one in that era would have said.

The current challenge in gay and lesbian (GL) fiction is to move with the times and write stories in which GL characters are no longer defeated victims—okay, that's a political challenge perhaps more than a literary one. Another challenge in both GL books and in serious contemporary fiction as a whole is not letting "message" overwhelm story. In any contemporary fiction for teens, too, the challenge is to keep up with the times or find believable ways to avoid them. I'm talking about the trappings of "teendom"—things like cell phones and clothes and music and dating behavior and slang (keeping in mind that the details of all of these, especially slang, change faster than most books' production schedules move forward).

How many rejections have you received in the course of your writing career? How did you deal with being rejected?

I've received many, but I've never kept count so I can't answer that question. At first, I was very upset at rejections, especially those that didn't offer helpful suggestions—I wanted to throw my typewriter (yes, typewriter, back then!) across the room or cry. But now I'm much calmer!

What's your approach to finishing a book?

I guess the best way to answer that is to sketch how I usually go about writing a book. Every book is different, of course, but each time when I start a new one, I wonder if I really know how. Then I work at ignoring that thought! I usually don't start a book until it's been gestating in my mind for a long time—frequently years—so I usually have a pretty good idea of what it's about, who's in it, and how it ends. I write a rough (very rough!) draft all the way through quickly, often outlining along the way and changing the outline as I go. I also write brief character autobiographies (I pretend to be the characters) at some early point as well, but usually not until I've drafted a few chapters or sections and seen a bit of how the characters behave.

I never stop work for the day until I know what I'm going to start with the next day—that's one thing that definitely keeps me going forward. And I rarely stop to perfect sentences, paragraphs, etc., until I'm revising. After the first or second revisions, I usually put the book away for a while—months or more—so that when I go back to it, I'll be able to see its flaws more clearly. At that point, I go on revising until, as a writer friend of mine once said, I can't see anything more to do. Then I give the manuscript to my partner, who's my first reader—and that usually leads to more revising, till it finally seems ready to send to my agent.

What's the most important thing you've learned as a writer?

I've learned many important things, but I guess the most important is that it's vital to try to keep on writing no matter what—even when one doesn't feel like it. And it's also important to remember that a writer's career—mine, anyway—contains both ups and downs, and that it's important to plow through the downs, keep writing, and have faith that the ups will return.

What is most rewarding to you about writing?

Getting a letter from a reader that indicates a book of mine has spoken to that reader, touched her or him deeply, and helped in some way.

What's your best advice for people who want to write for teens?

Read, read, read—and read some more. And write, write, write—and write some more!

Emmanuel Guibert

Published Graphic Novels:

Sardine in Outer Space; The Professor's Daughter;
Alan's War

Please say a few words about writing graphic novels.

I'm both a writer and an illustrator. I write for myself, I write for others, and others write for me. Each of these positions is interesting, and quite different from the others. The first one is like jogging by one-self in an unknown landscape. The second is like jogging side by side with a friend in an unknown landscape, pretending you're the one who knows the way. The third is like jogging side by side with a friend in an unknown landscape, confident that your friend knows the way, but memorizing it very carefully because you know that, on the way back, it will be your turn to lead.

Anyway, in the three situations, you're always running.

What's your approach to finishing a book?

A book is finished long before being finished. It's when you start thinking about the next one and preparing it. My oven is full of different pies, cooking at different speeds.

What's the most important thing you've learned as a writer?

To think about adults when I write for children, and think about children when I write for adults.

What is most rewarding to you about writing?

A 9-year-old reader, whom I met at an exhibition, once told me, "Your stories are good, because first I read them, and then they happen to me." I considered that quite rewarding.

Patrick Jones

http://www.connectingya.com

Published Books:

Things Change; *Nailed*; *Chasing Tail Lights*;
Cheated; *Stolen Car*; and others

Please say a few words about the YA subgenre in which you write.

I write a very narrow slice of the market: realistic fiction for older teens. It is narrow because many older teens (10th grade and up) no longer read YA fiction, and narrower yet, because to write for this age group, it means raw honesty. Raw in terms of language, themes, and subjects. This further narrows the market, since for many teens the gatekeepers for books are teachers who often shy away from using my novels. The primary challenge—other than writing for the narrow market—is working with editors on how honest to make the work: how much graphic sexual content, substance use, and profanity.

How many rejections have you received in the course of your writing career? How did you deal with being rejected?

My first novel, *Things Change*, was rejected three times. I avoided further rejection by not submitting it again for 10 years. My path to publication is a little different than most. Through my career working in a library, I'd made contacts in the book industry and thus was able to hand my manuscript to an editor without going through an agent. An editor rejected it the first time, and then the rewrite, until I got it "right" on the third try. My rejection is more post publication, which is dealing with my books being rejected by committees like Best Books for Young Adults or Minnesota Book Awards. I don't deal with it well, to be honest. I normally go back and reread some of the e-mails or MySpace messages from teens who tell me how much they enjoyed one of my books.

What's your approach to finishing a book?

A very important step for me is getting teens to read my work before I submit it to my publisher. I've worked with one particular high school nearby that gathers kids who want the experience of reading and commenting on a manuscript together. They read it, and then I go discuss it with them. I also make that offer to teens who e-mail me or that I meet doing school visits. I don't feel a book is "finished" anymore until I know that teens have given me the green light.

What's the most important thing you've learned as a writer?

As my editor would tell you, it is not how to punctuate! The real lesson is patience: This work takes time. That's not really a virtue I possess, and I also write my first drafts in huge writing jags over a couple of months. The patience comes with the rewriting, revising, and production from that "high" of getting it on paper for the first time until it comes out almost 16 months later.

What's your best advice for people who want to write for teens?

This work is about empathy. If you can't bring yourself to empathize with the journey that every teenager is taking, then writing successfully for this market will be very difficult. I'd also suggest reading a couple of the touchstone books in the field: *The Outsiders*, *Speak*, *Rats Saw God*, and a few others so you can discover the one thing that seems to join together the great works isn't theme or story, but voice.

Laurie R. King

http://www.laurierking.com

Published Books:

Mary Russell series (*The Beekeeper's Apprentice*) and others

Your Sherlock Holmes and Mary Russell series has found a wide readership among teens. In fact, I was first introduced to *The Beekeeper's Apprentice* through a mother/daughter book group. I was delighted to see the enthusiasm these teen girl had for your words, especially because you made full use of an extensive vocabulary in the character of Mary Russell. The mothers loved reading you too. Were you surprised to become a "crossover" success?

I was pleased when the first major review of *Beekeeper*, in *Publisher's Weekly*, gave it joint recognition in their YA section, and I was even more delighted the American Library Association named it a "notable book" in their YA category for the year. I hadn't expected it to be taken as a YA book, but looking at the story and the characters, of course it was. Girls like stories about strong young women as much as their parents (and grandparents!) do, and I'm afraid that a lot of deliberate YA titles write down to their vocabulary and interests. At least, that was true until recently. I think there's been a major shift in thinking since the first Harry Potter came out, and more books have been marketed for both audiences.

How many rejections have you received in the course of your writing career? How did you deal with being rejected?

All my rejections came early on, first when I was sending books out on my own (what is called "unsolicited"). Even when I had an agent, it took several years before my first book (*A Grave Talent*) sold, at which point I had two complete and two partial manuscripts on my desk. However, I sold all four of those stories, and since then everything has been under contract. Even more gratifying, every book I've ever published remains in print—I just heard that *A Grave Talent* has gone back for its 21st printing, after 18 years.

What's your approach to finishing a book?

I'm one of those writers who doesn't outline. This means that my first draft is almost always a complete mess; merely finishing it is the primary goal. Knowing that the writing is awful, the plot makes no sense, that I don't know who the characters are or where the story is going makes pounding at the keyboard a hard slog. However, I also know that until I have a rough draft (often *very* rough!) to work on, I can't make it into a proper book. So I close my eyes and push on to the end, and after that, after I know the outlines of where the story is going and what it's about, I can go back to the beginning and make it actually go there, make the people live and breathe, underscore the way the subplots tie in with the main plot, all that lovely tight complexity that makes for a satisfying story. But "finishing" a book is really a series of "finishes" that eventually leave me either satisfied, or more often, simply out of time to keep fiddling with it, since the publisher is pounding on my door with the deadlines.

David Lubar
http://www.davidlubar.com

Published Books:

True Talents; *Dunk*; *Hidden Talents*; *Sleeping Freshman Never Lie*; and others

Please say a few words about the YA subgenre in which you write.

My work is scattered across a variety of subgenres, including fantasy, science fiction, and horror. I guess the thing I'm best known for is humor. There are both external and internal challenges for writing humor. Externally, funny books don't get as much respect as serious books. (Balancing that, they can be pretty popular with readers and with the teachers and librarians who try to generate enthusiasm for books.) Internally, the greatest difficulty in writing humor for teens is making sure that the material is relevant to their interests, and that any references would be within their universe. You won't get many laughs if you make references to Eisenhower or slide rules. But you also can't fall into the trap of using contemporary references that might become meaningless in a couple of years. (Translation: No Sanjaya jokes.)

How many rejections have you received in the course of your writing career? How did you deal with being rejected?

I gathered more than 100 rejections before making any sort of sale. I tried to motivate myself by noting the slow improvement from form slips to jotted notes to actual letters where editors seemed sincere in their dismay about not being able to purchase my work. Even now, with 17 published books and tons of published short stories, I still don't like rejection.

What's your approach to finishing a book?

I keep banging at it until one of us dies. So far, when the dust has cleared, I've been the one still standing. I try to keep up a good pace each day. If I get bogged down, I'll take a breath and work up an outline. (I generally dive in without one.) If I get really stuck, I'll write a rambling dialogue with myself, discussing the problem. I keep talking on paper until an answer appears.

What's the most important thing you've learned as a writer?

You can always improve. There's no end to learning the craft.

What is most rewarding to you about writing?

Creating something from nothing. When a character speaks a great line, or a plot takes an unexpected turn, I feel grateful to my subconscious, or whatever mechanism is responsible for making things happen.

What's your best advice for people who want to write for teens?

Don't write down. It is crucial to respect the reader. Don't avoid complexity or depth. Don't treat a teen like a child. Write an amazing story, sharing something you've gained or learned in life. Oh—and don't kill the main character's best friend just because it's an easy way to create drama.

Barry Lyga
http://www.barrylyga.com

Published Books:

The Astonishing Adventures of Fanboy & Goth Girl; *Hero Type*; *Wolverine: Worst Day Ever*; *Boy Toy*; *Mangaman*; and others

You've written both prose novels and graphic novels for the YA market. What can you tell us about the differences between these two approaches?

They're similar only in that they both use the English alphabet . . . at least, when I do them. For one thing, in prose you can be very internal, very intimately tied to a character's innermost thoughts. You can do that in comics, too, but given their nature, comics work best when you emphasize external, visual elements. Don't tell us a character feels isolated through her internal monologue—show it via some sort of interesting graphic that communicates to the reader on a visceral level.

The act of writing a comic book is unlike writing in any other media. Some have likened it to screenwriting, and while it does share many characteristics with that medium, it is a unique form that stands on its own. When sitting down to write a comic book, you have to hold two mutually exclusive dictums in your mind at once: "Show, don't tell" and "Tell, don't show."

This is because you now have two audiences—the artist and the reader—and they each need different things from you. The reader just wants a good story; the artist needs instructions that will lead to that story. I can't expect my artist to divine the subtext and hidden meanings in the story the way a reader would. The artist is an ally; I can't hold back information or try to play coy. I just come out and say it: "Jane is angry in this scene." If I like, I can suggest to the artist ways to get her anger across, but it's my job to tell the artist that Jane is angry; it's the artist's job to show it to the reader.

Basically, with prose, you're telling your story directly to your audience. In comics, you're giving directions to the artist, who then goes ahead and figures out how to tell the story to your audience on your behalf. It took me as long to write the 100-page script to *Mangaman* (my graphic novel with artist Colleen Doran) as it did to write the 400-plus-page novel *Boy Toy*!

How many rejections have you received in the course of your writing career? How did you deal with being rejected?

Oh, wow. I have no idea! Hundreds? It's probably in the hundreds. You have to understand—I started submitting short stories to magazines when I was 12 or 13, so I've racked up a *huge* number of rejections, most of them quite richly deserved. I never dealt with rejection very well. It took many, many years before I could get a rejection letter without feeling depressed or angry or both. Eventually, as my writing improved, I started seeing rejections that said things like, "Hey, this isn't bad—keep trying." Or "This isn't right for us, but try again." And those made it easier.

What's the most important thing you've learned as a writer?

I'm not sure how to answer this. There are so many things I've learned, things about how to write and why to write. Things about the business of writing. Things about the nature of "being a writer." But the first thing that comes to mind is this: Trust your gut. If something just isn't working in a story, but you don't know why, trust your gut. Move on. Maybe later you'll come back to that troublesome part and figure it out. Or maybe you'll cut it. Or maybe you'll realize it wasn't a problem in the first place. But if you're all wound up over something, it's best to move on and not get your brain all in a tizzy over it. Trust me—the problems will still be there when you come back to them!

What's your best advice for people who want to write or illustrate books for teens?

Oh, boy. This one is going to sound sort of harsh, but I really feel strongly about this . . . Be sure your motives are pure. By this, I mean . . . Look, I see a lot of people who want to write for kids for all the wrong reasons. They think, "I don't approve of the books being published for kids . . . so I'll write some good ones!" Or they think, "These kids today need my perspective on things!" Or, "Today's teens should know what it was like when I was a kid!"

No, no, and no.

Don't be cynical. Maybe you don't like the books published for teens. And maybe you think today's teens are a rabble who need some stern adult guidance. Well, fine, but that usually means you're going to write lousy books that teens won't want to read. Ultimately, your goal *is* to be read, right?

If you write books for teens today, know this: Teens have many, many alternatives to reading your book. You need to speak to them in their language, about their world. Not about your world. Not in the language you used when you were their age.

Don't write a book you think kids "need to read" or "should read." Write a book teens will *want* to read.

Carolyn Meyer
http://www.readcarolyn.com

Published Books:

Young Royals series (*Duchessina*); Royal Diary series (*Anastasia: The Last Great Duchess*); *Marie, Dancing*; *Loving Will Shakespeare*; and others

Please say a few words about the YA subgenre in which you write.

I write historical fiction. Kids often ask me, "Is it true?" What they mean, I think, is, "Are your facts right?" And the answer is yes—insofar as I can find out the historical facts, and I spend a huge amount of time on research, gathering as many facts as I can. When the facts are not in agreement—and in history, they often are not—then I choose the facts that make the best narrative. I don't rewrite history, but once the known facts are in place, I invent like mad. One big challenge is finding the right voice for the narrator: How do you sound like Shakespeare without writing Shakespearean English? Another challenge is avoiding the Dread Anachronism, especially in language. I work hard at that, but I've been nailed a few times.

How many rejections have you received in the course of your writing career? How did you deal with being rejected?

When I first started to write 45 years ago, I sent all my marvelous short stories to *The New Yorker*, which promptly rejected them all. But when I found my niche, writing for kids (I started in how-to, progressed to more complicated nonfiction, then moved into fiction, and finally, about 15 years ago, into historical fiction), rejection was no longer the norm. I've written more than 50 books; only one has been rejected. The question I think you should be asking is, "How do you deal with criticism?" Because I get a *ton* of that. I've been fortunate to have excellent editors who hold the bar very high indeed, and I often have to go through three complete rewrites of my "perfect" manuscript before it meets their standards.

What's your approach to finishing a book?

I find that discipline compensates for brilliance and talent. I go for a 2½ mile walk every morning, eat my oatmeal, and sit down at my desk by 9 a.m. I quit at 5. I put in time on weekends. I drink a lot of tea.

What's the most important thing you've learned as a writer?

Mostly I've learned exactly who I am. I've been working full time at writing for 45 years, and I've gotten pretty good at it. There were times when I got discouraged (I wasn't making any money to speak of), but I've never wanted to do anything else.

What is most rewarding to you about writing?

Knowing that I reach kids, touch their lives, and maybe even expand their horizons—I know it happens, because I get a lot of e-mail from readers.

What's your best advice for people who want to write for teens?

Stomp on anybody who asks you at a party, "But when are you going to start writing for adults?" Writing for teens is the real deal. Satisfaction guaranteed!

Todd Mitchell

http://www.toddmitchellbooks.com

Published Books:

The Traitor King; The Secret to Lying; A Flight of Angels (coauthor)

Please say a few words about the YA subgenre in which you write.

Basically, I'm interested in intersections—stories where fantasy and reality cross over. The world is full of strange things. What some might consider fantasy often feels more true to me than strictly realistic fiction.

How many rejections have you received in the course of your writing career? How did you deal with being rejected?

I never counted my rejections, but there were many. Suffice it to say, I thought it would only take me a few years to get a book published. Instead, it took me over 10 years.

One thing that kept me going was when a friend of mine, who happens to be a completely amazing bestselling author, confessed to me that she wrote seven "practice" novels before getting one accepted. For me, the magic number was four. The good news, though, is that I got better with every novel, and when I finally wrote one that I knew was ready, it got accepted right away.

What's your approach to finishing a book?

I try to write the first draft fairly quickly (in around 4 months). I give myself a goal of 2–3 pages every day and try to keep moving forward without getting too obsessed about rewriting the beginning a hundred times. Even though I usually start off following some sort of outline with the first draft, things always change as I write. So this first draft is how I figure out what my story is about and who my characters are.

Once I've written a first draft, I might put it aside for a few weeks to gain perspective, then I'll come back to it and start rewriting. I tend to spend two to three times as long rewriting my books as I do actually writing the first drafts. This is where I tease the story out, explore my characters, and make things readable. Then I'll share the book with a few critical readers and revise it again. And, of course, when I finally send it off to editors, they'll request more changes.

What's the most important thing you've learned as a writer?

Stick with it. I can't tell you how many times I thought about giving up, but nothing else satisfied me as deeply as writing did. The beauty of writing is that the more you do it, the better you get at it. Being a writer has far more to do with perseverance than talent.

What is most rewarding to you about writing?

For years, I thought the most rewarding thing about writing would be to get letters from people who'd enjoyed my books. Now that that's happened, I can honestly say it's not the most rewarding thing. Don't get me wrong—I love getting letters. But the most rewarding thing is simply getting to write more stories. That's something I wish I'd known before I was published, because I think it would have helped me to stop worrying so much about publishing and instead focus on the writing. I strongly believe that publishing will come when the book is ready, but the act of writing itself is the greatest reward.

What's your best advice for people who want to write for teens?

Read a lot of young adult fiction. Spend time with adolescents. Revive your inner teen. And don't listen to people who suggest that writing for young adults is somehow lesser than "adult literary fiction"—they just haven't discovered how daring, complex, and truly amazing young adult fiction is these days.

Corinne Mucha
http://www.maidenhousefly.com

Published Graphic Novels:

*Freshman: Tales of 9th Grade Obsessions,
Revelations, and Other Nonsense*;
My Every Single Thought; and others

Would you tell us about your process as you write and illustrate your graphic novels?

I start out by brainstorming in my sketchbook or on loose-leaf paper. I scribble my ideas in a sort of loose grid, so it looks like I have nine tiny paragraphs on a page, knowing that nine panels is ideal for one page. Then I start editing, which means crossing lots of things out, drawing lots of arrows, putting some sequences in a different order, scribbling notes I won't be able to decipher 2 hours later. By this time, it all looks like a complete mess, so I rewrite it on a fresh piece of paper, and add in drawing scribbles to indicate what I'll draw to go with the captions or dialogue. At this point, I'd usually start working more with my editor to clean it up and make any additional changes. Once the content of a page is finalized, I start penciling it on bristol board. To help with my drawings, I use a lot of Google image search and take a lot of wacky pictures of myself and friends to use as photo references. When the pencils are complete, I start inking, with either pen and ink or fine-point markers. When I'm penciling and inking, I spend a lot of time listening to podcasts and books on tape, so searching for fun things to listen to can become a part of the process, too. It's fun.

How many rejections have you received in the course of your writing career? How did you deal with being rejected?

To be totally honest, I've been pretty lucky when it comes to rejection. Or maybe I just have excellent selective memory, and I can only remember the times that things went the way I wanted them to. When I started making comics, I self-published everything, which I still do some of. I love the process of self-publishing—everything from coming up with ideas to distributing books to stores. When you're your only editor, though, there's not a lot of rejection involved. Every book tends to get an automatic stamp of approval from the publisher. I've also done a lot of commissioned work, executing the visions of other people. Again, I've been lucky, because I've been asked to participate in some really great projects.

What's the most important thing you've learned as a writer?

I've learned a lot about what it means to have a good work ethic. It's easy to work too little, to say "I'll get to those ideas later," but it's also just as easy to work too much and get burned out. We all fall into the trap of thinking that working constantly is virtuous, but I find that overworking can be just as much a drain on my productivity as laziness. Balance is key! It's important to have a routine, and stick to it, and know when to use discipline to keep your butt glued to the chair. However, it's just as essential to include taking breaks as part of that routine.

What's your best advice for people who want to write or illustrate graphic novels for teens?

Draw as much as possible! Write as much as possible! And as soon as you can, get down a story down on paper, make a little book out of it, take it to the copy store, and give copies to all your family and friends. Don't wait until your work is "perfect" to show it to people. Don't be afraid to grow in front of people. Practice, practice, practice, and don't be afraid to let your work be vulnerable.

Lauren Myracle
http://www.laurenmyracle.com

Published Books:

Thirteen; *TTYL*; *The Fashion Disaster That Changed My Life*; *Peace, Love, and Baby Ducks*; *Shine*; and others

Please say a few words about the YA subgenre in which you write.

I write straight up contemporary fiction. Kind of. (Nothing in this field is totally straight up, I guess!) I write about girls and their daily lives and concerns, mainly. Sometimes it's hard, because the grown-up "gate-keepers" (teachers, librarians, parents) have a different take on what's appropriate to write about (and think about) than I do. But being fearless—and at the same time principled, of course, according to your own principles—just comes with the territory.

How many rejections have you received in the course of your writing career? How did you deal with being rejected?

Okay, um, ready? One hundred fifty-two rejections. You heard it right, baby. One hundred fifty-two rejections before I got my first novel accepted! At first each rejection devastated me, and I would fling myself on the couch and mope and feel sorry for myself. And then I got tough and realized that I could either quit, and guarantee that I'd never get published, or keep on struggling. I kept on struggling.

What's your approach to finishing a book?

Butt in chair. Just do it.

What's the most important thing you've learned as a writer?

To let my brain be open to possibilities—and to be willing to hurt my characters. Sounds awful, doesn't it? I don't mean I'm going to whack 'em over the head with a plank (though I might). I just means that I've finally learned that keeping my characters safe doesn't make for a good story. I've got to allow them to be hurt emotionally, so that they can grow.

What is most rewarding to you about writing?

Well, I do love the rush of having my brain engaged, once I get past the dragging of feet and doing of laundry that sometimes gets in the way. Other than that, I love having girls *read my stuff* and tell me that it meant something to them.

What's your best advice for people who want to write for teens?

Read books for teens! Seriously. Sounds like a no-brainer, but so many people I've met who say they want to write for teens aren't actually familiar with the (Awesome! Fabulous! *Not* dumbed-down!) genre.

Donita K. Paul
http://www.donitakpaul.com

Published Books:

The Dragon Keeper Chronicles (*DragonSpell*);
The Chiril Chronicles (*Dragons of Chiril*)

Please tell us about writing YA for the Christian market.

Whenever you write, you must remember your audience. My readers don't like what used to be called "blue" material. In some subcultures of our society, curse words, foul innuendoes, and blasphemy are part of the language. The use of these crudities does not impress YA Christians. It kills the pleasure they get from the story. And I don't dumb down my vocabulary by using "new" instead of "contemporary" or "shine" instead of "glisten." But I do respect their standards and leave out offensive words. That is one example of being aware of the perceptions of a particular audience, in my case, Christians.

As to purposely putting in my beliefs into my stories, I don't see how I could leave my Christianity out of my work. It would be easier to write in Chinese than to write without all the thoughts and feelings and values that make me who I am. It is especially rewarding when a reader takes the time to send me a card, letter, or e-mail telling me that through my novel, God has touched his life. People are kind enough to share encouraging words, saying that I have encouraged them. What goes around, comes around.

How many rejections have you received in the course of your writing career? How did you deal with being rejected?

Hundreds! They are par for the course. Professional rejection doesn't bother me. I am confident that my writing is well-done, and I trust the editors to know whether my work will sell to their readership.

But let's step over to being rejected through a book review. This is a little harder to handle. I would never write a nasty, personal, name-calling review of anyone's work, whether it was a novel, a song, or a hockey game. So it is difficult for me to understand why someone would trash me and my books.

I've found that the really negative reviews come from one of three types of reviewers. There is the frustrated writer who hasn't made it into print. I think Aesop labeled these "sour grapes." Second, there is the self-proclaimed authority. Without any credentials (such as a master's degree in literature), this person is out to show that he is thoroughly knowledgeable about the craft of writing. He uses big words like "conundrum" and trade phrases like "character arc." He really is less interested in the book he reviews than in the sound of his own voice. The third is a Christian basher. No need to take offense. They are angry at God and not me.

Now does this mean that I discount every negative review? Not at all. I find that some reviewers actually do nail me on certain aspects. My battles are wimpy. That's been pointed out numerous times, and I'm working on it. My endings sometimes are rushed. Yeah, I've got to admit that's true too. So, you guessed it, I'm working on it. Constructive criticism isn't really rejection. If I reject the spot-on evaluation, I'm the one who loses the chance to improve.

What's your approach to finishing a book?

I assume you mean finish a book I'm writing, not one I am reading. LOL. The one I'm reading would be easier. I don't finish it. I used to, but discovered I'm running out of time to read all the books I want to. But when I am down to the wire with a deadline staring me in the face, I make myself take my characters with me wherever I go. So I mull over their difficulties at the grocery store, at the dentist, in the car, and while washing dishes. The more they consume my life, the easier it is to get them down on paper.

What's the most important thing you've learned as a writer?

Read, read, read. Fill your creative tank. Watch movies, watch good television, watch people. See, really see, sunsets, traffic jams, flowers blooming. Hear babies cry and birds tweet, the dinger on the oven, and the doorbell. Touch, smell, and taste, grasping the ordinary and recognizing the infinite variations in the world around you.

What is most rewarding to you about writing?

Hands down, it's the readers. I love book signings where I meet readers of all ages. I love to get e-mails telling me something special that happened to my reader while engaged with my book. Looking at the computer monitor is boring, even with all the fictional characters to keep me company. I'd much rather be with real people, sharing my impressions of the story and hearing its impact on others.

What's your best advice for people who want to write for teens?

Don't write for teens. Write to express feelings in a story that teens and everyone else will appreciate. Librarians say that from sixth or seventh grade on, students wander from the YA section into the adult section. They read Stephen King as well as Steven Gould. And J. K. Rowling showed us doubters that young adults will read big books. By not specifically targeting the 13- to 18-year-olds, you avoid talking down to them, preaching, or missing the opportunity to stretch their abilities to embrace a "mature" concept.

Stephanie Perkins
http://www.stephanieperkins.com

Published Books:

Anna and the French Kiss; Lola and the Boy Next Door; Isla and the Happily Ever After

What drew you to writing YA romance? What can you share about this genre?

First loves and true loves are thrilling. There's nothing quite like them; the feelings that arise are as close to magic as real life gets. When I write romance, I like to think of it as a form of the fantasy genre. Not because big, passionate loves don't exist (they do!), but because it's satisfying to build upon that magical aspect.

How many rejections have you received in the course of your writing career? How did you deal with being rejected?

I have been very, very fortunate. I received three agent rejections, but the agent who did offer representation was my top choice. The first novel that went out on submission, *Anna and the French Kiss*, was sent to two editors, and they were both interested. I realize this is unusual, and I also realize that this won't always be the case for future projects. Rejection, unfortunately, comes in many forms—reviews can also be a painful form of rejection. I've learned to tread carefully around both good and bad reviews, as they can either swell or crush the ego. I'm incredibly sensitive, so I've found avoiding reviews altogether is the best move for me. My advice for dealing with rejection is to remember that: (A) even your favorite authors have been rejected, and (B) the only person who can make this career happen is yourself, so you'd better keep trying.

I've heard that National Novel Writing Month (NaNoWriMo) helped inspire you to finish your first book. What can you tell us about your experience with Nano?

I'm a terrible first drafter—I'm slow, and I loathe the process—so the competitive spirit of NaNoWriMo has been a blessing for me, for ripping out that first ugly draft. The light bulb went off when I realized that NaNo isn't about creating a *good* book, it's simply about creating *a* book. That took the pressure off. The sooner I have those first drafts out, the sooner I get to the fun part, which, for me, is revising. My books go through many revisions (so far, they've all been over 20), so the final product never looks much like its NaNo draft, but . . . without that crappy first draft, the final product would never happen.

What is most rewarding to you about writing?

Finishing. Getting a story out of my head and into someone else's.

What's your best advice for people who want to write YA?

My advice comes in two basic, complementary pieces:

➤ Read voraciously across the entire Dewey Decimal system. Not one genre, not one age level. Read anything that sounds interesting. Read as a writer—if you have any sort of reaction while reading a book, stop reading and think about what just happened. Ask yourself *how* the author accomplished this reaction. Keep pulling apart the text, keep asking questions.

➤ Write. Revise, revise, revise. Repeat.

Laura Resau
http://www.lauraresau.com

Published Books:

What the Moon Saw; *Red Glass*; The Notebook series (*The Indigo Notebook*); *The Queen of Water*

Please say a few words about the YA subgenre in which you write.

I write multicultural magical realism. *What the Moon Saw* and *Red Glass* were inspired by the 2 years I spent in rural Mexico as an English teacher and cultural anthropologist. Both books involve teens who are initially outsiders to the indigenous Mixtec culture, yet develop a strong connection with it. I think that spending time in indigenous communities helped me create authentic and vivid settings, characters, and imagery. In particular, participating in healing practices with curandera friends allowed me to naturally integrate spiritual or "magical" elements into otherwise realistic stories.

During the writing and revising process, I frequently fact checked details via e-mail with my Mixtec friends, who gave me feedback on everything from slang words to corn cultivation. My Mexican and Guatemalan friends here in the U.S. generously went through every bit of dialogue with a fine-toothed comb, offering their suggestions and thoughts. In gratitude to the countless people who contributed to my books along the way, I'm donating a percentage of my royalties to indigenous rights organizations. Writing these books has truly been a group effort.

How many rejections have you received in the course of your writing career? How did you deal with being rejected?

For my first book, *What the Moon Saw*, I received a total of about 12 rejections from agents and editors. In retrospect, I know that's not too bad, but every rejection caused me plenty of angst. I constantly wondered if the hours I spent writing every day were a giant waste of time. I felt guilty that I didn't have a regular 9–5 job, pathetic that I was depending on my husband to pay most of our bills, and even more pathetic that I couldn't find time to do my share of the dishes or housecleaning.

As I was battling doubts, one thing that worked well was imagining myself in 70 years, as an old woman looking back on my life. I would ask this old woman what mattered most at this time of my life. Her answer was never doing the dishes or cleaning the toilet. What always mattered most was writing.

What's your approach to finishing a book?

After I have a rough draft (basically an uncensored stream-of-consciousness piece of writing), I ask myself how I can bring the story's themes into greater relief, further explore characters and relationships, develop the story's natural structure, clarify subplots, and draw out emotional layers. Once I've dealt with these broad issues, I break the manuscript down into manageable 10-page chunks and try to revise a chunk per day. I do many revisions, continually tightening, cutting, and adding. My writing group and my mom give me invaluable feedback during this process, until we all feel that the manuscript is polished and ready to submit.

What's the most important thing you've learned as a writer?

My biggest struggle as a writer has been dealing with insecurities and anxieties surrounding writing. The specific nature of the anxiety has changed over the years, depending on my circumstances. What if this manuscript never gets published—have I wasted thousands of hours? What if I can't do the revisions my editor wants? What if I can never create another good book? And on and on.

By now, I understand that I can't escape these insecurities—I can only put them into perspective and choose not to pay too much attention to them. I conceive of them as a pesky, shape-shifting monster that's always trying to undermine my creativity. Now I can recognize the monster in his disguise and say, "Oh, it's you again," then do my best to ignore him and keep writing.

What's your best advice for people who want to write for teens?

I think that a powerful novel comes from a very deep, mysterious place. It doesn't result from analyzing market trends or intending to teach a lesson or trying to explicitly address a "teen issue." Good teen books are just as multilayered and resonant and deep as adult books, or even more so. In my experience, writing fiction for any age group is a dance between the dream mind and the rational mind—with the dream mind leading.

My advice is to respect this creative process and feel grateful you're part of it. The ancient poet-philosopher Rumi compared humans to hollow reed flutes—it is only when breath passes through that music is made. When I'm feeling stuck in my writing, I remind myself that I only need to be a hollow reed and let the story come through me.

Olugbemisola Rhuday-Perkovich

http://www.olugbemisolabooks.com

Published Books:

8th Grade Superzero

Your book *8th Grade Superzero* belongs to the multicultural subgenre of YA. Would you tell us a little about your process writing this book?

The story began as a bit of an accident. I wrote a couple of pages as part of an application for a writing workshop with the brilliant and wonderful Paula Danziger, who is one of my favorite authors. It was one of those night-before-the-application-was-due kind of things (a situation that I find myself in often), and I got an image of Reggie in my head—he was hiding in his bed, with the covers pulled up over his head—and I went with it for 3 pages. At that time, he was a 10-year-old boy tormented by an older sister. He grew a little over the years, became 13 so that I could explore some of the more middle school themes I was interested in exploring around race, spirituality, what it means to be an activist, etc. Paula really encouraged and supported me over the years; much later on, as I began to seek out Reggie's real story, I was inspired by people and moments in my life, and some of the teens that I taught and worked with—their desire to tackle big questions, to be thoughtful, and to be activists in many different ways.

How many rejections have you received in the course of your writing career? How did you deal with being rejected?

Many, of course! Usually, I lick my wounds for a bit, preferably with sweets, and then rejection usually spurs me on to keep working, to improve, to try again, in a bit of an "I'll show them!" way—I love a challenge. It's important for me to let any sort of critique sit for a bit so that I can get past my initial emotional reaction, positive or negative, and get to the soul, the "what makes this story the best it can be." I try to look at what's really "wrong," what can be improved or changed and made better, and what may be a matter of taste or opinion.

What's your approach to finishing a book?

Just getting through that first draft is the hardest for me. After that, revise, revise, revise. Even now that *Superzero* is published, I still revise it. At readings, I make changes all of the time as I read aloud.

What's the most important thing you've learned as a writer?

A few important things . . . that the process of writing is precious and beautiful and humbling and uncomfortable and shattering and edifying, no matter what, no matter how a work is "published" or recognized by others. That collecting, creating, listening to, and sharing stories is an amazing gift that I'm honored to take part in. That one's truth can be both unique and universal. And that writing and storytelling can build community in unexpected and lovely ways.

What's your best advice for people who want to write for teens?

Know and/or remember your teen self. Access those emotions, actions, and reactions that characterized your life during that period. Yes, times change, and some of the "props" in life change, but the essentials don't. Study your favorites in the genre. Dissect them, really look at why you enjoy them, tease out the elements of story that make them outstanding. "Craft" books can be a real boost, especially during the dry periods, and as opportunities to flex and use new writing muscles.

Challenge yourself. And . . . listen. Pay attention. Write often. Read. Repeat. Enjoy.

Amy Kathleen Ryan

http://www.amykathleenryan.com

Published Books:

Vibes; *Zen and Xander Undone*; The Sky Chasers series (*Glow*)

What drew you to write YA sci fi?

I like how science fiction is about big ideas. The science fiction I enjoy deals with how historical forces impact the individual in a society. I think stories like this reveal a lot about human nature.

What's it like to get a large advance for your work?

Oh, it's nice. I'm not going to lie. I'm not rich, not by a long shot, but I make a comfortable living as a writer, and it's very gratifying. A large advance also brings some pressure along with it. The first thing that happens after you agree to the sum: Your agent publishes an announcement in *Publishers Weekly* that trumpets how you just got a wad of cash. So people come out of the woodwork to congratulate you on your big fat raise. That can feel a little uncomfortable, if you're the sort who doesn't like to talk about money. Also, if your publisher asks you to do something, you do it, because they have a lot riding on your work, and you owe them your loyalty. I'm not talking about compromising your integrity; I'm talking about traveling to places you don't want to go and giving talks you don't want to give. And of course, I am always a little nervous that the book that got such a large advance will end up not performing like everyone thought it would. But that is always something I worry about. I do notice that the more I get paid for a book, the harder my publisher tries to sell it. Simple economics. As far as I can tell, a large advance can only be good for your career.

How many rejections have you received in the course of your writing career? How did you deal with being rejected?

I have received countless rejections. Every book I've sold has been rejected multiple times. I tried not to let this get me down, because if you want to be a writer, you have to accept that rejection is part of your job. You'll be rejected by agents and publishing houses; then when you're published, you'll sometimes be rejected by reviewers, bloggers, and readers in general. If you let rejection get you down for too long, you won't want to write, and your work will suffer.

What's your approach to finishing a book?

Short answer: I work on it, very, very, very hard, for a long, long time. Long answer: You finish a book several times over. First you finish a draft, then you finish your first revision, and your second, and you go on revising until the book satisfies your own high standards. Then you send it to your agent and you finish a rewrite for her. Then she sends it to your editor, and you finish another rewrite for her. Then your editor sends your book to a copy editor, and you finish going over those changes. Then you get the galleys and you finish reading through and correcting those. You finish a book so many times that ultimately, it never feels finished, because it's never really perfect.

What's the most important thing you've learned as a writer?

There is no substitute for hard work. You can be the most talented writer alive, but if you're not willing to work very hard, your talent means nothing. The only thing that matters is the finished product.

What is most rewarding to you about writing?

Probably every writer says this: I love hearing from readers who enjoyed what I wrote enough to bother writing me an e-mail to tell me so. Also, I absolutely love getting good reviews.

What's your best advice for people who want to write for teens?

Don't think of them as "teens." Think of them as adults who don't like to be bored with a bunch of wordy prose. That's how they think of themselves.

Lynda Sandoval
http://www.lyndasandoval.com

Published Books:

Who's Your Daddy?; *Chicks Ahoy*; "Party Foul," in *Breaking Up Is Hard to Do*; *Father Knows Best*; and others

Please say a few words about the YA genre in which you write.

I like to describe what I write as teens "who happen to be" fiction. Can I have my own genre? My books tackle universal, contemporary, realistic teen themes, but my characters often "happen to be" multicultural, or "happen to be" gay or lesbian. Why the "happen to be" designation? Well, because the fact that a character is Latina or Black or mixed-race ethnicity or gay/lesbian isn't what solely defines him or her, nor is it the sole focus of my stories. It's merely one facet of the teen experience he or she faces, one aspect of each book I write.

How did I end up in this non-genre genre? Well, I happen to be both mixed ethnicity (Latina/Scandinavian) and gay, but neither of these fully defined my growing up experience. It shaped it, sure. Like spices in a pot of paella, it gave my own coming-of-age a certain flavor, but for the most part, all the normal teen stuff in my life was . . . well, utterly, heinously normal! It's hard to describe it any other way. I wanted to write books, as an example, for Latinas who didn't grow up in the widely perceived stereotypical "Latina" situation. We didn't speak Spanish at home because my mom isn't Latina; however, I understand a lot of Spanish from having heard my father speak to my grandparents (when he didn't want me to eavesdrop—they all spoke fluent English, too). I actually speak English and German, and that's because I lived in Germany for 4 years in my early 20s. My gigantic family includes mixed-race cousins such as Latina/Asian (Korean), Latina/Black, and Latina/Caucasian. I have cousins with children fluent in English, Spanish, and Japanese. My world has never been a pure white canvas, and yet we were born and raised in mainstream America. So a rainbow cast of people is just reality to me. It wasn't something I decided to write because it was hot, it's just my world view.

I also wanted to write what my editor calls "fun gay fiction," because, although it's a crucial and defining step, the coming out experience isn't horrific for everyone—it certainly wasn't for me. It is for many, and I want to include that in my work as well. But what about those kids with enlightened and accepting parents, with support and unconditional love? Don't they deserve books they can relate to as well? I thought so—hence, my current editorial direction.

I volunteer in a GLBTQ (Gay, Lesbian, Bisexual, Transgender, Queer or Questioning) youth drop-in center, and those kids, whom I adore, are as diverse as any group of teens you might encounter. Trust me. They wouldn't all be interested in the same books. They—all of them—deserve a voice, and I hope to toss in my hat with the other amazing authors writing GLBTQ fiction, in order to do them justice, bring them to the forefront. They're just teens, struggling through the hell that is adolescence (I say that tongue in cheek) in the best way they know how. God bless them.

So that's my story. I write teens "who happen to be" fiction, and I couldn't be happier about it. I don't want to be locked in a box. I want to write fringe work that's also mainstream. Real life. The throughlines in my teen fiction, if I had to narrow them down, would be (1) snappy tone, (2) humor, (3) true teen struggles, and (4) wicked teen empowerment. I connect with teens so much. I really get them, and my respect for them is boundless. I only hope that comes through in my work.

What's your approach to finishing a book?

I have to write from the beginning to the end, revising as I go, and only one book at a time. I need to be immersed in that book. I'm not a draft writer per se. I don't write the full book and then go back and revise—way too daunting. I write-revise-write-revise-write-revise all the way until the end. My final read through is usually easy because, after all that, the work is pretty clean. I'm also a very deadline-driven author, which is to say, I need external motivation. Guilt, the need for cash—those work really well for me.

What's the most important thing you've learned as a writer?

To make peace with my crazy process, and not to compare it with any other writer's process. As long as you reach the peak of the mountain, the path you take is irrelevant. Whatever works.

What is most rewarding to you about writing?

I love working for myself, surprising myself with something I've written when I read it months later and think, wow, did I come up with that? I also love speaking to teenagers and hearing how a book touched them or made them laugh or got them through a difficult time. There are so many rewards from writing. It's hard to pare it down. I love it all!

What's your best advice for people who want to write for teens?

Remember that teens are—pause for collective gasp—just people. They are you, they are me, they are all of us. They're just younger. Don't be a separatist. Give them more credit for their insightfulness, sophistication, and intelligence. They are critically thinking, bright, open individuals and deserve fiction that respects all of that in them.

Denise Vega
http://www.denisevega.com

Published Books:

Click Here (To Find Out How I Survived Seventh Grade); *Fact of Life #31*; *Access Denied (and Other Eighth Grade Error Messages)*

Please say a few words about the YA subgenre in which you write.

I write contemporary fiction, where I do my best to reflect the lives and truths of today's teens authentically. I draw from my own middle school and high school experiences (which were often painful and some-times humiliating!), and I'm lucky enough to be around lots of teens to observe and talk about their experiences. I like to balance my pathos with a little humor, though, because if we can't laugh, we're doomed.

How many rejections have you received in the course of your writing career? How did you deal with being rejected?

Too many to count!

My best antidote for dealing with rejection is throwing darts at pic-tures of editors who've sent me such a horrid thing—kidding. Actually, I allow myself about 5 minutes of wallowing in self-pity, and then I decide if the manuscript needs to be revised or if it can go out again as is to the next publisher on the list. Once I do that, I get to work on my current project. I always have another book I'm working on that I'm in love with. That's the secret to not going crazy in this business: working on something that is fun and that you're passionate about while you wait for responses from manuscripts that are out with publishers.

What's your approach to finishing a book?

Crossing my fingers, begging the literary gods for help, and eat-ing lots of chocolate. Seriously, finishing a book for me means getting through the first draft, which is difficult because I tend to write by the seat of my pants. I get lost or come to a complete halt partway through. Recently I've done more planning—writing out bits of scenes and dialogue in some semblance of order, making sure I know the emotional growth arc for my main character, understanding where I want to end up—before I actually begin writing the first draft. I also try to resist the urge to go back and "fix" things as I write. If something comes up that I want to add or change, I make a note of it and keep going rather than take care of it right then. After I've revised the first draft about a zillion times, I offer it up to my critique group who slices, dices, and mixes it up into an unrecognizable blob that I must then reshape into something that resembles a decent book. I revise several more times until I feel it's ready to send to my agent so she can get it out to one of my publishers. Then I celebrate this milestone with something yummy!

What's the most important thing you've learned as a writer?

That the only thing in my control is the quality of the work. Everything else—getting the book accepted, how the publisher markets it (or doesn't—we midlist authors have to do a lot of our own marketing), book reviews, what readers think—is out of my control. The only thing I can do is write the best book I possibly can at the time, which for me means constantly improving my craft through reading YA lit, writing, and revising, revising, revising. It's important to remember that revising isn't about moving a sentence or deleting a word here or there. It's about re-envisioning the entire work—seeing it in a new way so you can really make the changes necessary to improve it.

What is most rewarding to you about writing?

Creating characters and situations that readers can relate to and hearing from readers about how the book moved them, made them laugh, caused them to behave differently in a situation than they would have before reading the book. Books have changed my attitudes about relationships and situations, and if at least one reader was touched by something I wrote, then all of the effort to get the book out there was worth it. I'm lucky to have heard from many readers who have enjoyed and been moved by my work.

What's your best advice for people who want to write for teens?

Don't be afraid. If you want to try something edgy, go for it. If you want to write a story with a spiritual or religious angle, do it. Teens come from a variety of backgrounds and experiences, and teen lit has room to reflect all their different realities. Write what you're excited about, not about what you think is the latest trend or what a publisher might want. In the end, it's just you and the page. Fill it with something that matters to you.

Allen Zadoff
http://www.allenzadoff.com

Published Books:

Hungry: Lessons Learned on the Journey From Fat to Thin; Food, Girls, and Other Things I Can't Have; My Life, the Theater, and Other Tragedies; Love and Sanskrit

Your YA books are contemporary novels, a rich mix of humor and pathos and coming of age. Would you tell us a little about your writing process?

I write from my heart. Luckily, my heart is immature, overly dramatic, and filled with longing. Perfect for a young adult voice.

The inspiration for my work is mysterious, but the process is not. The process involves hours of sitting in front of a keyboard, followed by hours of not sitting at a keyboard, distracting myself with walks, television, daydreaming, listening to music. That's followed by still more hours at the keyboard. I often compare writing to learning to fly a plane. You have to log a certain amount of hours in the pilot's seat to qualify, and there's no way around it.

How many rejections have you received in the course of your writing career? How did you deal with being rejected?

Thank you for bringing this up. It's been a while since I've had a good cry.

The truth is I've received more than my share of rejections. I think God may have made a mistake and given me the rejections from someone who became an overnight success. That guy got a pass, and I got his rejections on top of my own, sort of like being billed for your neighbor's cable television.

One positive note: Having been an overweight teenager, I'm very good at dealing with rejection. My adolescence was an excellent training ground for a career as a professional writer. I learned to take the hit and keep moving forward.

A few facts. I didn't start writing in earnest until my late twenties, and then I spent nearly a decade as a struggling TV and film writer in Los Angeles before my career as an author began. Even then, my first novel didn't sell. It was my second novel that became *Food, Girls, and Other Things I Can't Have*. It won the Sid Fleischman Humor Award from the Society of Children's Book Writers and Illustrators, and I found myself on stage receiving an award for the first time in my life. Or at least the first time since I won "Most Improved Tennis Player" at summer camp when I was 11 years old.

Awards, reviews, publication. It's all nice, but I spent over a decade writing without anyone much caring. This is a slightly embarrassing fact, but I think it's important for emerging writers to hear. When I was coming up, everyone who was successful seemed to have gotten it quickly and easily. That's not my experience, and it's not the experience of most writers I know.

I'm very grateful for the people who supported and encouraged me over the years. They thought I was talented when there was little real-world evidence to back them up. Nobody ever told me to stop writing, and I'm grateful for that, too. In hindsight, I needed a long time to grow, develop, and find my voice. I'm still finding it.

What's your approach to finishing a book?

Fear + Hard Work = The End. If I could do it without the fear part, I would. But at least for today, fear motivates me until the story takes over. That's when it's fun to be a writer, when curiosity about the story overcomes my natural fear of writing and looking bad. I get out of the way and let the story come through me. The story finishes itself, and I'm along for the ride. It's a great ride.

What's the most important thing you've learned as a writer?

Inspiration comes because I'm writing, not from waiting to be inspired. I consider it my job to show up for writing no matter how I'm feeling. I start work, and sometimes inspiration shows up, too. Sometimes it doesn't, but at the end of the day, I've got finished pages in front of me.

What's your best advice for people who want to write contemporary novels for teens?

Write zombies instead. No, that's terrible advice. Please don't do that.

I never wanted to write contemporary novels for teens. I just wanted to write my first book, and the main character came out as a teen, and the story happened to be contemporary and realistic. When I wrote my next book, *My Life, the Theater, and Other Tragedies*, I was dealing with my mother's death from cancer, and the book became a funny but serious exploration of how we rejoin the world after a tragedy. My next novel is about a boy's search for spirituality and connection in modern Los Angeles, where I live. My work is very much based on my life, my interests, my preoccupations. While it's a noble goal to want to write for teens and I'm a huge fan of contemporary realism, I don't have much choice in the matter. The work comes out like it comes out.

nonfiction authors

Christine Fonseca
http://christinefonseca.com

Published Books:

*101 Success Secrets for Gifted Kids:
The Ultimate Guide*

You write nonfiction for teens. What do writers in this genre need to know?

I think it is important to be well researched when writing nonfiction, and to have the ability to speak directly to your target audience. When I wrote *101 Success Secrets for Gifted Kids*, for example, I spent months talking with hundreds of gifted children from the ages of 8–18, asking them all about their lives as gifted kids. The things I learned from these focus-group discussions became the foundation for the book.

It is also important that writers understand the marketplace and exactly what niche their nonfiction book fills. By clarifying the market need, and working to fill that need, nonfiction writers ensure readership for their books—something that can be difficult in an increasingly crowded marketplace.

Finally, I think it is important that nonfiction authors try to make the information in their books as timeless as possible, so as to avoid sounding dated within a matter of months after hitting the shelves.

How many rejections have you received in the course of your writing career? How did you deal with being rejected?

With my nonfiction, the rejections have been minimal. However, this is partly because I was lucky enough to find a real void in the marketplace and fill it. I tapped into a niche—gifted students—where there was room for a new writer with my particular expertise and passion. However, I am currently moving into another genre in writing—YA fiction. And as an aspiring fiction author in a crowded YA market, rejections do come thick and fast!

Writers need to know that rejection is just part of the business. It does not define us, nor is it a personal attack. I know this is difficult; we pour our souls into each and every project. Being rejected for that work can feel tantamount to having our souls ripped to shreds. But it really isn't. Instead of looking at the rejection as saying "I am not interested in YOU as a writer," it's important for authors to view it more as "That particular project is not what I'm looking for right now." Then, go and write something new!

What's your approach to finishing a book?

Um, I write "The end." Just kidding. My writing process for nonfiction is to start with an idea and an outline. Then it's time for research. Typically the research takes me in a new direction somewhat, and I need to reorganize the initial outline. Once I've got a clear direction in mind, I sit down and write. It may seem strange, but with nonfiction I write very quickly—typically only taking a matter of weeks to draft the whole book. Then my trusted critique partners read it, I go through it once more, and then it's off to my editor. Fiction is a much longer process for me, but still starts with an idea, an outline, research, and a refined outline before I write the book.

What's the most important thing you've learned as a writer?

Tenacity and talent are everything in this business—with tenacity being the overriding *must have*. This is a tough industry and not for the faint of heart. It is hard work, often soul crushing, and sometimes painful. And so, so worth it! During my journey into publication, I have learned to be flexible, steadfast, and tenacious—all qualities that have benefited every aspect of my life.

What is most rewarding to you about writing?

There is nothing better than receiving an e-mail from either readers or emerging writers telling me that my book inspired or helped them in some way. Those messages give me a reason to keep writing.

What's your best advice for people who want to write for teens?

Hang out with teens. Really. Consider it research. The more opportunities you have to be around kids, the more likely you are to be able to both write from their point of view and connect to them in a way that is not pandering or preachy. I have a group of teens that read the openings of everything I write. Their purpose is simple: help me ensure that I am "speaking" to them, my audience. They are an invaluable source of inspiration and help throughout the writing process.

Zachary Hamby

http://www.mythologyteacher.com

Published Books:

Mythology for Teens; *Greek Mythology for Teens*; *Reaching Olympus: The Greek Myths* (Vols. I and II), *The Saga of the Trojan War*

You write nonfiction for teens. What do writers in this genre need to know?

I see two keys to writing for teens: Generate interest and avoid insult. Teen readers need to be hooked by your writing. As a teacher, I have the benefit of field testing my writing. When students respond negatively to a piece, it's often not because the piece was badly written or confusing; it's simply that they weren't interested. I didn't do a good enough job of connecting the subject matter to their life, their world, or their interests. I analyze the subject matter by thinking, "What points would most interest a teen?" and then accentuate those points. Julius Caesar wasn't just a potential dictator who was murdered for a political cause: He was a big man on campus who was stabbed in the back (literally) by someone he thought was a friend.

I also avoid insulting my readers by talking down to them. Teens will only feel patronized if you lower material below their level of comprehension. I try to respect my audience, and realize they are able to confront difficult or mature topics. Glossing over certain material because you think your audience is not mature to enough handle it often loses them. For example, I write about Greek mythology, and teens are often the most fascinated by the most grotesque myths. I don't dwell on the sordid details, but I don't leave them out either. This shows respect for my audience while still maintaining a boundary.

How many rejections have you received in the course of your writing career? How did you deal with being rejected?

In my short writing career, I've had many rejections. For my first textbook, I sent submissions to probably around 60 publishers and was rejected by nearly all of them. Through the process of getting published, I learned that rejections don't mean that your writing isn't good. Getting published is the complicated process of finding a publisher who is looking for the subject you're interested in writing about.

I also had to decide what I was willing and unwilling to change about my manuscript. One publisher wanted to publish my materials but remove some of the materials that they considered to be inappropriate for my audience. I knew what teenagers could handle, and I wanted to stay true to my work, so I turned down this offer. The next publisher was interested in the idea behind my material, but wanted me to develop it into a different style of textbook. While this wasn't how I had pitched the project, I realized that the publisher had a solid, marketable idea, and I went with it. It took extra work, but it became a textbook that was more beneficial to my audience, my publisher, and ultimately, me.

What's your approach to finishing a book?

Just do it! Others have said that the blank page is the writer's biggest enemy. For me, it's the blank screen and the blinking cursor. I just have to force myself to write, even when I don't exactly know what I'm going say. Getting *something* down on paper is the key; it doesn't have to be great; it doesn't even have to make complete sense the first time through. A messy first draft is much better than nothing. That's what revising is for—going back through, figuring out what I need to say with each chapter, each paragraph, each sentence, and making sure everything works together for the desired purpose. I can outline all I want, but until something is actually written, I have nothing to work with.

What's the most important thing you've learned as a writer?

One draft will never cut it. Rewriting the same paragraph for the 20th time has often driven me a little nuts, but if the end result is a better paragraph that's more easily understood by my readers, it's all worth it. Checking facts is also important in nonfiction. In first drafts I have sometimes included facts that I could have sworn were correct, but when I went back to check, I discovered that I had remembered or even learned things incorrectly.

What is most rewarding to you about writing?

Because my writing all has to do with education, I am always flattered by the thought that educational professionals around the country are using my book to teach their students. I love the feeling that my writing is helping young people learn! That's why I became an educator, and that's why I write.

What's your best advice for people who want to write for teens?

Today's teenagers will grow into adults running the world someday. They will need to be able to think, so that means they need to love to read. It's now—as their minds develop—that they need to be challenged. Don't talk down to them! They read to learn, so write to teach. If you do that, you will educate the future.

Sean McCollum

http://www.kidfreelance.com

Published Books:

The Fascinating, Fantastic Unusual History of Robots; History's Greatest Warriors series (*Vikings*); *Joseph Stalin*; *Volcanic Eruptions, Earthquakes, and Tsunamis*; and others

You've written more than 30 books and hundreds of articles for children and teens. How do you decide what to write about? How do you juggle so many projects?

I'm in the fortunate position now of publishers coming to me with titles they want written. We collaborate on an outline. Then it's in my hands. As far as deciding what to include in a book, in my research and writing I'm constantly asking, "What will a kid want to know about this? How can I unpack this subject so they'll have an 'Ah-ha, I get it' moment?" Those are common denominators in every paragraph. I also try to capture the excitement of any topic. If it's a story about slime mold, for instance, I'll search for the most passionate scientists on the topic and ask them to share what jazzes them about it. (Actually, that's not the best example—slime mold is pretty cool in and of itself.) Most experts are thrilled to share their interests with a young audience.

In regard to juggling projects, this is rarely a 9–5 job. Most weeks I'm at it 7 days a week—setting up interviews for an article due in a couple weeks, outlining a book with a deadline a couple months out, and protecting the hours for the actual writing. Time management is important . . . If I ever get good at it, I'll write a book about it.

What do writers who want to break into this genre need to know?

Any experienced editor or writer will tell you there's no substitute for researching the magazine or book publisher that you want to write for. Whenever I write for someone new, I'll read back issues, previous articles they've published on similar topics, or books in the same or similar series. I examine overall structure, sentence and paragraph length, vocabulary, transitions, use of quotations, etc. Throughout, I'm also "listening" for tone—is it playful, authoritative, or gee whiz?

That might sound like overanalysis, but especially when you're starting out, it can be helpful to deconstruct what you're going to replicate. With new writers, most nonfiction editors are not looking for someone who can wow them with a grand slam of unique writing brilliance the likes of which they've never seen; they mainly want to know you can touch the bases by writing clear, engaging prose.

Oh, and use topic sentences to guide readers into a paragraph. That might sound like a no-brainer, but you'd be amazed at how many articles leave out this high school level aspect of clear writing. Young readers are often developing skills of managing and processing the flow of information from text. Topic sentences offer the road signs to help them navigate.

Also, get interviews with experts if at all possible, at least on contemporary issues. Nothing makes an article or book more current than the views of people who are making things happen right now. It injects a story with authority and personality.

Lastly, read your story aloud to yourself. By doing this, I constantly catch redundant phrasing, passive voice, and other oopses that I otherwise would have skimmed over. Did I mention redundant phrasing?

You make a living writing nonfiction for kids and teens. How many hours does it take, and what tips can you offer about the business side of nonfiction?

I probably put in 45–60 hours a week, including cleaning the oven and other feats of procrastination. More hours than that and my writing gets stale. If you start earning enough that it affects your taxes, get a tax preparer who knows the ins and outs of the tax code in regard to freelance work. You'll be glad you did.

Much more importantly, cultivate a good relationship with your editors. Again, that sounds obvious, but too many writers view critical comments from an editor as a personal attack. It ain't. Writing is usually solitary, but publishing is a collaborative process. Once I got that—really, really got that—I was much happier and I started getting more work than I could handle. Want to win the devotion of an editor? Your first response to any feedback should be, "Sure, I can fix that." Later you can niggle about the details or come back with a well-considered counter-proposal—in a thoughtful and respectful manner, of course. I've worked with editors who at one time drove me batty, but later became the ones I trusted most because they pushed me to do my best work.

In my experience, there are three "abilities" of any successful freelancer, or perhaps of any successful anything: (1) *ability*—talent to write clear, engaging material; (2) *reliability*—the ingrained habit of getting quality work in on time; (3) *likeability*—the can-do character that makes an editor's job easier, not harder. Rule of thumb is that if you can master any two out of those three, you'll always have writing work.

What's the most important thing you've learned as a writer?

Love the story, whatever it may be. Find that aspect that speaks to your own passionate curiosity or observe the passion in others and lead with that. For example, I'm a big sports fan but had never gotten into motor sports. But when I was asked to write a series on racecars, I delved into the mindsets of the fans as well as the driving teams. By the time I started writing, I understood and resonated with their affection and devotion to what is a very demanding sport.

If you're going through the motions when writing something, then chances are your readers will find it boring, too. And I'm not talking about adding exclamation points in the text. (By the way—don't add exclamation points to try to manipulate readers into amazement! It doesn't work! It smacks of desperation!) Use story-writing skills to create characters, build suspense, and instill humor and surprise. In the end, good writing is good writing, whatever the genre.

What is most rewarding to you about writing?

I get a kick when I do school visits and the kids go "Ewwww!" when I tell them what a goat's eyeball tastes like. (Greasy and gristly, if you must know.) There are also the moments when I know the topic, I have found its heart, and the writing flows with little conscious effort. It's very Zen.

What's your best advice for people who want to write YA nonfiction?

Read the best stuff and practice the craft. Become active in a critique group that will offer constructive and honest direction. If you write consistently and court constructive criticism, you can't help but improve. Join SCBWI and learn how the industry works.

As far as writing for a young audience, I try to access the child and teen that still live inside me. Spending time with young people is valuable and insightful for getting a sense of who they are and where they're coming from. When I'm at my best, though, the material is being filtered and channeled through my own voice, not being forced into rhetoric that I think young readers want to, or "should," hear.

After I'd been at Scholastic for a while in the early 1990s, I realized that becoming a writer had much more to do with skill development than knowledge acquisition. I gradually improved because every day I had to write and write and write, and revise, revise, revise. It was an intensive apprenticeship, and I was fortunate enough to work among some very talented people who insisted on my best work and inspired me to produce it.

Josh Neufeld
http://www.joshcomix.com

Published Graphic Novels:

A.D.: New Orleans After the Deluge; A Few Perfect Hours (and Other Stories from Southeast Asia & Central Europe)

What can you tell us about writing and illustrating nonfiction YA in graphic format?

I've been writing and drawing comics pretty much my whole life, so it's exciting to see comics finally becoming embraced by educators and librarians. As much as I enjoyed heroic fiction when I was a kid, in my early adulthood I became much more interested in real-life stories. As the great Harvey Pekar once said, "Ordinary life is pretty complex stuff!" That was when I started doing comics about my backpacking adventures around the world, as well as illustrating other writers' true-life stories. I don't set out to do YA stuff in particular, but just tell straightforward stories as truthfully as I can. Also, the comics format—even though it's very effective in portraying big and dramatic moments—also often allows for the communication of subtle messages that might be too esoteric or complicated when described in straight prose.

After Hurricane Katrina, I volunteered with the Red Cross in the hurricane zone. That led to me doing the nonfiction graphic novel *A.D.: New Orleans After the Deluge* about five real people from New Orleans and their experiences with the storm and its aftermath. *A.D.* has been used in courses in both high school and college, and my wife, Sari Wilson, wrote the teacher's guide for it. One high school class in Ohio wrote me individual letters in response to the book, and I really treasure those kids' honest, idiosyncratic comments.

How many rejections have you received in the course of your writing career? How did you deal with being rejected?

Oh, I got more than my share of rejections, especially early in my career! One advantage of having worked in the field for so long—going as far back as high school—is that I'm pretty used to criticism, so I never got too discouraged. The thing that always drove me nuts was when I would get no response at all—I could deal with rejection better than being ignored. And I'm stubborn enough that I just kept going, doing my own personal work and trusting that one day someone would want to publish it. In the meantime, for a period in my 20s, I self-published to make sure it got out there. And of course the Internet was (and is) a great way to find an audience, and even in some ways to get around the traditional publishing model.

What's the most important thing you've learned as a writer?

Writing for comics is a unique task. You need to think visually and use words to augment the idea or story you are trying to tell. My challenge as a comics writer is to be as concise as possible, to make the pictures do the bulk of the storytelling. So I try to use captions and narration as little as possible, instead telling the story through action and dialogue. Which isn't to say I always succeed in my goal! I imagine the process is a lot like writing a play.

What's your best advice for people who want to write or illustrate nonfiction for teens?

As I talk about above, when creating comics, both tasks require the creator to think narratively *and* visually. The writer should try his or her best to imagine how the pictures might look, and the artist needs to always keep the story in mind. After all, the story is paramount: A well-written comic with subpar illustrations can still be an engaging read, while a poorly written comic with great art will always be a dud.

As far as content goes, teens are just as interested in the "big questions" as supposedly adult readers. In many ways, I am a proponent of novelist John Gardner's thesis that good art "attempts to test human values, not for the purpose of preaching or peddling a particular ideology, but in a truly honest and open-minded effort to find out which best promotes human fulfillment." So without being too conscious of that burden, that's probably the basis of my work. At the very least, I like to think that comics can teach people that the form is wide open to all sorts of stories, not only superheroes and funny animals, but history, journalism, biography, and all the other nonfiction forms.

Megan Nicolay
http://www.generation-t.com

Published Books:

Generation T: 108 Ways to Transform a T-Shirt;
*Generation T: Beyond Fashion: 120 New Ways
to Transform a T-Shirt*

Your book *Generation T* is written for teens, but it seems that adults love it too. I keep hearing from mothers who bought *Generation T* for their teen daughters and then fell in love with it themselves. What can you tell us about writing this book?

When I set out to write it, I was aiming more for the late high school/ early college crowd. Think about it in terms of the magazine model: Middle school girls read *Teen* magazine, 13-year-olds read *Seventeen*, and 17-year-olds read *Cosmo*. As a thirty-something, I'm not saying I'm reading *AARP* cover-to-cover, but the point is, everyone reads *up*. And it's come as a delightful bonus that the book has appealed to such a broad range of people. I've had 8-year-old fashion-designers-in-training approach me after events with a notebook full of sketches, I've had a 70-year-old grandmother inquire as to which sleeve style will be more flattering, and I've had mothers and daughters report on the ways in which they've been able to bond over making the projects. And let's not forget the guys: After my first book had only a few projects for the male contingency, we expanded to a whole chapter in the second book due to popular demand. The key is to have a very specific audience in mind (the specificity will aid in the writing as well as the marketing and selling), but recognize and be open to your book taking on a life of its own once it has reached that intended audience and been shared.

How did you go about finding a publisher?

I was in a unique position at the time that my book was published. I was working my first job out of college as an editorial assistant to the editor-in-chief at a publishing company (Workman) in New York City, and it was through that lens (and with the knowledge of what a good book proposal looks like) that I pitched the book to one of the senior editors at the company. Thankfully, they liked it! Had they not, I would have taken the proposal elsewhere, but the timing was right, and it was incredibly special to find the book a good home so close to home.

How many rejections have you received in the course of your writing career? How did you deal with being rejected?

Any rejection is disappointing (and if you're not disappointed, you probably didn't want it that badly). I try not to keep count, because it can become an unnecessary distraction—if not an all-out roadblock—when trying to move on to the next route. If I'm lucky, the rejection is a constructive one, and I can use it to build toward the next success, but if not, I just keep writing and getting stronger and celebrate the successes (however minor) in order to keep up the momentum and continue looking forward.

What's the most important thing you've learned as a writer?

First, say *yes*. Be open minded when you write—sometimes the narrative will surprise you, and take you in a direction you hadn't expected. Go with it. Like coloring outside the lines, don't be afraid to write off the map (you can always go back to an outline, but those natural divergences are too valuable not to explore). My tendency is to edit myself as I write, but it's more important to write freely in order to get it down on paper, and try not to worry about revisions until it's time to polish. Then be diligent in revision, and accept that an editor is your friend. A good editor will bring that needed new perspective to the text, work with your voice rather than against it, trim it where it's too indulgent, and encourage you to expand it where it's too slim—all in order to enhance the story, subject, or message you're trying to express. Despite the negative reputation of the red pen (or red track changes nowadays) that an editor wields, he or she *is* actually on the same team as you, working *with* you to present the best piece of writing possible.

What is most rewarding to you about writing?

I love working with and playing with words, and that's what keeps me engaged in the day-to-day process, but what really gets me emotionally is when I hear from folks who have read what I've written and have been moved enough by it to let me know. It's especially meaningful for me because the types of books I write aren't expected to engender passionate response. After all, it's not tragic memoir or suspense-filled mystery: My books are step-by-step guides to cutting up T-shirts!—so it's rewarding to know that there is an impact: that I've written instructions that are clear enough to follow, that I've created projects that inspire variation and experimentation, that I've created an environment within the pages of the book that empowers readers to go beyond the pages to create art and messes—and artful messes! Ultimately, writing is meant to be read, so it makes me positively giddy when that interaction happens.

What's your best advice for people who want to write nonfiction for teens?

The key is to know your audience, identify with them, and *respect* them. When writing for teens, treat them and talk to them as you would your close friends. We're actually the only ones who categorize them as teens (very few teens identify that way, and cringe at anything labeled with the word "teen")—from their perspective, they're maturing and making that adjustment to young adulthood, and as awkward as the process may be, they want to be listened to, taken seriously, and engaged with in real ways. I'm reminded of how my dad, who has taught at the high school level for nearly 40 years, describes what he loves so much about teaching that age group: Those 4 years see such major transformation in terms of development of self-identity and awareness, establishment of social and political views of life, and a general figuring out of how one fits in to the larger picture (more so than during the middle school or college years)—they're absorbing and growing a lot more than people give them credit for! For me, writing for people who are in the throes of that transition is exciting—and if you write with respect, honesty, and a healthy dose of *real*, you gain your readers' trust and are, in turn, given that rare opportunity to make an incredible impression on a fresh young mind.

Janet Price

Published Books:

Take Control of Asperger's Syndrome (coauthor); *Take Control of Dyslexia and Other Reading Difficulties* (coauthor)

You write nonfiction for teens. What do writers in this genre need to know?

I think the most important aspect of writing nonfiction for anyone is to be able to clearly express the information in a way that is meaningful to your audience. The key to doing this for teens is to find a hook to make the information relevant to them. When writing *Take Control of Asperger's Syndrome*, one of the most important things we did was to survey teens with the disorder and find out what was important to them, what worked for them, what didn't, and why. This way we knew that our information would definitely be useful and interesting. Another hook was in our presentation. I have a teenage son who was really into video games during the time I was writing the book, and I noticed how he spent hours poring over his strategy guides. That's what gave me the idea to organize the information as a strategy guide, with challenges identified as "missions" and strategies offered as "tips and tricks," so that it would be a familiar and accessible format for teens.

How did you decide to write a book?

It wasn't until I entered my 40s that I finally had an opportunity to write a book. By this point I was working as an educational consultant and was very experienced in the areas of autism spectrum disorders and Nonverbal Learning Disorder. My boss, Rich Weinfeld, had authored four books on various educational topics and had connections in the publishing industry. I had mentioned to him that I'd always wanted to write a book, and when a need arose for a book for teens about Asperger's syndrome, he asked if I'd be interested. Of course I was, and collaborated with my good friend and colleague Jennifer Fisher to make it happen. Our second book was published in late 2011. This is really an unusual way to write your first book, but perhaps it's also a lesson to aspiring nonfiction writers. Rather than focusing on getting that book deal, work on becoming really well known in your field, and perhaps a book deal will come to you.

What have you learned by writing a collaborative book? How did you organize the collaboration? Who did what?

When writing a collaborative book, it's important to choose someone to work with who shares your vision and voice, and with whom you can be completely honest. Because I was collaborating with a good friend who is also a colleague (so we were familiar with each other's work habits already), it was a very comfortable arrangement. Jennifer and I have confidence in each other's abilities, and are both able to offer and receive constructive criticism in a positive way, although Jennifer has occasionally referred to me as a "taskmaster." I definitely try to keep us focused and keep the train running on time!

We organized our collaborative efforts by essentially dividing our books in half, each taking the chapters in her areas of interest and expertise. If we were both interested in a topic, we wrote together. This was the case for our chapter about self-advocacy in *Take Control of Asperger's Syndrome*. We also edited each other's chapters after the first draft.

What's the most important thing you've learned as a writer?

Trust your instincts. Really.

What is most rewarding to you about writing?

Honestly, I thoroughly enjoy the process of writing from start to finish. While I compose mostly on a laptop these days, I still love the feel of a pen gliding across a piece of paper, and I do most of my brainstorming and outlines this way. I love going to bed thinking about a chapter I'm working on, and waking up at 3:00 am with a sudden burst of inspiration or a great idea. I quietly steal out of bed, trying not to wake my husband, fumble for a pencil and paper, and jot it down so I can get back to work in the morning. It sounds silly, but awake or asleep, I'm always a writer. And of course, seeing my name in print is fun! There is certainly a great reward in being able to share my ideas with others, although with blogs, Internet outlets, and do-it-yourself e-publishing, it's not such a rare thing to be able to do that anymore. I love writing just for the intrinsic joy, and would continue to do so even if nobody ever read the words but me.

What's your best advice for people who want to write nonfiction for teens?

Respect your audience, and remember what it feels like to be a teenager who wants to be taken seriously. Don't underestimate a teen's ability to understand complex information, and just as you wouldn't want to "talk down" to a teen, don't "write down," either!

Cheryl Miller Thurston
http://www.cherylmillerthurston.com

Published Books:

Unjournaling; *Yoga for the Brain*; *Captain Intro and the Conclusionator*; and others

You write nonfiction books for teens on the subject of writing. What drew you to this genre?

As a former teacher of students, grade 7 through college, writing was always my "thing" in the classroom. I loved getting young people excited about playing with words, experimenting with words, and seeing the power of language. I especially loved working with students who thought they hated writing—and then roping them in and changing their minds.

How does writing nonfiction for teens differ from writing for adults?

Honestly, I don't think there is much difference, at least for me. Maybe that's because my style involves making things clear and easy to understand, and that style is suitable for people of any age. I think good writing can appeal to just about any age level, within limits.

My writing often involves humor, and I don't think I really change my voice for young people. If something is unlikely to make an adult smile, I think it's unlikely to make a teenager smile, either.

Some of your books are collaborations with Dawn DiPrince. How did you organize the collaboration? Who did what?

Dawn and I have a long history of working together, and we collaborate rather effortlessly because we think so much alike. We share the same philosophy about the teaching of writing, so that helps tremendously.

We came up with what we call the "not this, but . . ." technique, which helps us a lot. We developed it when we were both working on a monthly newsletter of reproducible activities for teachers to use in the classroom. In trying to come up with a lesson idea, one of us would throw out something vague and say, "Not this, but . . ." For example, I might say, "Not this, but how about something about how the smell of English leather always reminds me of my high school boyfriend Jesse?" I'd essentially be saying, "This may be a stupid idea, but maybe it will take us in a direction that might be interesting."

We soon learned that with "Not this, but . . ." brainstorming, we could *always* come up with something, and on time. That's very empowering—it gave us confidence and an ability to work quickly as well.

Although we started out working in the same office, we have worked together via e-mail for at least 10 years now, living in different cities far from each other. We write things independently, and then give feedback to one another. I can't exactly say how it works, but it does.

What sorts of rejections have you received in the course of your writing careers? How did you deal with being rejected?

Rejection? Well, I papered one wall of my office with rejections years ago. A big moment early on was getting a hand-written rejection that said the magazine *almost* bought my piece. Almost. Hey—that was progress, and I rejoiced.

How do I deal with rejection? About as well as anyone—you know, wallowing in the slough of despond, being convinced that I have no talent whatsoever, that I'm a worthless human being, that I might as well give up even trying—that sort of thing. Like many writers, I turn rejection inward, blaming myself. I'm not recommending this attitude, but I don't think it's uncommon. Writers at least need to know they aren't alone in their despair.

I cope by allowing myself one day to wallow. Popcorn (with butter), a chick flick, copious complaining, maybe a margarita with my husband, and a little voice in my head that tells me to enjoy the wallowing because tomorrow I'm going to be over it. I usually am.

What's the most important thing you've learned as a writer?

Cut it in half. Years ago, I wrote a piece for a very specific market, and it was rejected. There was only one other place that could possibly publish the piece, but the word count limit was just over half the length of my piece. Could I cut it in half?

I could, and I did, and I saw how much better it was. I'll always remember the editor saying that the piece was so tight that he couldn't really find anything to edit. Now I try to keep that in mind. I tend to overwrite at first, and when I start chopping, the work improves.

What is most rewarding to you about writing?

What is most rewarding is being able to say I'm a writer. I was a writer for years, many years, before I could ever say so. Because I admired writers so much, I had a hard time putting myself in the same category. I always felt I was pretending, playing at the art, not worthy. It took a long time for me to realize that I *am* a writer. That somehow just thrills me to death.

What's your best advice for people who want to write nonfiction for teens?

Like teens. Respect them. Remember being a teen yourself. I would never have written for teens if I hadn't gotten to know about a gazillion of them through teaching. I think that when you actually get a kick out of a certain age group, your warmth and respect will shine through your work.

Sari Wilson

http://www.sariwilson.net

Published Graphic Novels:

Forward, 54th!: The Story of the 54th Massachusetts Regiment; State of Emergency

What can you tell us about writing nonfiction YA in graphic format?

First, I'm a writer. So I really enjoy writing nonfiction comics for a YA audience because I think this group is so perceptive about their literature. They're still connected to the live-or-die necessity of stories in our lives, how they allow us to make meaning of our world.

As a culture, we've moved away from the large tale—the heroic, the epic—toward the subtle, quirky, the sophisticated. Of course comics can be that—and are that—but one thing I like about the graphic form is that it lends itself to powerful visual imagery and to action sequences. One graphic book I published this year is about the 54th Regiment, an all-African American Union Army regiment that fought incredibly bravely in the Civil War. It was illustrated by Aaron McConnell, who did a great job incorporating historical reference and giving the story a vibrant humanity. It's an amazing story that works really well in the graphic form.

Another book of mine, *State of Emergency*, combines prose and the graphic form to tell a story of two authors and Hurricane Katrina: Dave Eggers and Josh Neufeld (my husband!). We used graphic sequences from Josh's book about Katrina, *A.D. New Orleans After the Deluge*, to retell parts of the story of Katrina survivors. It's like a story within a story—and I think it works really well. I enjoy exploring how different formats for storytelling work together and are entwined.

How many rejections have you received in the course of your writing career? How did you deal with being rejected?

Hundreds. Literally. I have folders and folders. These books were a bit different, but for a lot of my stories I received more than 20 rejections before they were published. One thing I learned is to just keep going no matter what, because you don't want to look back later and say, "If I had just kept trying!" That, and make charts for your submissions. When a rejection comes in, you just check a box and send out your story again.

What's the most important thing you've learned as a writer?

To be open to the world in all its aspects and paradoxes. At the heart of stories is tension between things—counterpoint and opposition. That's why we keep reading—to see if there can be resolution among the tensions, because that's so difficult in all our lives.

What's your best advice for people who want to write or illustrate nonfiction for teens?

Just do it. Try it. Fail. Try again. Then fail again. And find a writing community or group of some sort to help be your guide. Writing is solitary, but the writing life shouldn't be.

The End

Writing a book is such a journey. If this were fiction, it would be time to check in with the characters one last time. I'd be looking back to the first chapter and all that had happened since it began. Nonfiction is different. Instead of the presence of characters, I've imagined readers beside me, chapter by chapter. And now that the book is done, I don't really like saying goodbye.

So I'll look forward to meeting you again in the form of an excellent novel or nonfiction book—written by you.

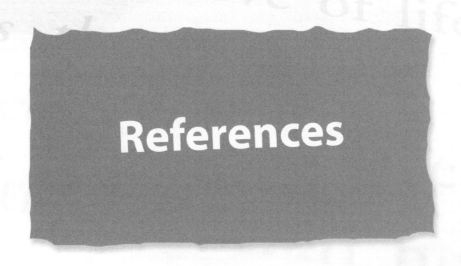

References

Anderson, M. T. (2002). *Feed.* Somerville, MA: Candlewick Press.

Austen, J. (1996). *Pride and prejudice.* New York, NY: Book of the Month Club. (Originally published 1813)

Bachorz, P. (2009). *Candor.* New York, NY: Egmont USA.

Barron, T. A. (1999). *The mirror of Merlin.* New York, NY: Penguin.

Barton, C. (2011). *Can I see your I. D.?: True stories of false identities.* New York, NY: Dial Books.

Bauer, J. (2008). *Peeled.* New York, NY: Penguin.

Bell, H. (2003). *Goblin wood.* New York, NY: HarperCollins.

Booker, C. (2004). *The seven basic plots.* New York, NY: Continuum.

Calhoun, D. (2000). *Aria of the sea.* New York, NY: Farrar, Straus, Giroux.

Collins, S. (2008). *The hunger games.* New York, NY: Scholastic.

Crutcher, C. (2001). *Whale talk.* New York, NY: Random House.

Garden, N. (2006). *Endgame.* New York, NY: Harcourt.

Godberson, A. (2009). *Envy.* New York, NY: HarperCollins.

Hamby, Z. (2009). *Mythology for teens.* Waco, TX: Prufrock Press.

Hanley, V. (2000). *The seer and the sword.* New York, NY: Laurel-Leaf.

Hanley, V. (2005). *The light of the oracle.* New York, NY: Laurel-Leaf.

Hanley, V. (2012). *Seize the story: A handbook for teens who like to write.* Waco, TX: Prufrock Press.

Jones, P. (2007). *Chasing tail lights*. New York, NY: Walker and Co.

King, L. R. (1994). *The beekeeper's apprentice*. New York, NY: Bantam.

Lubar, D. (2003). *Dunk*. New York, NY: Clarion.

Meyer, C. (2007). *Duchessina*. New York, NY: Harcourt.

Mitchell, T. (2010). *The secret to lying*. Somerville, MA: Candlewick Press.

Mucha, C. (2011). *Freshman: Tales of 9th grade obsessions, revelations, and other nonsense*. San Francisco, CA: Zest Books.

Myracle, L. (2005). *The fashion disaster that changed my life*. New York, NY: Puffin.

Paul, D. K. (2004). *Dragonspell*. Colorado Springs, CO: Waterbrook Press.

Paul, P. (2010, Aug. 6). The kids' books are all right. *New York Times*. Retrieved from http://www.nytimes.com/2010/08/08/books/review/Paul-t.html

Perkins, S. (2010). *Anna and the French kiss*. New York, NY: Penguin.

Resau, L. (2009). *The indigo notebook*. New York, NY: Delacorte Press.

Rhuday-Perkovich, O. (2010). *8th grade superzero*. New York, NY: Scholastic.

Rowling, J. K. (2007). *Harry Potter and the deathly hallows*. New York, NY: Scholastic.

Ryan, A. K. (2011). *Glow*. New York, NY: St. Martin's Griffin.

Sandoval, L. (2006). *Chicks ahoy*. New York, NY: Simon Pulse.

Vega, D. (2008). *Fact of life # 31*. New York, NY: Alfred A. Knopf.

Zadoff, A. (2009). *Food, girls, and other things I can't have*. New York, NY: Egmont USA.

About the Author

Victoria Hanley loves to nurture emerging writers. She is the award-winning author of the bestselling book *Seize the Story: A Handbook for Teens Who Like to Write*. She is also a YA novelist published in 13 languages. Her books have received awards and honors in the U.S. and abroad, including the International Reading Association Young Adults' Choices, the Colorado Book Award, Kallbacher-Klapperschlange Award (Germany), Colorado Authors League Top Hand Award, Publishers West Silver Award, and New York Public Library Book for the Teen Age. Her work has also been placed on state award lists in Texas, Oklahoma, Utah, and Colorado and has earned a Carnegie Medal nomination in the United Kingdom. Victoria is an active speaker and workshop leader and the recipient of the Colorado Broadcasters Association Award for Best Regularly Scheduled Feature. She has been a featured speaker for the Young Adult Literature Conference, the Colorado Chapter of the International Reading Association, the High Plains Library Association, the Rocky Mountain chapter of the Society of Children's Book Writers and Illustrators, Colorado Association of Libraries, Pikes Peak Writers Conference, Rock Solid Writers Conference, Big Sur in the Rockies, and Rocky Mountain Fiction Writers. She has been published in the *ALAN Review* and has also led workshops for thousands of teens at libraries and schools across the mountains and plains region.

Growing up, Victoria lived in California, Massachusetts, Wisconsin, New Mexico, and Oregon. She now lives with her family in Colorado at the foothills of the Rockies.

You can visit her online at http://www.victoriahanley.com.